SATURDAY AFTERNOON MADNESS

Bob Waldstein & Phil Silverman
with Wayne Ellis

Four Horsemen Press

Photo Credits
p. 19: Big Chief Knucklehead; p. 31, 42: Penn State University; p. 41: S. Fong; p. 47 Yale University; p. 54: Guts and Glue Photographics; p. 51, 68, 68: University of Michigan; p. 82 Chinese Bandits Archives; p. 87 Louisiana State University; p.96, 99, 102, 105: Clemson University; p. 99 Dino J. Dog; p. 115, 119: University of Georgia; p. 133, 142 Jefferson Y. Peters; p. 161: *Dothan Eagle*; p. 163: Dr. Frederick Crawford; p. 173, 176, 177, 180, 182, 187, 192: Notre Dame University; p. 193: Vincent E. Welby Jr., Notre Dame University; p. 208, 209, 209: University of Colorado; p. 217: Bob Brooks, MIT Museum; p. 221, 222: University of Washington; p. 229, 243, 244, 245: *The Stanford Daily*; p. 235: Stanford University; p. 250, 253, 257, 262: Glen Johnson Photography, Texas A&M

Layout: Steve Rothenberg
Cover Design: Susan Sutherland

ISBN 0-9648571-0-3
LCCN 95-71499

Four Horsemen Press
Box 213, Boston University Station
Boston, Massachusetts 02215
Email: Sataftmad@aol.com
Saturday Afternoon Madness Hotline: (617) 527-7971

Table of Contents

Editor's note...

This book is the result of two separate series of events. The first consists of a six-month tour de farce perpetuated by a couple of escaped lunatics: Phil Silverman and Bob Waldstein. Their story, a modern day pilgrimage to escape reality and re-enter the frenzied world of college football, provides the factual and fictional basis for this book.

The second string of events began approximately 18 months after Phil and Bob's journey began when I was asked, coerced and groped into their service. Having known these two for close to a decade, I was familiar with their trip and, more importantly, with their severely warped perspective of the world. In turn, Bob and Phil were aware of my writing background (Masters in English from an academic institution of questionable repute) and my penchant for the bizarre, obscure and stupid. More importantly, they knew that I, like them, was straining to bend my creativity into some sort of marketable avenue. So these two colossal egos (and waistlines) grappling for literary supremacy came to me. Because neither would take a narrative back seat, I suggested the splintered voice of "we, Bob and Phil." They grudgingly agreed to this after I convinced them that the only reason they hadn't seen this literary device before was that nobody had the balls to try it. In reality, it offered them a compromise and me a way to keep their crap separated. With that said, this book is intended to be three people's salvation.

We Blame It All
On Chinese Food

We blame it all on Chinese food. Well, that may not explain everything, but it helps account for the most bizarre 18 months of our lives, so far. It helps explain why Phil is a 32-year-old attorney making a lawyerly wage and yet teetering on the edge of financial ruin. It helps explain why Bob, a 28-year-old Ivy Leaguer, was holed up in Charlottesville, Virginia, frantically trying to turn our journeys into a book.

Bad things tend to happen when we get near Chinese food, and April 22, 1993 was a perfect example. We were sitting in the lounge of Tang Dynasty riding the synergistic effects of mixing MSG and Mai Tais. After a quarter century of Chinese food gluttony, we've learned that we do our best thinking with our mouths full.

There we were, as always, pondering creative ways to leave behind our mundane lives to do something really remarkable. The get-rich-quick schemes we usually devised were invariably discarded as impractical, illegal or immoral (usually all three), leaving our ever-expanding waistlines as the only concrete result from all of this plotting. But that fateful April night, oh that perfect night, as Bob struggled to say, "Geez, aren't these hot" in reference to his latest mouthful of ribs, he mumbled what sounded like: "Gridiron Jihad." We both sat in stunned silence, literally chewing on the possibilities of a college football "holy war."

For us, "gridiron jihad" came to mean an almost religious trek across the country to participate in, and write about, the revelry surrounding football, not professional football with its dollar-lust, but college football, steeped in tradition.

We planned to live out and write about the ultimate sports fan's dream — and yes, with the mantra, "If ESPN will broadcast it, and the breweries will sponsor it, we will watch it," we are the ultimate sports fans.

For most, this type of dream would have actually involved participating in a sporting event with the athletes themselves and then writing about it, a la George Plimpton. Unfortunately, we weren't nearly athletic enough to attempt that. More importantly, though, we didn't want to expose innocent women and children to the sight of us in shorts. If we knew nothing else, we knew our physical limitations.

With participation out of the question, we chose the only real aspect of sports in which we excelled: watching. Having come of age at the end of the sequin-infested '70s and the beginning of the sitcom-heavy '80s, we had plenty-o-expertise in watching. When college instructors were asking for volunteers to solve troublesome problems, we sat there watching. When college campuses were torn apart by students protesting the cause du jour, we sat there watching. Finally, when our local cable affiliates starting broadcasting Nickelodeon, we sat there watching and watching and watching. We have raised watching to an art form. If you don't believe us, try sitting through one of our day long *Leave it to Beaver* debates: "Query: Are urban gang wars a predictable result of the Eddie Haskellization of society during the 1960s?" Our book explores and glorifies the watcher and the art of watching.

That same wonderful, horrible April night, we made the first of many, many wrong assumptions. In our MSG-induced delirium, we assumed that publishers would line up for the rights to our book. We reasoned that because the entire sports industry revels in, and caters to, the high-density watcher, the fanatic, and yes, the couch potato, our book would surely sell, and then be turned into a miniseries, as well as a highly successful line of Phil and Bob figurines, complete with the Kung Pao grip. The terminology surrounding today's sports telecasts plays up to the spud-like watcher identity. Commen-"taters" broadcast games to spec-"taters." What could be easier to understand? This "Russet-Roulette" principle of sports broadcasting emphasizes the eternal truth that sports are tailor-made for the watcher. For this reason, our book would be topical and therefore marketable. Right?

*   *   *   *

At this point, you may be wondering, what the hell would send two young professionals on a gridiron jihad across the heartland of America, especially two guys who were the products of comfortable middle-class upbringings and supposedly educated enough to know better than to take such an ill-advised risk. Each of us, in our own way, did it because it felt like the most logical alternative at that point in life.

Bob first realized he wasn't cut out for the corporate world when he felt stifled by the bureaucracy at his first job, and that was at summer camp. Nevertheless, after graduating from the University of Pennsylvania, Bob traded in his Frisbees for three-piece suits and joined a Big Six accounting firm. Unfortunately, his tenure was doomed from the start. In reflection, Bob realizes that sending a stripper to his training class probably wasn't the most prudent career-building maneuver. After an unspectacular year as an auditor, the higher-ups called him in for his annual review and obligatory promotion. But Bob had a surprise for them. During that winter, he had been inundated with postcards from friends living in the Caribbean. Demonstrating his usual flair for diplomacy, Bob graphically told the partners what to do with their promotion (it had something to do with mayonnaise and wine corks), and then purchased a one-way ticket to St. Thomas.

Upon arrival in St. Thomas, Bob received two job offers. As a loan officer for the Federal Emergency Relief Agency, he could have gained invaluable professional experience helping the islanders rebuild their shattered lives in the wake of Hurricane Hugo. Instead, the movie *Cocktail* inspired him to choose the other option and become a pool waiter — not the worst decision of his life, but certainly right up there. We're sure Tom Cruise never had to rub lotion into some 320-pound behemoth's acne-infested back.

Bob's other jobs in paradise were just as fruitless. Working the floor of the island's busiest toy store, he had the unenviable task of convincing vacationers that their grandchildren's affections were contingent upon purchasing overpriced, battery-operated stuffed animals. After a couple of weeks of prancing around in a parrot costume and answering every price request with, "I'm sorry, Mr. Bananas isn't for sale, but for a $29.95 adoption fee...," Bob finally cracked, drop-kicked Mr. Bananas into a display of chirping parakeets and was kindly asked to leave not only the store, but the island.

Bob's talent for finding horrendous jobs didn't end with his return to civilization. Having always dreamed of pressuring elderly white trash into purchasing overpriced "sleep systems," he sank to the depths of an adjustable bed salesman. Frustrated with his career path (more of a career foot trail), Bob decided that some additional education (and maturity) might better acclimate him to the corporate world. It never really did. After receiving an M.B.A. from Duke, the best job he could muster was as a glorified clerk helping one of New England's most notorious deadbeats worm out of his debts. Bob was just itching for a change.

Phil's story ends in the same state: vocationally dysfunctional. His inability to accept conventional wisdom and ultimately live out the life of a bankruptcy attorney began at an early age. At eleven, he was thrown out of religious school because of his class project. Using a fish tank filled with Cherry Kool-Aid and his hands, he attempted to demonstrate that it was physically impossible for Moses to have parted the Red Sea.

Phil's dysfunctional lifestyle continued at Dartmouth College, where he was quite rightly accused of not embodying the gung-ho, workaholic, Ivy League image. Inadvertently, he scheduled a couple of classes that conflicted with *Andy Griffith* and the *Space Ghost/Frankenstein Junior Power Hour*. Even though he would have received an "A" from Aunt Bea, he barely received a diploma.

After graduation, Phil became a paralegal. His effectiveness in this job was summed up by the office managing partner who called Phil "the single greatest obstacle to productivity since organized labor." Still, there was something about the law, or possibly the avoidance of the law, that inspired him to pursue the legal profession. Despite parental pressures to pursue a law degree at some eastern bastion of higher learning, Phil enrolled at the University of San Diego. Three years later, he returned to Boston with a law degree, a tan and a beautiful wife.

Unfortunately, the tan lasted longer than the marriage. So there he was, four years later, an MSG junkie, busting his ass to help the bankrupt live like the non-bankrupt...and hating it. Phil needed a change.

                     *   *   *   *

We first met while sharing responsibility for evening programs at the same summer camp during the mid-'80s. While the other counselors were busy with the kids, we were usually squirreled away at the local Chinese restaurant trying to dream up entertaining evening activities to break up the monotony of camp. While most of our ideas were deemed to be too dangerous, degrading or deviant to get beyond the planning stages, we did come up with a few doozies. If William Golding had witnessed our pagan, organ-burning ceremonies or ritualistic milkshake-drinking festivals, *Lord of the Flies* would have been even more pessimistic about the fate of poorly supervised children.

For a couple of former camp counselors, the whole concept of cruising the country, watching football, partying and writing about it sounded like the trip of a lifetime. Hell, if we could make a few bucks in the process, we might even be able to avoid having to hire our own bankruptcy attorneys. We slowly began thinking of ourselves as a modern day Lewis and Clark, blazing a trail of viewership and cholesterol consumption across the country. Boldly going where svelte men feared to travel, we would bench-mark a path of watching for all the slugs out there who dream about leaving their listless careers behind and doing something incredibly stupid.

Exploration metaphors aside, we knew there were some serious problems with our initial concept. Our topic, "college football," was so naively wide-open that even Marcel Marceau could ramble on incessantly about it. Our idea needed to be streamlined, so we went back to the drawing board, or chaffing dish as it were. After a dozen trips back to Tang Dynasty, we finally realized that the key to unlocking our topic-block was always there, right in front of us. To make sense of our adventure, we simply had to put the theme into a culinary perspective:

Our trip and resultant book would actually be very much like the egg rolls we had been gorging ourselves on. On the outside, holding the whole mess together, was a travel log account of two guys wanting to sample some of the best sports fare this country has to offer: college football and all that accompanies it. With that as the crispy outer shell, the real meat of this book would be a mixture of strips of juicy football trivia, marinated in spicy social commentary, maybe with a pinch or two of subjective observations on pop culture.

Simply put, we would write about the wildest, wackiest and most wonderful characters and traditions surrounding college football. By arriving a week before the game and immersing ourselves in the ambiance of the host school, we hoped to unearth enough material for an entertaining book. And, if we couldn't? We would just make stuff up.

*   *   *   *

We had to name our book. Originally, we liked the name that had given rise to the whole sordid idea, *Gridiron Jihad*. But with the Moslem holy warlike overtones, we decided to forego that route, lest our relatives disown us. We came upon the name *Saturday Afternoon Madness* while trying to sum up the general attitude that pervaded college football.

However, the term "madness" created a different challenge because there are a hundred different meanings for the word. To further narrow our scope, we settled on aspects of the definition as it appears in *Webster's Ninth New Collegiate Dictionary*, even though we weren't quite certain why Emanuel Lewis had published nine dictionaries:

The quality or state of being mad, extreme folly... ecstasy, enthusiasm, any of several ailments of animals marked by frenzied behavior.

Extreme folly, ecstasy and animal-like frenzied behavior — all qualities and traits that could easily be recognized on any given Saturday. Then again, we never really had to look much farther than ourselves for the majority of this behavior.

*   *   *   *

Title and target in hand, we still had to find a suitable cross-country vehicle. We originally planned to take Phil's Acura Integra, but there just seemed to be something blasphemous about living our version of the American Dream in a Japanese car. But what other logical choice did we have? Bob's "Stinkin' Lincoln" had 120,000 hard miles on it and when the engine was turned off, it made the same high pitched "bee-bee-bee-bee" noise that Shemp Howard made while snoring. Still, if logic had ever entered into our thinking, Phil would have continued bending deadbeats under the limbo stick of financial obligation, and Bob would still be trying to fake gastritis to weasel out of a morning analyzing balance sheets.

Just as we became resigned to traveling in the Acura, we received some news that forever reshaped our trip, our friendship and our bank accounts. Bob's (now former) favorite cousin had found us a limousine that a financially distressed funeral home was willing to unload for the meager sum of $2,800.

Unwilling to be made fools of (at least knowingly), Phil begged Bob to hold off buying the limo until a mechanic could examine it. The mechanic was very helpful. He started hitting Bob upside the head and screaming, "Whaddaya got rocks in ya head kid?"

Editor's note... *Actually he does. Phil put them there while Bob slept one night at camp in 1979. Nothing real big, just some pebbles so they would rattle around when he walke*d.

That was all the encouragement we needed. The black 1979 Cadillac Sedan-DeVille 6-door limousine gave us an air of legitimacy where previously there had existed a legitimacy vacuum. Anybody seeing us driving cross-country in potentially the least economical, non-RV ever built would have to think we were either very important or very stupid. Of course, we hoped to come off as the former, or at least we hoped to advance along the stupid-important continuum as the trip progressed. That black monstrosity must have weighed at least 5 tons: 10,000 pounds of gas-guzzling, environment-choking Cadillac.

Ominous you say? We thought just the opposite. Sure it was used in funerals, but it didn't actually carry the dead people. It wasn't a hearse, and it didn't have those tinted "we-have-some-thing-to-hide" windows. We figured that since so much sadness had existed in this vehicle, it had to undergo a positive karma swing at some time. It never occurred to us that this car looked so good because it had never been driven over 50 mph for an extended period of time. To ask this car to do what we had planned was like asking us to share our last egg roll. It wasn't going to happen, and somebody would probably get hurt.

*   *   *   *

And so, before you could say, "heinous career decisions," we quit our jobs, said good-bye to our loved ones (read: Chinese food chefs), and not-so-coincidentally, watched our mothers begin their quest to shatter Ethel Rosenberg's world record for the most "oy veys" in a three-month period.

The day before leaving, we stocked the car with junk food and stopped off at the local AAA office to chart our journey. Two hours, 24 maps, three magic markers and one frustrated travel agent later, we were finally asked to leave.

As we rumbled out of Newton, Massachusetts, we were sure of only one thing: we had too many damn maps! On the other hand, we were unsure of lots of things. Most notably, assuming we could make it cross-country without getting lynched or imprisoned, just what made a couple of white-collar slugs think they could write an entertaining book? A combined 13 years of higher education provided enough of a solution: ignore the issue.

We simply convinced ourselves that we were underestimating our writing skills. Phil reasoned that his four solid years representing bankrupt clients who didn't have an economic or legal leg to stand on had given him a certain amount of "creative" writing experience. Bob was certain that his stint as the restaurant critic for Duke's student newspaper was a laudable foray into the world of journalism, even if he only had detailed the trials and tribulations of a Jewish kid who discovered that pork was his favorite of the four food groups. That still counted as writing experience. Right?

Editor's note...*Wrong! Wrong! Wrong! After the trip ended, they realized that for all of their notes on cocktail napkins and crumpled Big Mac wrappers, they really didn't have one page of publishable material. They both tried to create their own versions of what had happened, but they ended up with two very different eye-witness accounts of the same accident. They resolved their writing experience problem by coercing me into serving as their editor / referee / nursemaid. What follows is the result of nearly three months of working with Bob and Phil in their realm, the Chinese restaurant. Our discussions, interviews or whatever you want to call them, took place in this environment in the hope that I would be caught up in the same level of Szechwan consciousness that gave birth to their trip. The reader will be the ultimate judge as to whether I did reach their level, but one thing is certain: Upon finishing the book, I was ready to write another one a half-hour later.*

Why College Football Is Better Than The Pros

In this age of professional sport free-agency, no one can ever tell what the make up of a pro team will be from year-to-year. But with college football, there is a serious sense of identity that breeds fierce loyalty to the team. The institution remains, even after the player has given his four, five (or in the case of Jackie Sherrill's Texas A&M teams, seven) years. In an era of Andre Agassi-esque "image-is-everything" emphasis, college football is a brief time-out, a chance to return to the world of consistent identity and comfortable expectation. That said, the following are other reasons why we chose to pursue Saturday Afternoon Madness on the collegiate level:

Pro football is a sport. College football is a religion.

College players never have and never will go out on strike.

The University of Michigan has, is and will always be in Ann Arbor. The Chicago/St. Louis/Phoenix/Arizona Cardinals would move to Baghdad if the price were right.

The Seattle Seahawks play in the Kingdome, a sterile mausoleum where fans watch tiles whiz by as they drop from the dome's ceiling. Just a few miles away, the University of Washington plays at Husky Stadium, a place where fans enjoy panoramic views of the Cascade Mountains, sparkling Lake Washington and Seattle's distinctive skyline.

No one ever got a degree from the Minnesota Vikings or spent the best four years of their lives at the Meadowlands. The Raiders don't have home-coming and the last time we checked, SAE didn't have a chapter at Soldiers Field.

Professional football is played in big cities like New York, Detroit and Chicago. College football is played in charming college towns like West Point, Ann Arbor and South Bend.

Colleges have cheerleaders and huge marching bands that play school songs that send goose pimples running up and down your spine. The pros have dancing bimbos and stale Adam Ant tunes piped over the PA system.

The Cadets from Army have stolen Navy's goat on countless occasions. A depraved New England Patriots fan once stole another fan's wheelchair.

College football rivalries are the products of decades of animosity with deep underlying sociological implications. The intensity inherent in Alabama-Auburn, Army-Navy, Texas-Texas A&M, or for that matter, Amherst-Williams is independent of either team's record. With all but a few exceptions, NFL rivalries are completely dependent on the strengths of the competing teams. Let either Dallas or San Francisco slip a notch and see what happens to that rivalry.

Even if Wisconsin is losing by five touchdowns, Badger fans will stay to celebrate the "Fifth Quarter," a raucous polka festival in which the fans sing and dance in the stands following the game. NFL fans often leave close games during the fourth quarter to beat the traffic.

Bear, Bo and Woody never coached in the NFL... Keith Jackson, Keith Jackson, Keith Jackson... Lafeyette-Lehigh, Depauw-Wabash, Southern-Grambling... Chief Osceola, Script Ohio and the Sooner Schooner... Collegiate announcers are unashamed to use the word "we" when calling their team's games.

Before each half, Ralphie, Colorado's Buffalo mascot, runs a ceremonial lap around the field while the Buff faithful wildly cheer him on. During NFL games, some drunkard invariably does a lap around the field while obese security guards attempt to wrestle him to the ground.

At Texas A&M, thousands of Aggies chop down 10,000 trees and build the world's largest bonfire to symbolize their burning love for their school. The only bonfires in the pros involve cars overturned during riotous victory celebrations.

Before every home Ole Miss game, the Rebel players walk single file through the Grove, as thousands of adoring fans wildly shout encouragement to them. Before Jets games, players drive their BMWs to exit 16W of the New Jersey Turnpike and park their cars in a special lot where they are protected from disgruntled fans.

The NFL decides its championship on the field. The colleges let a bunch of fat manic pollsters choose their champion... Well, there may be some advantages to the pros

East Rutherford, New Jersey
Kickoff Classic: Florida State vs. Kansas

And Away We Go

On a humid August morning, we embarked on our safari into the magical world of Saturday Afternoon Madness. The first stop on our pigskin pilgrimage was the Kickoff Classic, the football season's inaugural game, contested each year at the Meadowlands in East Rutherford, New Jersey. This year's "classic" featured a match-up between top-ranked Florida State and Big Eight also-ran Kansas.

Despite the nearby toxic waste dumps, there was no better place to start our journey than East Rutherford, for just a few miles away, Rutgers and Princeton played the first ever intercollegiate football game in 1869. In a soccer-like game that bore as much resemblance to modern-day football as *Hogan's Heroes* does to *Schindler's List,* Rutgers prevailed — six goals to four.

During that game, the Princeton players deployed "scarers," yells copied from Civil War regiments, meant to frighten the Rutgers players. Instead, the constant screaming only winded the Princetonians, contributing to their defeat. For the rematch, Princeton brought some extra students to do the yelling; thus, the birth of cheerleading. With cheerleaders on the sidelines, Princeton avenged their loss. A deciding match was canceled due to concerns that athletics were being overemphasized.

While Princeton-Rutgers may have been the first intercollegiate contest, various forms of football have been played since the beginning of recorded history. While there is evidence that every culture (with the exception of the French) played some sort of football-like game, the modern game traces its roots back to Britain. According to John McCallum's *College Football U.S.A.*, football was introduced to Britain during the Danish occupation of the first half of the eleventh century. Resentment toward the Danes was so fierce that it became a popular activity to unearth Danish graves and kick the skulls about. Even after inflated cow bladders were adopted as a more durable ball, the game was still called "kicking the Dane's head."

From this game evolved the British "melees." With as many as a few hundred men on each side, teams attempted to move a ball across goal lines that could be as far as a half mile apart. As the name indicates, the melees were particularly brutal contests, with the players often destroying everything in their paths. In 1069, in an effort to reduce the carnage and calm the local merchants, the game was revolutionized, renamed "futballe" and restricted to marked-off fields away from town.

Even with such refinements, futballe remained a rough sport. The penalty for being offside was a kick to the shins! Nevertheless, this new sport gained such immediate popularity that King Henry II banned futballe because it was detracting from compulsory archery practices. Hank's royal edict sent the sport underground for almost four centuries.

By the 18th century, futballe had lost its mass appeal and was played exclusively by British schoolboys. With kicking the only permissible way of moving the ball, futballe bore a great resemblance to modern-day soccer. Not surprisingly, most of the children without ties to Third World countries found the game to be quite boring. But on a fateful day in 1823, William Webb Ellis, a student at the Rugby school, picked up the ball and ran with it, scoring history's first touchdown. While some of his classmates criticized Ellis' blatant disregard for the rules, others praised him for enlivening an otherwise dull game. Eventually, the sport split into two distinct games: association football (its abbreviation "assoc" is the origin of the word soccer) and rugby, the father of American football.

           *   *   *   *

The engine purred as we headed south on I-95, or at least Phil thought it was the engine. It turned out to be Bob making yummy sounds as he finished off his second bag of salt-n-vinegar potato chips. Two-hundred miles and two tanks of gas into our trip, we rolled into the Meadowlands. For about ten minutes, we stood there in the vast concrete parking lot, half in disbelief that the limo actually made it out of Massachusetts without falling apart and half in confusion about how we were going to uncover the wildest, wackiest and most wonderful characters and traditions surrounding college football.

As we stood there sweating through our clothes, a noise off in the distance gave us hope. It was difficult to make out at first; it sounded like either the Seminole War Chant or a bunch of guys waking up from a terrible hangover. It was probably a little of both. Nonetheless, we were drawn to the sound, like two dogs drawn to one another's asses: uncontrollably, almost instinctively.

As we weaved through the maze of conversion vans and family wagons, the sound became clearer. Finally, the Winnebagos parted as if Moses himself were casting them aside, and we came upon a truly remarkable sight. High above the Jersey landfills stood a majestic structure screaming skyward: a forty-foot tall teepee. And milling around it were the shapes and figures that we had envisioned from the moment the fateful phrase "gridiron jihad" was first muttered. Football fans. Saturday afternoon warriors. And better yet, the tribe was sending smoke signals, begging us to join them. Then, beyond our wildest dreams, we realized the smoke was not from ordinary wood burning. No, it was the sweet smoke of barbecue grills going full blast. The fumes urged us onward and indicated that chicken wings were on the menu. Not since the Grinch unleashed himself on Whoville had anybody been as wanderlusty as we were when we entered the Seminole Valhalla.

Just then, an imposing figure emerged from the delicious blue smoke. With a handshake that nearly cracked our white-collar wrists, Chief Gary Valinoti welcomed us into his domain.

And what a domain it was! The hoards of smiling faces dancing around the majestic teepee seemed scripted from a light beer commercial. Apparently, the warrior-Gary's alter-ego was a successful Wall Street businessman. But this Gary, the devout Seminole and Florida State alum, had purchased 100 cases of beer and enough food to feed Rhode Island in an effort to appease the angered Seminole football gods. Gary said that two consecutive heartbreaking losses to Miami had left his gods with the taste of turf toe in their mouths. It had to be cleansed, and he had been chosen to provide the cleansing fodder.

Chief Gary Valinoti takes refuge from the heat inside his tepee

Editor's note... It suddenly dawned on me, Chief Gary was Bob and Phil's true introduction to that rare breed of man, the college football fanatic. Born and bred in the Northeast, and schooled at four less than football-powerful institutions, these guys had never met a certifiable Division I football lunatic. Of course, they would be amazed. With nothing in their backgrounds with which to compare him, Gary was impossible for them to explain.

From my perspective, growing up under the giant red shadow of one of the truly great college football powerhouses, Nebraska, I easily conjured up a mental picture of Gary, especially since Florida State had perpetrated so many recent thrashings on the Huskers. I knew that even though each Saturday afternoon warrior would be as distinctive as the team that he or she followed, common denominators existed that transcended team and school: the warrior's unbridled loyalty to his or her alma mater and a seriously warped system of priorities centered around the school. Phil and Bob expressed a certain degree of astonishment when they learned that Gary's particular brand of Seminole pride included spending his forthcoming honeymoon at the Florida State-Miami game in Tallahassee. I took it as a gaffe on his part for scheduling his wedding during football season.

Along with a couple hundred of his closest friends, we followed Chief Valinoti into the stadium. Nobody really expected much of a game, so when the Seminoles began pounding an undermanned Kansas team, no one was disappointed. Given the cornucopia of food and grog that remained at the teepee and the oppressive heat in the stadium, it's not surprising that most of Gary's tribe had returned to the tailgate before the end of the first half.

After the victory party broke up, we contemplated our next move. Bob was anxious to get on the road to Penn State, which was about a five hour ride west. Phil countered that Atlantic City was only about an hour south, and since our budget was going to be a little tight later on in the trip, winning a few extra dollars in the casinos might be a good idea. This was the first of what would become a long and brutal series of impasses, but we were prepared. We had decided to settle all of our differences with board games. While a few rounds of Hungry Hungry

Hippos seemed more appropriate, we settled our first dispute with a game of Twister, a contest of skill, flexibility and guts.

To make a long story short, Phil pulled an Achilles tendon when forced to attempt left-foot-blue while precariously perched on right-hand-green, right-foot-yellow and left-hand-red. Anyone experienced in Twister knows that not even Slinky-Jim, the side show contortionist from the Maine State Fair, could have pulled that one off. Although he had prevailed, Bob has always been one to appreciate a valiant effort in the face of horrendous odds, so he acquiesced and we headed for Atlantic City.

Once in town, we hit the roulette table like two hillbillies hittin' shine. Four hours later, we finally grew tired of being the economic whipping boys for the state of New Jersey and decided to hit the road for Penn State.

Perhaps it was fate, but a torrential thunderstorm forced us to seek refuge at the Park Inn -- a seedy motel featuring sixteen red-shag carpeted rooms, each with a panoramic view of Big Al's Truck Stop. Ours featured turquoise walls, velour bed spreads, and a tastefully artistic masterpiece on the wall: a black velvet portrait of Jesus playing golf with Elvis. Despite the over-whelming stench of chutney and the Chia Pets growing in the shower, the motel possessed a certain indescribable charm.

After a fitful night of sleep, we awakened early to begin our trip to State College, but the limo gods were not smiling on us. The limo wouldn't start. No, worse, it wouldn't even begin to start. Instinctively, we popped the hood and started examining the engine. Considering our combined automotive knowledge could fit on the top half of a football ticket, this maneuver seemed futile at best. Eventually, Phil called AAA and in his best Humphrey Bogart imitation, told the operator, "This could be the start of a beautiful friendship."

Two hours passed before the mechanic arrived. Those were the worst couple of hours of our lives. Well, maybe not as bad as when Bob was hit in the groin by a discus, but definitely worse than when Phil chugged a cup of sour milk on a dare. We were just hours into our once-in-a-lifetime journey and the limo was already broken down. Given our limited budgets and the financial sodomizing administered by Atlantic City, this mechanical nightmare could have ended the trip. Luckily, the AAA mechanic told us he only needed to replace the battery. Upon hearing this, we both took off at a dead sprint (waddle) for the truck stop across the street and bought six D-cells. By the time we returned, the guy had already jumped the car and warned us not to stop until we reached State College, or we might not get it started again.

We followed his advice... sort of. We couldn't possibly drive through Philadelphia without wolfing down a few cheesesteaks at Pat's and Geno's — Philadelphia's two most legendary cheesesteak emporiums, both of which happen to share the same South Phily street corner.

As we pulled away from Pat's and headed toward beautiful State College, Phil felt a wave of excitement running down his leg. Then he looked down and saw that it was actually only a gob of cheese making the transition from his thigh to the seat cover. But it felt great. We were living the American dream.

Ten College Football Events
to Witness Before You Die

Texas Aggie Bonfire: To symbolize their undying love for Texas A&M (as well as their burning desire to beat the University of Texas), thousands of Aggies spend the better part of a semester chopping down 10,000 trees and building the largest bonfire this side of Waco.

Saturday Afternoon with Touchdown Jesus: Because of the scarcity of tickets, every game is like homecoming. Just walk through the picturesque campus for a couple of hours, visit the Grotto, chat with the alumni and follow the Irish Band from the Golden Dome to Notre Dame Stadium. Never mind the fact that you'll be whistling the *Victory March* for the rest of the afternoon, you just might find yourself in church the next morning.

The Iron Bowl: Alabama-Auburn: Karl Marx would have loved this one: the agricultural school competing against their snobby rivals for gridiron supremacy of the most football-crazed state in the nation. This is the ultimate 365-day-a-year rivalry. Tune in any sports radio station in March, and assuming they're not talking about football recruiting, they'll probably be talking about the Iron Bowl. If you do go, be prepared to pick a side. Much like World War I Germany, they don't respect the rights of neutrals.

Any Florida Intrastate Battle: Florida State, Miami and Florida just may be the three best football programs in the country. Furthermore, Florida's Swamp and FSU's Doak Campbell were the two loudest stadiums that we experienced, and the Orange Bowl is so imposing that the Canes lose there only a couple of times a decade.

Tailgating on Lake Washington: After spending a few hours floating on these scenic waters, you get to watch the most exciting team in the Pac Ten play in a stadium that offers views of Seattle's skyline, the Cascade Mountains and Lake Washington. If you can't make it to the Pacific Northwest, floating down the Tennessee River on an autumn Saturday is a more than suitable replacement.

Saturday Night on the Bayou: Nothing like letting the LSU fans get liquored up for a full day before a game. An opposing coach once said, "The worst thing about night games in Death Valley is not being able to see the whiskey bottles flying at you." Saturday Night on the Bayou had been described as "a combination of Mardi Gras, the Coliseum during Rome's halcyon days, an early-day Fourth of July celebration, New Year's Eve in Times Square and Saturn Three blasting off." It's also college football's greatest tailgate. Saturday Afternoon on the Bayou and Friday Night on the Bayou were honorable mentions for this list.

Second Saturday in October at the State Fair in Dallas: Although some of the luster has slipped from this game because of recent lackluster teams (as well as a slowdown in the petroleum-based economy), the potential is still there. With 700 fans being arrested before one game, Dan Jenkins declared this rivalry to be "the equivalent of a prison riot with coeds." Veterans of this rivalry still reminisce about the "Night it Rained Furniture," in reference to a particularly wild pregame party at a high-rise Dallas hotel.

The Fifth Quarter at Camp Randall: We liked Wisconsin more when they sucked. Where else would thousands of crazed cheese-heads remain in the stadium dancing to polka music after a five touchdown defeat?

The Army-Navy game: Unlike traditional rivalries, Army-Navy is really one team split into two. Watching the Cadets and Midshipmen march in before the game could make even Saddam Hussein shiver with patriotism. Furthermore, it was the upsets in this rivalry that inspired the cliché, "You can throw the record books out the window..."

Florida-Georgia at the Gator Bowl in Jacksonville: "The World's Largest Cocktail Party" Enough said.

State College, Pennsylvania
Penn State vs. Minnesota

A Case Study in College Football

Penn State was a fitting first campus for us to visit. Just as we began new chapters in our lives, Penn State embarked on a new era in its gridiron history. After 106 years as an independent, Penn State became the eleventh member of the Big Ten conference. This move brought a completely new identity to the Nittany Lions, and vice versa. No longer were they the "Beasts of the East," feasting on the likes of Syracuse, Pitt and Boston College. They were now a midwestern school battling other large public institutions such as Wisconsin, Michigan and Ohio State.

The East had certainly lost its most prized pigskin possession. If you had asked students from any of the eastern football schools who their biggest rival was, they probably would have said Penn State. But any Penn Stater could tell you that these eastern "rivals" were just warm-ups for their intersectional match-ups against the Notre Dames and USCs of the gridiron world. Given their outstanding record against the current members of the Big East (116-19-1 during the Joe Paterno era), you can't really blame them for seeking out new challenges.

Besides offering Paterno the opportunity to win his first conference championship and the accompanying Rose Bowl berth, the new conference affiliation allowed Penn State to bask in the glory of Big Ten football. As Bob Wood so eloquently wrote in his book, *Big Ten Country:*

> Football in the Big Ten is magic. It's sunny, blue, crisp autumn afternoons freezing your rear off — nipping on some schnapps and hot chocolate. It's tailgating for five hours talking football, munching dogs, brats, burgers... It's that explosion, that roar of the crowd that greets the opening kickoff, and the marching band fight song that blasts out a celebration of each home team's score. It's loyal alums head-to-toe in their school colors, and crazy, screaming end zone student sections... Big Ten football is passionate. It's friendly. It embodies the good things that college football is all about.

If you think you picked the wrong college football travelogue, it's not too late to trade this book in.

*   *   *   *

Four hours and a six-pack of Strawberry Yoohoo into our New Jersey-Happy Valley jaunt, signs for Nittany everything started appearing: Nittany Jim's Steakhouse, Nittany House of Pancakes, Nittany Burger... We pulled into lion country knowing full-well that the limo-beast would die once we stopped. Luckily, the Nittany service station was right across from the Nittany Budget Motor Inn, which was just a stone's throw from the Nittany campus.

After parking the car, Bob got choked up, and not because we had to shell out another hundred dollars for a new battery. He told Phil that there was something very special about Penn State. Bob explained how, even as a child, he could sense that games between Jackie 's Pittsburgh and Joe Paterno's Penn State were battles between darkness and light. And when Penn State beat those trash-talkin' hoodlums from Miami in the 1987 Fiesta Bowl, he knew that Joe Paterno and Penn State stood for all that's right about collegiate athletics. Tears were streaming down Bob's face as he expressed how heartbroken he was when he arrived at the University of Pennsylvania expecting big-time football, only to discover that he had accidentally enrolled at the wrong school. Just as Phil was beginning to fear that he was traveling with Alan Alda's soul brother, Bob faked an attack of Tourette's Syndrome at the Nittany convenience store.

*   *   *   *

Penn State is a place where the game is played the way it's supposed to be played, unchanged from those halcyon days of old, when the games were played on natural grass by players with crew cuts named Chuck, Chip and Charlie, who probably celebrated a hard fought victory by downing some of mom's milk and cookies. No decorative patches grace Penn State's nameless blue and white uniforms, the most basic in all of college football. After all, what's the point of decoration when you're fully expected to emerge from the field of battle caked in mud anyway?

*   *   *   *

We got out of the car, told the mechanic that we needed a new battery and asked him where the closest restaurant was. We knew Happy Valley was aptly named, when Hank (his shirt said) told us of the Nittany Szechwan Palace two blocks away. He must have been psychic, for he seemed to anticipate what else we needed to know. "Oh yeah, it's a buffet," he said. Suffice to say, the Szechwan staff applauded when we entered, and hurled Asian curses at us as we left.

We emerged from our afternoon binge ready to begin conducting the fieldwork for the greatest college football book ever. Unfortunately, we didn't have any idea where to begin. After months of debating such pertinent issues as how much lawn furniture we should pack and what we should nickname the limo, we had no clue as to how we were going to uncover the characters and traditions surrounding Penn State football.

Penn State's Football Hall of Fame seemed like a logical starting point. You can watch hundreds of games on television and listen to Beano Cooke wax philosophic about the legends of the game, but it can't quite capture the feeling of seeing the old uniforms, viewing the trophies and watching the old videotapes. Nonetheless, trophies and awards can't tell stories, and the oral history of Penn State football is what we were really after. We left the museum feeling somewhat unfulfilled.

We felt that as long as we had a starting point, a base of operations, we would eventually stumble on what we were looking for. Instinctively, we approached the grubbiest student we could find and asked him to direct us to the darkest and dingiest bar on campus. He burped and pointed toward the All-American Rathskeller.

The Skeller has become a Pennstitution. Despite its grunge, the Skeller exudes an indescribable wholesomeness, seemingly capable of hosting a bachelor party, 50th anniversary party and polka-party all at once. In part due to its antiquity, the Rathskeller forms a bridge between Penn Staters of all ages, perhaps, more so than anything else on campus, with football being the lone exception.

Back in Boston, we were lucky to find a bar that served pitchers of beer, but patrons of the Rathskeller can have entire cases of 7-ounce Rolling Rocks delivered to their tables. The Skeller even earned a spot in *The Guinness Book of World Records* when 932 cases of Rolling Rock were consumed on a single day in 1987. The bar still holds its annual "Case Study" on the Saturday after St. Patrick's Day and attempts to shatter the previous year's record. Penn Staters are so enthusiastic about Case Study that they have been known to camp out on Friday night in anticipation of the bar's 10 a.m. opening. Unfortunately, Guinness no longer publishes records involving gluttony or alcohol consumption. This doesn't dampen the students' enthusiasm for Case Study, but it did quash our planned assault on the record for the most trips to the Jade Island luncheon buffet (non-bulimic division).

As dilapidated and history-laden as the bar is, it pales in comparison to its most dilapidated and history-laden customer: Harry Neideigh. Harry has had an off-and-on association with the Rathskeller since he began washing dishes there in 1948. Since then, he has been fired and rehired more often than Billy Martin, Dagwood Bumstead and Fred Flintstone combined. Despite a fiery temper that caused his frequent dismissals, he was always rehired because the Rathskeller just wasn't the same without him.

Long since retired, Harry serves as the bar's goodwill ambassador. He can always be found on the same bar stool, drinking the same drinks, telling the same jokes and probably wearing the same underwear. When the bar was sold a decade ago, a clause was inserted into the deed that required all future owners to give Harry perpetual free food and drink. The management, aware of Harry's legendary temper, won't serve him alcohol until after lunch, at which time they usually slip him watered down drinks. Few people enter the bar without paying homage to Harry. Unfortunately, years of hard-living have severely slurred his speech. No matter what he says, his muttered rumblings always sound vaguely like, "Paul is dead. He had no shoes. I am the Walrus — Coo coo ca choo."

We wish we could describe Penn State's picturesque campus, but we spent almost every waking hour holed up at the Skeller. It's not easy researching a book in a bar. Not only was it hard to make sensible notes on beer-soaked napkins, but as the evening progressed, and the stories grew and grew, it became impossible to discern fact from fiction, legend from infamy and the women's bathroom from the men's.

Nevertheless, we heard some great football stories. One of our favorites involved a wild postgame celebration following Penn State's 1990 victory over top-ranked Notre Dame at South Bend. When Craig Fayak kicked a 34-yard field goal to give the Lions a 24-21 upset victory, the Nittany campus went berserk. Thousands of jubilant students spontaneously swarmed Beaver Stadium and attacked the goal posts in a frenzy akin to that of a starved Dom Deluise attacking a ten course meal. With the goal posts hoisted overhead, the exuberant mob started screaming for "Old Main," the venerable building which stands as the spiritual and geographic epicenter of campus. Unable to fit the goal posts through the stadium tunnel, they carried them up through the stands and tossed them over the top of the stadium. After an impromptu pep rally at Old Main, the revelers joyously carried their trophies over to Joe and Sue Paterno's house and planted the goal posts on their front lawn. (And according to one of the Skeller's drunken patrons, when Joe Paterno returned from South Bend, he single-handedly picked up the goal posts, and used his teeth to bend them into the shape of a balloon-dog.)

Even though we seemed to spend half our time at the Skeller and the other half sleeping off our Skeller performances, we were actually learning a lot about the aura surrounding Penn State football. Still, there were some colossal wastes of time along the way. Nickelodeon couldn't have picked a worse time to broadcast an *F-Troop* marathon.

Joe Paterno's mid-week press conference also proved to be a waste of time. Initially, we were overjoyed to be invited. Just a few weeks before, we had been pencil-pushing cogs in the vast white-collar machine; now we were in the presence of Joe Paterno, listening to him espouse his philosophy about football and life. Better yet, he had to answer all our questions, no matter how ridiculous. Would he know the sound of one hand clapping? Could he sing the *Mr. Ed* theme song? Just think how stunned the other members of the media would have been if we had gotten this Brown University classics major sidetracked on a debate concerning Cicero's views on Stoicism. Because we were hoping to be awarded press passes for the game, we decided to remain as inconspicuous as a pair of loudly dressed 230-pound men could be.

When Coach Paterno took the podium, we both froze. There he was, the Yoda of college football coaches, the master. We were overcome with awe. Looking at the guy, you would never realize that you were in the presence of one of the game's most legendary figures. With his dark Coke-bottle glasses and flood pants, Paterno bears more resemblance to a stadium usher than a football coach. It didn't matter to us that he stood there kvetching for a half hour about how banged up his team was and how poorly they matched up against mighty Minnesota. Nor did it matter to us that Paterno named John Sacca as his starting quarterback. Nothing mattered, nothing at all.

Unless we were having a bad reaction to the day-old falafels we had eaten earlier that day, Joe Paterno was somehow controlling our minds. Neither of us could break his hold; his will was our will. We didn't know if everyone else in the room was being controlled like we were, but then again, our mental endurance has been substantially worn down by *Lucy* reruns. Paterno seemed to look right through us, as if we were immaterial. In that instant, he was revealed to us as "The Paterno," super-being, mental giant. As the press conference ended and he left the building, our brains were finally freed. We slumped to the floor.

After awakening two hours later in an alley somewhere on campus, we realized that the next time we came across The Paterno, we had to be prepared. As for Coach Paterno's announcement that Sacca would start, it swept through Happy

Valley like a tidal wave. Despite the Mideast peace summit and the threat of a huge hurricane hitting the Carolina coast, Paterno's selection of Sacca was the headline story in the local *Centre Daily Times*, even supplanting the discovery of "Batboy's Recapture" as reported by the *World Weekly News*.

Aside from The Paterno's awesome display of power, the press conference may have been the biggest letdown since *Caddyshack II*. How many questions can be asked about some second-string center's sprained ankle? The press conference experience reinforced the notion that if we wanted to uncover the characters and traditions surrounding college football, we should be hanging out with the residents of the Rathskeller, instead of wasting our time at officially sanctioned events.

＊   ＊   ＊   ＊

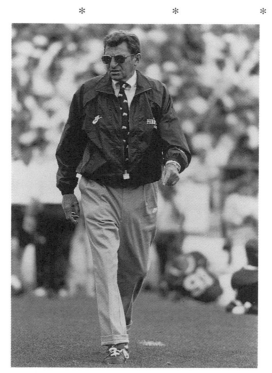

The legendary Joe Paterno stalks the sidelines

From all accounts given to us at the Skeller, Joe and his wife Sue are the first family of Happy Valley. Having been at State College since 1950, they are so integral to Penn State that many graduates are shocked upon discovering that the Paternos' signatures don't grace their diplomas.

Joe Paterno's impact on Penn State extends far beyond the gridiron. It wasn't enough for him to lead a recent $10 million library fund-raising campaign, so the Paternos donated $250 thousand of their own money for good measure. According to Ronald Reagan, "Joe Paterno has never forgotten that he is a teacher who is preparing his students not just for the season, but for life." To underscore his educational commitment, Paterno's academic All-Americans enjoy equal billing with the football All-Americans in the Penn State Hall of Fame.

Paterno demands that his players exhibit the same zeal for achievement both on and off the field. Mike Reid may have been the consummate Paterno player. Despite the fact Reid was Penn State's best lineman, Paterno gave him his blessing when he decided to skip his sophomore season to take a lead in a campus production of *Guys and Dolls*. Reid went on to win the Outland Trophy his senior season and all-pro honors with the Cincinnati Bengals before embarking on a Grammy Award winning country music career.

Still, as ex-Oklahoma coach Gary Gibbs painfully discovered, they don't sculpt statues of football coaches for graduating their players. Paterno is the only coach to achieve 250 victories while winning 80 percent of his games and graduating 80 percent of his players.

Due to his immense popularity, Paterno's image adorns everything from life-size cardboard cutouts ("Stand-up Joes") to golf balls guaranteed to go straight up the middle three out of every four times.[1] He is so respected that the Republican party has been urging him to run for political office for years. Joe must realize that anything short of the oval office would be a step down in power.

But the Paternos haven't let success go to their heads. They have lived in the same modest house since 1967. They don't drive fancy cars and they even have a listed phone number. How

---

1. Despite Paterno's reputation for conservatism, the 1982 Lions were the first national champions ever to gain more yardage passing than on the ground.

many Pitt fans do you think have called asking if Joe had leather balls?

With Penn State's victory in the 1995 Rose Bowl, Joe Paterno became the first coach to win all five major New Year's Day bowl games (Rose, Orange, Sugar, Fiesta and Cotton). Still, he wasn't the first coach to guide Penn State to Pasadena. That honor belongs to Hugo Bezdik, whose Nittany Lions faced USC in the 1923 Rose Bowl. Penn State had accepted the Rose Bowl invitation before the season started and despite a 6-3-1 record, headed west to Pasadena. Due to heavy parade traffic, they arrived at the stadium an hour after the scheduled kickoff time. In a game finished in complete darkness, Southern Cal prevailed 14-3.

---

*　　　　*　　　　*　　　　*

Just for kicks, we decided to call up the Paternos. When Sue answered, we expected her to quickly shoo us off. Even our own parents refuse to talk with us for more than three minutes at a clip. Instead, she entertained us for almost half an hour. In between some pretty decent football stories, she bragged about all her children, nephews and nieces. Not surprisingly, she seemed prouder of their educational accomplishments than her husband's national championships.

When the conversation shifted back to football, Sue had many interesting anecdotes. While most fans rely on some great play or a great game to jog their memory for the details, Sue told us that she relies on her past pregnancies. One of our favorite stories involved the now legendary desecration of the Nittany Lion Shrine. Sue explained that she remembered that event by focusing on a particularly difficult pregnancy, during which she "vomited for nine months." When Bob told her that reminded him of his freshman year in college, Phil was sure she would hang up. Fortunately, she didn't and began relating the sordid details.

It was 1966. The Beatles had conquered America and Joe Paterno was sporting a mop-top haircut and John Lennon Glasses, so we later heard. It was Paterno's first season as head coach, and Sue wanted to do something to inspire the apathetic Penn State students. Along with the wives of several other assistant coaches, Sue targeted the Nittany Shrine, a statue of a nittany lion to which Penn Staters have developed a strong sentimental attachment. A few nights before the Syracuse game, Sue and her cohorts covered the shrine with orange water-based paint, knowing full well that Syracuse would be blamed.

On game day, the largest crowd of the season watched Penn State attempt to avenge the desecration of their shrine. Although they fell short, losing 12-10, Penn State's football fortunes soon began to rise. The following season, Paterno led the Lions to a seven-game winning streak and a top-ten finish, thus awakening the slumbering Nittany Lion pride.

Few people realize that if not for Sue, Joe may have left Happy Valley to become coach of the New England Patriots back in 1972. It was considered to be such a done deal that a press conference was scheduled to announce the move. But after Sue let her feelings be known to Joe, they decided to stay in Happy Valley. In the end, they realized that the satisfaction they received from being able to influence the lives of the students was far greater compensation than the monetary riches that the NFL offered.

*   *   *   *

The Skeller denizens told us that if we wanted to learn all there was to know about Penn State football, we had to seek out retired play-by-play announcer Fran Fischer, which we did. Apparently, he hadn't been tipped off that we were coming because when we arrived, he graciously invited us in.

This was our first real interview and it took us some time to get things going. Here we were with this walking, talking encyclopedia of Penn State football and all we could initially think to ask him was "Where's the best late night food in State College?" After recommending the grilled sticky buns at Ye Olde College Diner, he entertained us for hours with the legends and lore of Penn State football.

Fran has seen the team emerge from a virtual unknown to the perennial powerhouse that it is today. He recalled the early days in 1967 when the team traveled to Kansas, where the Big Eight's myopic view of football led the master of ceremonies at a pregame banquet to wish Penn State, "Good luck in the Ivy League." With all due respect to the two-time defending Ivy

League champion Quakers, confusing Penn's and Penn State's football program is like confusing the acting abilities of Pee Wee Herman and Marlon Brando.

Fran also had fond recollections of the 1982 team's triumphant return from its Sugar Bowl victory over top-ranked Georgia. Upon arrival in Harrisburg, the team was welcomed by thousands of adoring fans. That was to be expected. They were finally bringing their first national championship home to Happy Valley. What was truly amazing, though, were the throngs of cheering fans who lined the 100 miles of Rte. 322 from Harrisburg to State College. Fran loaned us a videotape that captured the trip so that we could view it for ourselves. In what may have been the longest parade in Pennsylvania history, fire engines and police cars with sirens blaring escorted the team busses from one town to the next. If there was an award given to the school with the most devoted fans, this championship parade would ensure at least a nomination for Penn State.

Fran told us that the intensity of this celebration was probably the result of Penn State's numerous near misses at attaining college football's top prize. Despite finishing both the '68 and '69 seasons as undefeated Orange Bowl champions, the pollsters relegated them to the status of bridesmaids each year. Before the '69 Arkansas-Texas game, President Nixon declared that the winner would be national champion. After Texas beat Arkansas, but before the pollsters could decide for themselves, Nixon presented a national championship plaque to Texas coach Darrell Royal. At Penn State's 1973 commencement, Joe Paterno asked the graduating seniors, "How could Nixon know so much about football, but so little about Watergate?" After finishing the '73 season as undefeated Orange Bowl champions, Paterno told reporters that there was only one poll that mattered, the Paterno Poll, in which Penn State had finished number one. The polls that didn't matter had Penn State finishing fifth. Nevertheless, the '73 team still proudly wears their championship rings.

Perhaps the most painful of the near misses came in the 1979 Sugar Bowl against Alabama. Trailing 14-7 late in the fourth quarter with the ball inside the Bama 1-yard-line, only a couple feet and a two point conversion stood between Penn State and the national championship. After their third down rush left them a few inches short, Alabama's Barry Krause warned Penn

State's Chuck Fusina, "You better pass." Penn State ran and the hearts of Lion fans everywhere were shattered as the immovable object withstood the irresistible force.

It was happening again. Only this time, because The Paterno was not around, it again caught us off guard. Fran Fischer also had the ability to control minds. We had been sitting there for hours and hadn't been able to utter a word. The only explanation was that he was like The Paterno. Did everyone associated with Penn State have the ability to control the feeble-minded? Was this the reason that the area was called, "Happy Valley?" Unable to break Fischer's spell, we continued listening.

Fran continued by saying that if the 1982 national championship got the monkey off Penn State's backs, the 1986 championship propelled the Paterno legend to dizzying new heights. The Penn State-Miami Fiesta Bowl was far more than just a championship showdown between the two top-ranked teams in the nation. It was a battle between what collegiate athletics should be and what they have become.

The differences between the two teams were amplified when the Penn State players arrived in Phoenix wearing coats and ties while the Miami players wore battle fatigues and menacing sun glasses. At a pregame banquet for the two teams, Jerome Brown posed the Blutarski-esque question, "Did the Japanese sit down and eat with Pearl Harbor before they bombed them?" He then led Miami's hasty departure, later dubbed the "Steak-Fry Walkout."

Fran then told us about the game, but all we could think about was all of that red meat that had been left untouched, uneaten and unloved. Our eyes started to lose their glaze as we formed mental pictures of the unequaled beauty of almost 250 steak dinners being abandoned: juicy and meaty, with home fries and perhaps a vegetable or two just waiting...

Just like that, we were out of the trance. However, Fran was unaware. From that point on, Bob dug his nails into his palm until blood squished between his fingers to keep Fran out of his head. Phil just kept clenching and unclenching his butt cheeks.

Fran told us that some Hurricanes even downplayed the match-up, boasting that Miami had already won the national championship when they defeated Oklahoma back in September. They claimed that the Fiesta Bowl was just the final game of the season, and they had good reason to be confident. This may have been Miami's best team ever, and in the minds of some pundits, the best team in college football history. Led by Heisman Trophy winner Vinny Testaverde, the Hurricanes featured seven future first round draft picks. On the other hand, Penn State only had six players who were eventually drafted in the first three rounds. Despite Penn State's perfect record, many experts compared this match-up to racing basset hounds against greyhounds.

Fortunately for the Nittany Lions, Miami was too busy yapping to review the game films from Penn State's 1981 victory over Dan Marino's top-ranked Pitt Panthers. In that game, Penn State dropped six linebackers into pass coverage. The confused Marino played the worst game of his collegiate career. Penn State used a similar strategy in the Fiesta Bowl, baffling Testaverde all game with a myriad of zone defenses. Testaverde, who had previously amassed streaks of 114 and 116 passes without an interception, threw five of them that day. Despite being outgained 445 to 162, Penn State prevailed 14-10, capping off its centennial season of college football with its second national championship.

With the end of that story, Fran noticed Bob's bloody fists and the sweat running down Phil's thighs and knew his spell was broken. He didn't seem too upset, just a little sad that we would not know the blissful existence enjoyed by those he controlled. Needless to say, we left our interview with Fran saturated with Penn State images and words, but the strongest memory for both of us was of those 250 lonely steaks.

           *   *   *   *

The true low point of the entire trip occurred on Friday. After four grueling days and nights at the Rathskeller, we both woke up hung over and suffering from horrible chest colds. But the fluids we were coughing up couldn't compare with the green ooze seeping from our limo. We weren't certain whether the car was possessed or merely leaking fluid from the radiator. After checking the prices for an exorcism, we revisited our friend Hank at the Nittany service station. We were completely crushed when he warned us that it might be a blown gasket, which would take several days to fix at a cost close to a thousand bucks. It seemed appropriate that a torrential rainstorm started as we walked up the road to Champ's Sports Bar to mull over our predicament.

We were anything but champs when we entered, soaking wet, sick as dogs and doomed to an economic hell by the 10,000 pound anchor tied to our wallets. Our once-in-a-lifetime football odyssey was in jeopardy because that damn limo had broken down three times during the first six days. We decided that if the repairs were insanely expensive, we would abandon the limo and complete the trip in Bob's "Stinkin Lincoln." We were so despondent that we could barely polish off two burgers apiece.

As if our situation wasn't already bleak enough, a bulletin flashed across the television about a wacko who had fired shots at the workers of a nearby construction site before escaping into the woods. With our luck, the psychopathic sniper would soon burst into Champs and start shooting at the largest targets he could find.

After a couple of hours wallowing in our misery, we ventured back to the service station. It turned out that the problem was merely a popped radiator hose, a quick $50 repair. Hank mentioned that it was quite common for old radiator hoses to break and offered to replace all our hoses and belts for a couple hundred bucks. In yet another display of poor judgment, we told him that wouldn't be necessary. Then, after learning that the armed psycho had been apprehended, we walked over to the campus. Strangely enough, the sun had come out.

*   *   *   *

Because we were unable to find affordable lodging for Friday evening, we planned to camp out with the Winnebagos (the vehicles, not the Native Americans) in the shadows of Beaver Stadium. Given our nasty colds, irrational fear of wild animals and general disdain for the whole camping experience, we were looking for another alternative. As luck would have it, Fran Fischer's son was the manager of the luxurious Toftrees Hotel and Resort, the same hotel that houses the Nittany Lion football team on game nights. When Fran's son offered us a significantly discounted room, we had to make the difficult choice between freezing our butts off sleeping on a bed of sticks or room service and remote control cable television.

As we sipped pina coladas in the hot tub, we observed what a difference a few hours makes. The despair of the afternoon at Champs had become a fading memory. Now everything was right again in the universe. After relaxing in those soothing bubbles for a couple hours, we descended on the lounge for happy-hour appetizers. And we're not just talking about a hot dog steamer either. The Toftrees was serving a complimentary flock of chicken wings. If only they had a more liberal credit policy, we might still be there.

The whole concept of a football team shacking up in a hotel the night before a home game was quite foreign to us. It's actually quite a common practice among big time football schools, especially those without athletic dorms. Having witnessed football Friday at State College, it's not surprising that Paterno would want to sequester his players.

Staying at the same hotel as the Penn State football team presented us with some interesting financial opportunities. We contemplated a plan in which we would repeatedly pull the hotel fire alarm during the wee hours of the morning. Sluggish from the evacuations, the Nittany Lions would never be able to cover the 21 point spread. Luckily, better judgment, as well as a healthy fear of being raped in prison, kept us away from the alarms. Besides, we had already decided to bet on Penn State. In fact, we had decided to bet $100 on every home team during our trip. Notre Dame's legendary Gipper always claimed that he played better when he had money riding on the game. Likewise, we could probably cheer and write better with a little financial incentive. And how much money could we possibly lose over the course of a season anyway?

*   *   *   *

Finally gameday arrived. Hoping to avoid retribution for the previous evening's wet toilet paper fight, we made an early exit to campus. State College comes alive on gameday. By 10 a.m., the Rathskeller was packed tighter than a three-day-old burrito, with revelers lining up for their infamous Bloody Marys. Harry Neideigh helped concoct the Bloodies with the care and precision of a nuclear chemist. The owners even let old Skeller alumni relive their collegiate glory by tending bar. One guy, known as Rabbit, said he has been coming back to every home game since graduating in the sixties. He even made Harry show us the pictures of his kids that Harry carries around in his wallet. As much as any place on the trip, this place gave us the feeling of family, if only because every booth in the place was packed with families working their way through cases of 7-ounce Rocks.

Before leaving, we traded bar tricks with members of the Rathskeller family. One of the managers taught us how to speed chug bottles of beer by strategically placing straws in the bottle to let the air escape. We, in turn, taught her the famed Statue of Liberty shot. A longtime favorite of the Buddhist Monks, the Statue of Liberty shot requires you to dunk your fingertips in Sambuca and light them on fire. As the crowd sings *God Bless America*, you hold the flaming finger torch above your head, and chug the Sambuca shot. Our legal consultants have urged us to warn you not to try this at home.

In the Skeller, we met one deranged but incredibly likable psychopath who claimed to be John F. Kennedy. He dismissed the Statue of Liberty as a "pussy drink" and proceeded to pour a shot of Sambuca on his forearm, light it and demonically laugh as the flames rose high into the lights. Claiming to own a hearse, he insisted that we screwed up by buying a limo instead of a hearse. With his backwoods drawl, he told us, "It's tough to get women into the hearse, but the ones who do come in... they party!" By that time, his arm had already broken into festering welts, so we bid him and his charred flesh adieu.

Along with 94,000 other fans, we made our way toward the stadium. Nothing could have prepared us for the awesome sight of our first big-time campus football game. Land that had been pasture just a couple of days before was now blanketed with a seemingly endless supply of blue and white RVs and conversion vans. We spent hours wandering through the myriad of tailgates, talking with fans and scarfing their food.

We especially enjoyed following Joanne Shorr and her Kazoo Marching Band. These pied pipers of Penn State serpentined their way through the endless maze of tailgates, stirring up the fans with snappy renditions of marching band classics. To be kind, the tunes were, at best, vaguely recognizable. One guy just kept playing *Pop Goes the Weasel* regardless of what the rest of the band was playing. Nonetheless, we've always been fans of enthusiasm rather than execution.

We finally scalped a pair of tickets and made our way into Beaver Stadium. Although the name Beaver Stadium may not inspire the same intimidation as Clemson's Death Valley or Florida's Swamp, Penn State enjoys one of college football's best home-field advantages. With average attendance close to 95,000, only Michigan and Tennessee play before larger crowds. (Unless you measure crowd size by girth per individual spectator, in which case Iowa wins hands down.) For a couple of guys who had never been inside a stadium that could seat more than 60,000, it was truly an overwhelming sight.

1994 Average Attendance Leaders

1. Michigan *Michigan Stadium*   105,867
2. Tennessee *Neyland Stadium*   95,924
3. Penn State *Beaver Stadium*   94,866
4. Ohio State *Ohio Stadium*   92,650
5. Florida *The Swamp*   83,804
6. Georgia *Sanford Stadium*   83,194
7. Clemson *Death Valley*   76,789
8. Alabama *Bryant-Denny Stadium*   76,752
9. Nebraska *Memorial Stadium*   76,187
10. Auburn *Jordan-Hare Stadium*   72,936

Prior to the game, Penn State's Blue Band marched onto the field for a few pregame selections. Expecting to hear wild stories about band pranks, we actually attended their rehearsals

a couple of days earlier. Unfortunately, it was a waste of time. Once you've heard one salute to Ethel Merman, you've heard them all. Still, it was a nice moment when everyone stood to sing the alma mater, *For the Glory of Old State.* Unfortunately, nobody seemed to know the words. Instead, many fans sing the alternative lyrics, "We don't know the Goddamn words," which fits the cadence of the song surprisingly well.

Before the kickoff, there was a ceremony to commemorate Penn State's admission into the Big Ten. During the ceremony, it was announced that the winner of all Penn State-Minnesota games would be awarded possession of the "prestigious" Governors Cup. What is it with Minnesota and silly trophies? They battle Michigan for the Little Brown Jug and Wisconsin for Paul Bunyon's Axe. The winner of their annual showdown with Iowa receives the bronzed pig, reported to be named Floyd of Rosedale. Don't get us wrong, we're as much into tradition as the next guy, but if you're going to play for a pig, it might as well be barbecued and served with plenty of cole slaw, cornbread and sweet tea.

TRASH or TREASURES?

The following is a sampling of some of college football's more notable trophies:

Trophy	Rivals
Axe	Stanford-Cal
Enterprise Bell	Army-Navy
Tobacco Bowl	Virginia-Virginia Tech
Victory Bell	USC-UCLA
Golden Egg	Ole Miss-Miss State
Rag	Tulane-LSU
Old Oaken Bucket	Indiana-Purdue
Soiled Undies	Duke-UNC
Brass Spittoon	Michigan State-Indiana
Platypus Bowl	Oregon-Oregon State
Illibuck	Illinois-Ohio State
Indian Princess	Dartmouth-Cornell
Tea Cup	Clemson-South Carolina
Little Cannon	Purdue-Illinois
Locomotive Bell	Nevada-Pacific
Buffalo Head	Colorado-Nebraska
Natalie Wood	Sharks-Jets
Tydings	Maryland-Virginia
Beer Keg	Kentucky-Tennessee
Old Frying Pan	TCU-SMU
Peace Pipe	Oklahoma-Missouri
Outhouse	W. Virginia-Virginia
Tech Bell Clapper	Oklahoma-OK State

Source: *Saturday's America*

Once the game began, we quickly realized that many Penn State fans were quite fickle. One fan sitting behind us was complaining that quarterback John Sacca had the same bad tendencies as his older brother, Tony, who had quarterbacked the Lions only a couple years before. We had a hard time figuring out why this guy was complaining, and mentioned to him that Sacca had just completed his third first-quarter touchdown pass to Bobby Engram. Not to concede a point easily, the guy countered, "See, he can only focus on one receiver, just like his brother."

As the game got out of hand, so did the student section, bombarding each other with marshmallows and plastic cups, creating what appeared to be a mini-snowstorm within their section. When we asked a student why they threw marshmallows, she said they were the all-weather weapon. During muggy September games, the marshmallows get all gooey and stick to everything. By November, they freeze and make awesome projectiles.

Another great aspect of Penn State games involves the lion mascot. The section that chants, "We want the lion!" loudest is rewarded with the opportunity to pass the lion hand-by-hand overhead up to the top of the stands. While watching this ritual, we thought ahead to our scheduled visit to Madison. Passing students up the Camp Randall stands has become synonymous with Wisconsin football. One time, some clever Badger fans sat in the final rows of the stadium with a stuffed dummy. When an attractive coed was passed up to them, they threw the dummy over the top of the stadium walls. The entire Camp Randall crowd gasped before realizing they were the victims of a devious prank.

Despite a game that was never really close, we were mesmerized by watching Coach Paterno roam the sidelines. He stormed up and down the sidelines ranting and raving at the officials, even though his Lions held a comfortable second-half lead. Somehow, the referees appeared to be immune to The Paterno's persuasive powers. We can't say the same about ourselves. During a particularly heated harangue of the referee, The Paterno let loose such a powerful psychic blast that we passed out in our seats.

We awoke in the middle of a truck stop parking lot on what looked to be the outskirts of Happy Valley. The sun was just coming up. We must had been out for almost 15 hours. We found all of our luggage and gear had been neatly packed in the car and that our motel bill had been paid. We each thought the same thing: The Paterno.

We pointed the limo down Interstate 90 toward Ann Arbor, and put some distance between us and Happy Valley. Later that day, we read in the paper that Joe Paterno and his Penn State Nittany Lions had earned a 38-20 victory. Unfortunately for us, Minnesota scored a couple of meaningless late touchdowns to bust the 21 point spread, putting us down $110.

Early American Football

While viewing the ancient photographs and misshapen footballs at the Penn State Football Hall of Fame, our minds wandered back to the earliest days of college football, a game that bore far more resemblance to a violent form of soccer than modern-day football. Forward passes, running with the ball, and tackling below the waist were all prohibited on the field, but in the stands, anything went. Teams of anywhere from 15 to 100 players scored goals by kicking the ball across the opposing goal line.

The game didn't begin to resemble football until Yale's Walter Camp instituted his revolutionary rule changes in 1880. Camp established the concept of possession with a system of downs as opposed to the soccer-like continuous battle for the ball. Under Camp's original rules, scoring went as follows: five points for field goals, two for touchdowns, four for point-afters, one for a safety, and according to our unreliable editor, 17 points for head-butting the referee in the groin. In recognition of his contributions to the game, Camp has been anointed as the "Father of American Football."

Even with Camp's rules changes, early football was markedly different from the modern game. For one thing, the officials were usually incompetent (maybe the game wasn't that different after all). It wasn't uncommon for teams to select the referees from the stands. These amateur refs often officiated with rule book in hand and kept track of the line of scrimmage by dropping a handkerchief. There were arguments after virtually every call and a good orator was every bit as important to a team as a good back.

Much like today's game, gambling was prevalent. When the prospects seemed bleak for the home team, fans often stormed the field, forcing the referees to cancel the game, thus nullifying all bets. According to John McCallum's book, *SEC Football*, these disruptions became so frequent that officials from the University of Alabama were forced to line the field with barbed wire and armed guards to prevent the hooligans from interrupting play.

The peril that the referees and visiting teams performed under may have been best illustrated during the 1908 Georgia-Tennessee game. After Georgia had driven down to the Tennessee 2-yard-line, one of the Volunteer fans brandished a .38 revolver at the Bulldog players and declared, "The first man who crosses that line will get a bullet in his carcass." Georgia fumbled on the next play.

The early game obviously wasn't for the faint of heart. Once a game started, a player couldn't leave unless he was hurt, or at least feigned injury. John Heisman once returned to a huddle only to have his captain instruct him to "get your neck broke."

These were also the days of the tramp athlete. There were no eligibility rules and athletes often jumped from school to school in search of the best financial package. It wasn't uncommon for players to "transfer" to other schools for just a single important game before returning to their original schools. Before inspiring the trophy, John Heisman played for nine seasons at Brown, Penn, Oberlin and Akron.

Still, many of the game's most enduring traditions originated during this primitive era. When Walter Camp proposed lining the field with horizontal lines every five yards, one of the members of the rules committee gasped, "The field will look like a gridiron." The term stuck. Likewise, the huddle also traces back to this era. Between plays at Gallaudet College, a small Washington DC school for the deaf, the players huddled around the quarterback to read his hand signals. The rest, as they say, is history.

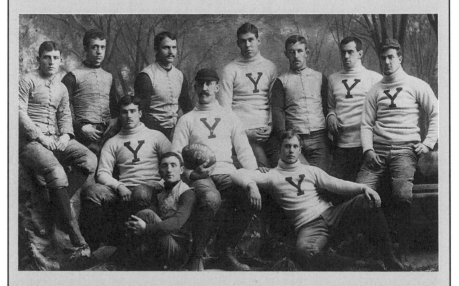

Yale dominated 19th century football, losing only once from 1879 to 1889. Their 1888 squad amassed a 13-0 record while outscoring their opposition 698-0. Amos Alonzo Stagg is farthest left. Coach Walter Camp isn't pictured.

Ann Arbor, Michigan
Michigan vs. Notre Dame

Because Michigan is Michigan

For the entire ride from State College to Ann Arbor, Bob rambled on incessantly about his desire to finally see and touch the one great Ann Arbor icon ingrained into his being. Was he talking about Michigan Stadium? No. Michigan's distinctive winged helmet? No. Bo Schembechler? Not even close. It was Crazy Jim's quintuple blimpy burger with cheese. But of course!

Ever since being forced to memorize a Crazy Jim's menu while pledging his fraternity, Bob had harbored a not-so-secret yearning to visit the spot of the quintuple with cheese. He was finally getting his chance. So when we entered Ann Arbor, we asked the first student we came upon to direct us to Crazy Jim's. The student directed. We went. Bob ordered.

It's not often that Bob is disappointed with food, not often at all, but this was different. Instead of validating the image he had been cultivating for nearly a decade — that of five burgers piled on top of each other in a mountain, glued together with more cheese than anyone's arteries could handle — he received five wafer-thin, half-dollar-sized burgers with more cheese than anyone's arteries could handle. Sure it was good, very good in fact, but it simply didn't live up to the hype. Bob's Blimpy Burger experience turned out to be a microcosm of our Michigan football experience.

For months, we had looked forward to joining 107,000 maize and blue fanatics in Michigan Stadium for college football's largest love-in. But much like the quintuple with cheese, experiencing football at Michigan Stadium was good, very good in fact, but not as awesome as you would expect, given the humongous crowds.

Surprisingly, Michigan has never had the reputation as one of college football's louder stadiums. Opposing players have dismissed the Michigan crowd as the quietest 100,000 they've never heard. The explanations for this lack of crowd noise all seem to be cop-outs. Supposedly, the Michigan fans are spoiled by success. They've been so good for so long that they have a hard time getting excited for anything less than a national championship. That's all well and good, but success has only made the fans of Penn State, Alabama and Notre Dame all the more rabid. Some say that the fan base is too geriatric to cheer loudly. Tell that to the 70-year-old grandmother we saw on all fours barking for her Dawgs at Georgia. Some pretentious observers have even declared the Michigan boosters to be too educated and refined to worry about such trivial matters as football. But education hasn't dampened the enthusiasm of the hockey fans at Cornell or the Cameron Crazies at Duke.

While there's no denying the lack of crowd noise, we're not ready to label Michigan fans as passive. Like every other place we visited, we met both diehards and softies. Apparently, the best explanation for the lack of crowd noise may be acoustics. The cavernous single-decked, bowl-shaped stadium tends to funnel noise upwards away from the field.

Whatever its cause, the lack of crowd noise at Michigan Stadium was one of the biggest letdowns of the trip. Still, if we were to make this trip all over again, we would most certainly visit Michigan. Why, you may ask? Quite simply, Michigan is Michigan, and any book seeking to do justice to college football would be woefully inadequate without a substantial section about the Wolverines and their part in the history of the game. Furthermore, they were playing arch-rival Notre Dame. We wouldn't have missed this game for all the duck sauce in China.

*　　　　*　　　　*　　　　*

We spent our first morning in Ann Arbor exploring Michigan's Hall of Champions sports museum. This museum went above and beyond what any school could rationally be expected to do to display its history and traditions. Every sport is covered, from its crude origins at the school, through its historic triumphs, to its most recent events. Still football is clearly the centerpiece. From the 1-0 victory in the first game ever played against Racine in 1879, through Gerald Ford's days as an all-conference center, to Desmond Howard's Heisman Trophy, the place captures the Wolverine grandeur and captivated us for hours.

From the endless supply of old film footage to the astronomical amount of Wolverine memorabilia, we gained an appreciation for how integral Michigan has been to the history of college football. For instance, it was Michigan that broke the eastern stranglehold over college football at the turn of the century.

Harvard, Yale, Penn and Princeton dominated 19th-century football. They won every national championship, and most All-American teams were comprised exclusively of players from these schools. But this era of eastern domination ended when Fielding H. Yost's Point-a-Minute teams went unbeaten for 56 consecutive games from 1901 to 1905, outscoring their opposition 2,832-42 (an average of 50 to 3/4). The Buffalonians may not have invented the chicken wing, but they certainly took it to all new heights. The same can be said for Michigan and football.

One of the greatest exhibitions of Michigan's dominance occurred in the first ever Rose Bowl held in 1902, when the Tournament of Roses Committee decided that football would make a better sporting highlight for their parade than polo. A boisterous crowd of 8,000 witnessed the most lopsided rout since Little Big Horn. The game was mercifully called with eight minutes remaining and Michigan leading Stanford 49-0. Out of fear that such lopsided contests would scare spectators away, football was scrapped in favor of chariot races for the next 16 years.

The lone blemish during Yost's unbeaten streak was a 6-6 tie at Minnesota. That game provided the genesis for the Little Brown Jug, college football's most famous trophy. Fearing that Minnesota might doctor their water supply, Yost sent a student manager into town to purchase a water jug. He returned with a five-gallon putty-colored jug he had purchased for 30 cents. If the game had been played in the tea-sippin' town of Ann Arbor, we're sure he would have returned with little clear pints of Evian purchased for $1.69 apiece.

With two minutes remaining in a savagely fought contest, Minnesota scored the game-tying touchdown. In the ensuing pandemonium, the fans swarmed the field, causing play to be discontinued. As the Michigan squad hurried off the field, the jug was inadvertently left behind. When Minnesota's equipment manager found the jug, he sent the following message to Yost: "We have your little brown jug. Come and win it." The game had been so brutal that the two schools severed athletic relations for six years, but the challenge was remembered. Michigan won the 1909 game, thus regaining possession of the Little Brown Jug. Since then, the jug has been awarded to the winner of their annual showdown. Because Michigan has beaten Minnesota in 24 of their last 26 meetings, the jug seems to be on permanent display in Michigan's Hall of Champions.

Since the days of Yost, Michigan's program has thrived. There have been four national championships, a string of 21 consecutive bowl appearances and over one-hundred first team All-Americans. Furthermore, Michigan has led the nation in attendance every season since 1973.

*   *   *   *

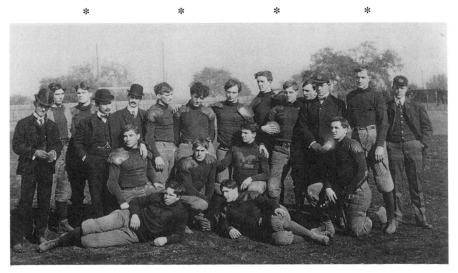

1901 Michigan Team -- outscored their opposition 550-0

Even if Michigan fans as a group are not all that rabid, we certainly found pockets of insanity. There is no better example of the extremes that Michigan-mania can take than the self-anointed "Guts and Glue of the Maize and Blue," Scott Kelsey and Paul Mrozinski. Scott and Paul are by far the most fiendishly twisted and blindly devoted fans that we met during our journey, and we mean that as the highest compliment.

Don't take our word for it. Their coworkers can attest to their Guts and Glue outlook. Upon learning that a fellow employee supports any squad other than their beloved Wolverines, Scott and Paul quickly jump into action. They baptize the perpetrator's blasphemous cubicle by singing *The Victors* and sprinkling it with holy soil taken from Michigan Stadium's grounds. It's not an antagonistic ceremony, but rather an honest effort to correct what they perceive as an uninformed choice. They even offered to attend a coworker's wedding and provide good luck by throwing Michigan Stadium turf instead of rice.

It's not as if they leave their psychosis in the office either. Scott and Paul have willingly forced their families to endure more than their share of Wolverinitis. Just moments after the birth of his son, Scott blessed him by rubbing a piece of Michigan Stadium turf on his leg. The insanity didn't stop in the delivery room. Scott's son is regularly subjected to an ongoing battle between his day-care providers, devoted Ohio State boosters, and Scott. It's not unusual for Scott to send his son to school dressed from head-to-toe in Michigan regalia, only to have him returned in Ohio State garb.

While their antics have become a full-time pre-occupation, their fervor reaches an apex for the Notre Dame game. They constantly refer to Notre Dame as "vermin." Actually it's a bit more involved than that. The exact phrase they used over and over was "Notre Dame-vermin-swine-scum-pig-dogs," with equal emphasis on every word.

Notre Dame's Lou Holtz has long been one of their favorite targets. Paul repeatedly told us, "Even on steroids, Lou Holtz couldn't carry Coach Moeller's jockstrap." Just ask Lou Holtz what it's like trying to play golf with two lunatics in trench coats shadowing you for eighteen holes. When they can't annoy Holtz, they're more than happy to pester his superior, Athletic

Director Dick Rosenthal. They have deluged Rosenthal with angry letters demanding the discontinuance of the Fighting Irish nickname, insisting that it constitutes a derogatory ethnic slur. Just to be constructive, they have suggested an alternative nickname: The Squirmin' Vermin.

These guys don't need much inspiration to set them off. Take, for example, their response when Desmond Howard won the 1991 Heisman Trophy. Howard had forever won a place in the hearts of all Wolverines with his fourth down reception ("The Catch") against Notre Dame. Clutching a 17-14 fourth quarter lead, Michigan had the ball fourth and a foot from the Notre Dame 25. 107,000 fans and 11 Irish defenders expected a plunge up the middle, but Coach Gary Moeller called a pass into the end zone. Although the Irish were caught completely off guard, the play wouldn't have meant a thing if not for Howard's spectacular diving, fingertip catch. With The Catch, Howard staked his claim to the Heisman and ended four years of Michigan frustration against Notre Dame. Somehow, Scott and Paul got a hold of Desmond Howard's Heisman Trophy. Desmond, if you're reading this, look on the lower half of your trophy for a small "V" etched into the player's body. Courtesy of Scott and Paul, it stands for "Victory over the Vermin." If Notre Dame's Touchdown Jesus ever gets a big blue "M" painted across His chest, you know who to blame.

The night before the Notre Dame game, Scott and Paul bring their followers into the woods for an evening of incantation and ritual to drive off the vermin spirit. The climax of the festivities involves the burning of Notre Dame paraphernalia in the "holy grill." One year, they even burned a Notre Dame football helmet. Paul nostalgically compared the eerie green color in the flames to the color of the vermin's uniforms when Gerry Faust was coaching them, no doubt giving him some pleasure at the memory of those down years for the Irish.

While lunching with Scott and Paul, a bulletin flashed over the radio that a Notre Dame fan had transplanted sod from Ireland into Michigan Stadium's north end zone, supposedly in the precise location where Desmond Howard made The Catch in the 1991 game. There was no way that Scott and Paul would stand for this "soiling" of the soil. Leaping into action, they raced over to the stadium with us in lukewarm pursuit. By the time we had caught up with them, they had found and removed the offending grass. To "rebuke the vermin," they sprinkled some holy dirt, cursed Lou Holtz and sang *The Victors*. As we were leaving the stadium, Paul called out, "Turf check!" They each whipped out a piece of Michigan's old astroturf. Neither of them go anywhere without their mobile pocket shrines. They also left some light reading for the Notre Dame coach. While Coach Holtz is leading his team from the locker room on to the field, he can search the walls for the minute inscription, "Lou is a weasel." Nothing major, just a subtle reminder to Holtz that he was on Michigan turf.

*   *   *   *

**The Guts and Glue of the Maize and Blue,
Paul Mrozinski and Scott Kelsey**

Scott and Paul may be a little on the left side of right-minded, but they are certainly not in the minority in their hatred of the vermin. Representative of the overall Michigan-Notre Dame milieu at Ann Arbor, we begin this section on their intense rivalry with this Wolverine jewel:

A Michigan fan is hanging out in a bar talking football with a Notre Dame fan. The Notre Dame fan claims to be so devoted to the Fighting Irish that he has a tattoo of Joe Montana on his right buttock and one of Rick Mirer on his left. The Michigan fan says no one could be that committed. To convince the skeptical Wolverine, the Notre Dame fan dropped his drawers. While staring at the tattooed derriere, the Michigan fan says, "I can't quite make out Mirer or Montana, but that's definitely Lou Holtz in the middle.

In many ways, this joke best communicates the animosity that most Michigan fans harbor toward Notre Dame. Move over Buckeyes. Notre Dame is now Michigan's number-one rival. As Scott and Paul proclaimed, "We respect Ohio State, pity Michigan State, but absolutely despise Notre Dame."

Ever since those barnstorming Michigan players taught the game of football to the Notre Dame students in 1887, their boosters have been arguing about which school possesses the pre-eminent program in college football. The evidence is inconclusive. Michigan and Notre Dame are the two top programs in terms of victories and winning percentage, with Michigan holding the edge in victories and Notre Dame leading in winning percentage. Although Michigan leads the head-to-head series 15-10, Notre Dame has only lost twice in their last eight meetings.

WINNINGEST TEAMS
(Division 1-A)

Victories		Winning Percentage	
Michigan	731	Notre Dame	.761
Notre Dame	712	Michigan	.745
Alabama	682	Alabama	.734
Texas	682	Oklahoma	.720
Penn State	664	Texas	.711
Nebraska	662	Southern Cal	.702
Oklahoma	650	Ohio State	.699
Ohio State	640	Penn State	.689
Tennessee	627	Nebraska	.688
Southern Cal	622	Tennessee	.685

Both schools like to take credit for every important innovation to the game, ranging from two-platoon football to the forward pass. They even argue about music. Both schools claim to have the quintessential college fight song. Michigan's *Victors* was written by South Bend resident Louis Elbel. Notre Dame's *Victory March* was written by Michael and John Shea after repeatedly being subjected to *The Victors* during a 23-0 loss to Michigan in 1902. John Philip Sousa called *The Victors* the greatest fight song in the history of collegiate sports. On the other hand, when music historian Bill Studwell selected the most inspiring fight songs, *The Victors* finished second behind Notre Dame's *Victory March*.

The Ten Most Inspiring Fight Songs

1. *Victory March* Notre Dame
2. *The Victors* Michigan
3. *On Wisconsin* Wisconsin
4. Cole Porter's *Bulldog Bulldog* Yale
5. *Maine Stein Song* Maine
6. *Anchors Away* Navy
7. *Fight On!* Southern Cal
8. *Ramblin' Wreck from Georgia Tech*
9. *Fight Texas* Texas
10. *Across the Field* Ohio State

Source: Bill Studwell

Despite their geographic proximity, these two gridiron giants rarely played each other until the '80s. Allegedly due to anti-Catholicism, Michigan only played Notre Dame twice from 1910 to 1977. Naturally, this resulted in plenty of arguments concerning which school had the better team. After both schools finished the 1947 season undefeated, the Associated Press selected Notre Dame as their national champion. Legendary sportswriter Grantland Rice created a national stir when he called the poll a disgrace. To settle matters, a United Press reporter polled the Southern Cal players who had been soundly thumped by both Michigan and Notre Dame that season. When the Trojans overwhelmingly declared Michigan the tougher opponent, the UP declared the Wolverines to be the national champions.[1] This was the birth of the UP poll, which eventually evolved into the CNN/USA Today coaches' poll.

---

1. Because of Rice's protest, the AP revoted. In that second poll, Michigan displaced Notre Dame in the top position, making 1947 the only season in which the AP actually selected two national champions.

With a career that spanned 53 years and 67 million words, Grantland Rice was the dean of American sports journalism. The verbose, yet poetic Rice is arguably the individual most responsible for the spread of football's popularity. He nicknamed the '24 Notre Dame backfield as the "Four Horsemen," Georgia's Sanford Stadium as "Between the Hedges" and Red Grange as the "Galloping Ghost." Still, the gentlemanly Rice was probably best defined by the final lines of his poem, *Alumnus Football*:

> *For when the One Great Scorer comes*
> *to mark against your name.*
> *He writes, not that you won or lost,*
> *but how you played the game.*

In many ways, this rivalry transcends football. It's a battle between a mammoth public institution and a Catholic private school. Michigan has the Diag, a campus center bustling with student activity and counterculture. Notre Dame has the Grotto, a sacred shrine where the devout go to pray and light candles. Furthermore, the closest thing to counterculture at Notre Dame is the young accountant's society. Notre Dame has priests while Michigan has Preacher Mike. Michigan has the Hash Bash, a giant smoke out that takes place every Spring on the Diag. The only Hash Bash at Notre Dame is a breakfast special at the Morris Inn.

Still, despite their obvious differences, these two majestic institutions are far more similar than they are dissimilar. Both universities are driven by an unwavering commitment to excel in every endeavor they undertake, whether it be academic or athletic. In fact, this shared desire for preeminence may be the single greatest underlying factor in their rivalry.

*   *   *   *

Arising from our sleep on Tuesday morning, we were faced with another mechanical mishap. Having popped yet another radiator hose, the limo was sitting in a puddle of green slime. Despite being only ten days into a 20,000 mile trek, our vehicle had already broken down four times. The limo had quickly transformed itself from a delightful conversation piece into an agonizing financial and environmental nightmare.

If we were mechanics and two clueless slobs pulled a limousine with Massachusetts plates into our station and started rambling about the "green gook oozing from the wahuzit," there would be dollar signs flashing in our eyes. Surprisingly, we were treated quite fairly by most mechanics. The lone exception occurred at an unnamed Ann Arbor service station where an unscrupulous mechanic insisted that the reason we kept popping hoses was because our radiator was too hot. The remedy? Paint the radiator black so it would dissipate heat better. The only thing it dissipated was $75 from our wallets.

*   *   *   *

Undeterred by our mechanical difficulties, we made the two-mile hike to campus. Unfortunately, we wasted the better part of the day in a futile search for a bar dark and dingy enough to serve as our headquarters. There were certainly plenty of campus bars, but no place you could walk into during the early afternoon, wallow in the stench of stale beer, and find a bunch of characters waiting to be culled for information. What we did find was a frightening over-abundance of espresso bars and coffee houses: additional insight into Michigan's disturbing lack of crowd noise.

There was no way that either of us were going to spend any time at a place where the strongest drink on the menu was *cafe au lait*, so we headed back to Crazy Jim's. After engulfing a few more Blimpy Burgers, we set out on a quest for local blues impresario/street dude, Shakey Jake. We wanted to jam with Jake in one of his free outdoor concerts. With only his failure to learn a second chord keeping him from the big time, Jake's minimalist style has been compared to everyone from Robert to Navin Johnson. But much like the equally talented Barry Manilow, Jake does have his detractors. One guy, who introduced himself as the Leprechaun (probably because he talks to them after a second bottle of Wild Irish Rose), told us, "Jake can't sing a lick." Others claimed that Jake was an eccentric financial wizard who sang only as an avocation. Whatever his musical talents may be, there's no debating that Jake is a beloved local legend. We found plenty of cars with "I Brake for Jake" bumper stickers, but unfortunately, no Jake.

We also checked out a few of the more interesting campus spots, most notably, the two old-fashioned barbershops located on South State Street. Although they seem out of place on a this cappuccino-sipping campus, both barbershops have become institutions. Like a cut from Floyd's of Mayberry, a haircut at either of these places is far more than just a trim and a splash of tonic. It's a place to wallow in the glory that is Michigan athletics. Most interesting is the picture in the "Coach Four" of USC's phantom touchdown in the 1979 Rose Bowl, a play that is still remembered with intense bitterness by many Wolverines.

As the Rose Bowl's first half came to a close, USC's Charles White scampered in for the go-ahead touchdown that eventually provided the margin of victory. Michigan fans still insist that White fumbled the ball before crossing the goal line, a position which appears plainly justified by the picture we saw, in which the ball is clearly lying on the 1-yard-line as White is about to cross the goal line. The best part of the picture is the referee who can be seen in the background staring directly at the grounded ball. An arrow has been drawn toward the referee, and the question written in at the tail end of the arrow asks, "Is this man blind?" The author of that question has signed his name below — legendary coach Bo Schembechler.

It seems that a bit of fatalism has permeated the collective psyche of Michigan fans. Although they've finished in the top-ten for 20 of the past 25 seasons, Michigan's last national championship came during Truman's first term. Several times they have stood at the precipice of glory, only to be doinked by the fickle finger of football fate. As lifelong citizens of the Red Sox Nation, we fully understand how pessimism can blossom from a lengthy history of near misses and dashed dreams.

Bostonians blame their 75-year championship draught on the "Curse of the Bambino," which refers to the Red Sox selling Babe Ruth to the hated Yankees for chump change. Additionally, a legacy of racism (they were the last team to integrate), ridiculous personnel decisions and assorted bonehead maneuvers have doomed the Sox to a cycle of mediocrity. If any organization deserves to be cursed, it's the Red Sox.

Conversely, Michigan has made few compromises in their pursuit of excellence. Ann Arbor is a place where the term student-athlete isn't an oxymoron. In fact, Michigan's only blemish may be its racially motivated blockage of Notre Dame's admission into the Western Conference during the '20s. Could Michigan's misfortunes somehow be attributed to a "Curse of the Irish?"

What, you don't believe in curses? How else could you explain all those Michigan misfortunes? On the eve of the 1970 Rose Bowl, Bo Schembechler suffered a mild heart attack. The next day, a demoralized Wolverine squad lost to Southern Cal. The Wolverines went on to lose nine of their next ten bowl games. They also shared three consecutive Big Ten championships from 1972-74 without being invited to a single bowl game. During the late '80s, Notre Dame saddled Michigan with four consecutive heartbreaking opening-day losses, blemishing those seasons before they could even get started. And it wasn't Canadian whiskey that led to Gary Moeller's downfall. The Curse of the Irish is the only possible explanation.

*   *   *   *

Although the Kickoff Classic is the formal beginning of the college football season, Michigan-Notre Dame is the season's first significant game. The winner moves to the forefront of the national championship race, while the loser must redefine their goals for the rest of the season. Since 1978, the winner of this game has always finished above the loser in the final polls.

These games are invariably hard fought, close contests usually decided by a couple bounces of the ball. Whether it be a Reggie Ho last minute field goal in 1988, a Rocket Ismail touchdown kickoff return in 1989, or a Lake Dawson immaculate reception in 1990, the ball always seems to be bouncing Notre Dame's way. Forget about this Catholic vs. public school stuff, the most fundamental difference between Michigan and Notre Dame is that the Wolverines always find bizarre ways to lose, while the Irish always find amazing ways to win. Going into the '93 contest, Michigan had beaten Notre Dame in only one of their last six meetings.

Despite Notre Dame's recent domination of the series, optimism pervaded the Ann Arbor campus. Led by Tyrone Wheatly, the third-ranked, five-time defending Big Ten champions were legitimate national championship contenders. Conversely, Notre Dame had been so decimated by graduation that even the most enthusiastic Golden Domers were conceding this to be a rebuilding season. A pessimistic Lou Holtz questioned whether his team would even win a single game.

As devastating as the graduation of Rick Mirer and Jerome Bettis may have been, Notre Dame's on-field problems paled in comparison to their off-field controversies. In their shocking expose, *Under the Tarnished Dome*, Don Looney and Don Yaeger presented strong evidence that Notre Dame is far from the beacon of integrity that it is portrayed to be. They alleged, among other things, that Lou Holtz physically and emotionally abused players, had knowledge of widespread steroid use at Notre Dame and committed and covered up NCAA rules violations while he was coaching at Minnesota. About the only thing these guys didn't insinuate was that Chris Elliot was the model used to design Touchdown Jesus. Despite threats of American intervention in Serbia, the *Tarnished Dome* allegations received headlines across America. *Nightline* devoted an entire program to the accusations and the book was perched atop the *New York Times* best seller list.

It has been said that the two most important jobs in the Catholic church are the Pope and football coach at Notre Dame, not necessarily in that order. Holtz definitely seemed to be succumbing to the pressure of the most difficult coaching job in America. A year earlier, he protested an official's non-call by throwing the referee into a headlock. Just a week earlier, Holtz had checked himself into a hospital complaining of chest pains. Certainly, the *Tarnished Dome* controversy couldn't be helping the diminutive general's constitution. This, coupled with the pressure of the annual Michigan showdown, had the potential to send Holtz back to the emergency room.

To top it all off, the Irish looked less than scintillating in their opener. While struggling to a 27-12 victory over lowly Northwestern, the offense looked completely inept. The punchless Irish seemed no match for a loaded Michigan juggernaut. Optimism, bordering on cockiness, was prevalent in Ann Arbor. A few students told us that it was a shame that such a great Michigan team was being wasted on a mediocre Notre Dame squad. Las Vegas had installed Michigan as a 9 1/2 point favorite, a margin unheard of in this series. A few of the more sensible fans warned us that Notre Dame is most dangerous as an underdog.

*   *   *   *

The night before the supposed shellacking of the Tarnished Domers was to take place, we found ourselves in the midst of our first and only camping experience. Before purchasing the limo, we conducted exhaustive financial analysis and determined that the money we could save by cooking for ourselves and camping-out would more than offset the added expense in gasoline and repairs. After wasting an hour cooking some sticky spaghetti with a soupy tomato sauce, we junked most of our cooking equipment in State College. From that point on, the make-your-own sundae bar at Ponderosa was the closest we ever came to cooking. We didn't have much better luck with camping.

Considering our forefathers wandered through the desert for forty years (they must have been too stubborn to ask for directions), it seems improbable that we were such lousy outdoorsmen. It's really not our fault. Our entire camping experience came from our years at summer camp in Maine. Do you remember the camp from the movie *Meatballs*? Well, we worked at the camp for rich kids across the lake. As you can imagine, any camp that sports several big screen TVs, batting cages and a fully stocked game room isn't going to let their kids rough it in the woods. Our "camping" trips consisted of driving a busload of pampered kids to a fully equipped campground, located within walking distance of a Dairy Queen.

Given our background, it only seemed appropriate that our one camping experience came in the backyard of Wolverine alum, Tom Kladzyk. For one weekend each season, dozens of Tom's college buddies descend upon his home for one wild evening of reliving their collegiate glory. Through mutual acquaintances, we were invited to enjoy the festivities. Every corner of the house was taken up by sleeping bags, and tents were pitched all over his backyard. Considering they partied until dawn, the tents seemed rather unnecessary.

While everyone else was preoccupied with tequila shots, we blitzed the two ice chests filled with succulent Maryland crabs. After polishing off a half-dozen hard-shells apiece, we both decided to get some rest for what promised to be a very long day. But first, we had to endure a very long night. We're not sure whether it was because the music was loud enough to have coaxed the Branch Davidians out of their compound or if it was the selection of the music itself, but sleep was definitely out of the question. To this day, Phil still claims to have recurring nightmares about being the guinea pig in a sleep deprivation experiment in which the entire discographies of Culture Club and Men at Work are continuously blared into his eardrums.

*　　　　　*　　　　　*　　　　　*

The next morning, we scraped the crab shells off our bodies, piled the tent and half a dozen people into the limo, and ventured back to Ann Arbor. The stadium parking lot was abuzz with anticipation, and we embarked on our usual attempts to scarf free food and meet interesting characters. We stumbled on one elaborate tailgate complete with china, Waterford crystal and a silver candelabra — further evidence as to why crowd noise is rarely a factor in Michigan Stadium.

We quickly found the dynamic duo of Paul and Scott, who introduced us to Art Wahl. Because Art is the son of a Lutheran Bishop, he has been designated as the group's spiritual leader. Wearing an oversized blue cape emblazoned with a maize "M" and a wool hat, knit to resemble the winged Michigan football helmet, Art's clerical garb was far more reminiscent of a second-rate superhero than anything sacrosanct.

Being a man of the cloth, Art couldn't just stand by and idly watch the sin around him continue unabated. Art explained: "A doctor heals the femur; I heal the blasphemer." And just who are the blasphemers? Any Notre Dame fan unfortunate enough to pass by, of course. Art rose upon his alter (the tailgate of his station wagon) and preached from *Under the Tarnished Dome*. Unless hurling a pickle at Art was a sign of their redemption, we don't think any Notre Dame fans were converted.

We asked Scott and Paul what inspired their seemingly unnatural loyalty towards the Maize and Blue. We knew that Bruce Wayne became Batman after witnessing the brutal murder of his parents; Knute Rockne received the inspiration for his Notre Dame shifts from the rhythmic precision of a chorus line; and that Charles Foster Kane was driven to create a vast empire after his favorite sled was taken from him as a youth. But we didn't know what could have shaped our dynamic duo into such fanatical Wolverine fans?

They told us that as far back as they could remember, autumn Saturdays meant Michigan football. When they weren't attending the games with their families, they were watching them on television or listening to them on the radio, and more often than not, a combination of the two. Like countless other Wolverine fans, they always turned down the television volume so they could listen to Bob Ufer's play-by-play call. In fact, they credit listening to Ufer as being the single greatest contributing factor to their Michigan psychoses. Apparently, they aren't alone.

Although he's been deceased for over a decade, Bob Ufer's recorded voice still provides the soundtrack to countless tailgate parties. With his voice blaring from fraternity windows, it was obvious that the Ufer phenomenon extends far beyond the alumni. According to the consensus opinion, listening to Bob Ufer is the best way to get psyched up for a game. One alum told us about his nephew who was grappling with the difficult decision between enrolling at Michigan, Emory or Virginia: "I sent him a Bob Ufer tape. If listening to Ufer couldn't turn his blood maize and blue, he didn't deserve to be a Wolverine." Needless to say, he made the right decision.

Bob Ufer was, is and will always will be the voice of Michigan football. For almost four decades, he ruled the Michigan airwaves. Stylistically, Ufer was to radio what Grantland Rice was to print. He combined an impeccable knowledge of Michigan football that could be recalled at a moment's notice with a gift of gridiron prose that often sounded like a 33 album being played at 45 speed. Yet, despite his formidable linguistic skills, it was Ufer's passion and enthusiasm that defined him. His unbridled love of Michigan shone through with every word that emanated from his heart.

Aside from having witnessed a half-century of Michigan football, Ufer's association with the legendary Fielding Yost made him the "Moses of Michigan Athletics." After track practices (Ufer once held the world record for the 440), Ufer spent many afternoons listening to the aged Yost weave stories of Michigan glory. In this respect, Ufer serves as the bridge between Michigan's storied past and its contemporary fans.

Ufer concluded his 37-year Michigan broadcasting career at half time of the 1981 Iowa game. As the band spelled out "Ufer," he told the crowd: "Besides my family, there are two things that are important in my life: Michigan and Michigan football." Ufer then led the emotionally charged crowd in one final chorus of *The Victors*. Two weeks later, Bob Ufer succumbed to cancer. Fielding Yost's gravestone reads, "I want to rest where the spirit of Michigan is warmest." Fittingly, Bob Ufer is buried next to Yost.

Although Ufer was certainly one of a kind, there's no doubting that collegiate announcers are more colorful than their professional counterparts. How would you like a game described? By some faceless announcer objectively describing a touchdown run or an ecstatic Bob Ufer screaming at the top of his lungs: "Anthony the Darter Carter went down that tartan tarp like a penguin with a hot herring in his cummerbund! God bless his cotton pickin' maize and blue heart!"

*   *   *   *

On we went into Michigan Stadium, or as Ufer would have said, "The hole that Yost dug! Crisler paid for! and (Athletic Director) Canhum carpeted!" As awesome as it was empty, it's truly a sight to behold filled. We'll let Bob Ufer describe the atmosphere that surrounds Michigan Stadium on football Saturday:

> You can feel the excitement! the tension! and the charisma! Especially ten minutes before kickoff when a hush settles over the stadium, and we all anxiously wait for that simple four word command to emanate over the PA system: Band Take the Field! Out of that eastern tunnel pour 235 well drilled! well disciplined! Michigan bandsmen! They pour over the eastern sideline! They form the Big Block M and they play the greatest college fight song ever written! *The Michigan Victors*! That's when the chills go up and down your spine! You get goose pimples all over! Your blood turns maize and blue and everyone out there becomes part of the winningest tradition in the history of Big Ten football, as well as the history of Big Ten athletics!

At that moment, the maize and blue coursed through even our cholesterol-clogged veins and we're unashamed to admit that we joined along in an emotional chorus of *The Victors*:

> *Hail! To The Victors Valiant*
> *Hail! To The Conqu'ring Heroes*
> *Hail! Hail! To Michigan*
> *The leaders and the best*
>
> *Hail! To The Victors Valiant*
> *Hail! To The Conqu'ring Heroes*
> *Hail! Hail! To Michigan*
> *The champions of the West*

Unfortunately, Conqu'ring Heroes is hardly the image Michigan projected as they played more like Hogan's Heroes that day. Furthermore, as expected, the stadium really wasn't that loud. For a while, we even thought the official school cheer was "Down in Front."

To add insult to injury, the Michigan Band's half-time salute to Phil Collins just may have been the greatest musical abomination since Tiny Tim mothballed his ukulele. When they played *The Victors*, we got goose pimples all over, but rock just wasn't meant to be performed by three-hundred polyester-clad tin soldiers marching in formation, and in our humble opinion, Phil Collins wasn't meant to be performed by anyone.

After Notre Dame's shocking victory, the Irish players triumphantly carried Lou Holtz off the field. The 1993 upset of mighty Michigan was another chapter in Notre Dame's storied history. *Under the Tarnished Dome* became an afterthought as Notre Dame moved to the forefront of the national championship picture.

*   *   *   *

The Michigan fans were despondent. An ominous gloom set over those same tailgaters who had been so boisterous just a few hours before. Subsequent losses to Michigan State, Illinois and Wisconsin caused many fans to lose all hope. The Preacher, Art Wahl, was one of them, at least until Scott and Paul rifled off the following letter to him:

Dear Ms. Wahl:

The Magnified Despair of Defeat has reduced you to making a damn fool out of yourself! Those who stay WILL be Champions! Those who don't are nothing but yellow-bellied, sap-suckin', cowardly, fair-weather, gutless, spineless traitors!! You, ma'am, appear to be in the latter category. If you expect to revel in the joys of victory, you must be prepared to face the aforementioned Magnified Despair of Defeat like a man. Gary Moeller is a man. Bo Schembechler is a man. Fielding H. Yost was a man. Bob Ufer was a man. What does that make you?

What are your alternatives? Become a Buckeye (they won last week)? Become Vermin? How about a Sparty Maggot? What are you thinking, ma'am? A Michigan Man never, never, ever gives up. It seems you have a choice to make: be part of the winningest tradition in the history of man's inhumanity to man, or get a Neiman-Marcus card and spend your Saturday afternoons at the mall with your lovely wife.

Yours in Yost,
The Guts and Glue of the Maize and Blue.

Scott and Paul were happy to report that Art made the right choice. Every sports fan should be required to memorize these words of wisdom. You can say what you want about the dynamic duo, but just remember this: After big victories, it's a tradition for fans to leave roses on the graves of Bob Ufer and Fielding Yost. Scott and Paul also leave roses after big losses. God bless their cotton-pickin' Maize and Blue hearts.

Baton Rouge, Louisiana
LSU vs. Auburn

Let the Good Times Roll

Editor's note...When I asked Bob and Phil about the most immediately noticeable difference between football in the North and the South, aside from the food associated with each, they both said, "the food." After I explained what I had meant with the phrase "aside from the food associated with each," Bob answered, "the Cajun food," and Phil added, "the drinks." Changing my tactics, I asked, "What was the most noticeable difference between the people preparing the food in Michigan and the people preparing the food in Louisiana?" Phil said the people in Michigan didn't know how to cook jambalaya, and I almost gave up. But after hearing the sordid details of their southern swing (LSU, Clemson, Georgia, Florida State, Alabama and every county fair in between), I understood why they considered the South to be the epicenter of Saturday Afternoon Madness.

LSU marked the beginning of our five week swing through the heartland of southern football. The culture surrounding football in the South is markedly different from that of any other region of the country.

Aside from being friendlier (assuming that you're wearing the proper colors), southern fans tend to be much louder than their northern counterparts: by a three-to-one ratio, according to most accounts. This hootin' and hollerin' actually dates back to the "rebel yells" and "scarers" used by Confederate soldiers to psych themselves up during Civil War battles. If the War Between the States had been a yelling contest, we'd all be eating grits and watching *Dukes of Hazzard* reruns.

But describing Southern football fans as friendly people who like to cheer doesn't tell the whole story. According to the gospel of southern-fried college football:

> *In the Northeast, it's a cultural exercise,*
> *In the Midwest, it's a slugfest,*
> *Out West, it's a tourist attraction,*
> *In Texas, it's for big stakes,*
> *But in the South, it's a religion.*

If southern football is a religion, then Saturday is the holy day of obligation. As sportscaster Tim Brando told us, "Weddings, funerals, and everything else all take a back seat to football." In the South, an unplanned pregnancy is one that results in a birth on a football Saturday, and mixed marriages are those between Alabama and Auburn fans. We even heard one booster brag about his favorable divorce settlement: "She got the house, the boat, and the kids, but I got the [football] tickets!"

Clemson Sports Information Director Emeritus Bob Bradley, who has attended 440 consecutive Tiger games, told us about a woman who was sitting in the midst of three empty seats, with her jacket draped over two of them and her lunch bag on a third. When someone asked whose seats she was saving, she replied that they belonged to her husband, her daughter and her son-in-law. The puzzled fan asked why they were late coming to what promised to be an exciting afternoon of football. The woman explained: "My husband just died, and my daughter and son-in-law are at the funeral."

Other regions may match home attendance figures, but southern fans are legendary for taking their enthusiasm on the road. Officials at Raleigh were once forced to halt a game because the visiting Clemson fans were drowning out the North Carolina State quarterback's signals. Southern schools accommodate their legions of nomadic fans by rarely scheduling games outside the region. Then again, the real reason for this premeditated myopia may be simpler; southerners just don't care about football played anywhere else!

We experienced this *confederocentrism* first hand. Everywhere else we visited, fans seemed preoccupied with Notre Dame. But during our southern tour, we barely heard mention of them. NBC paid millions for the rights to broadcast Notre Dame home games, only to have a good portion of their southern affiliates opt to carry the SEC telecasts instead. Of course, when Notre Dame does make one of their rare Dixieland appearances, the games are no less than holy wars.

Perhaps the feelings of most southerners were best summed up by the Tennessean who wrote, "Southerners don't think anybody else can *really* play football. Even when they're losing to a team from the North or the West, they still don't believe that those people truly understand the game. I think it goes back to the Civil War. We lost, but we had the best soldiers. Ohio State and Southern Cal and all the rest of them have the big stadiums and lots of money and millions and millions of boys playing high school ball, but we got the players."

*   *   *   *

As anxious as we were to experience the lunacy of southern football, we must admit to fretting over how a couple of loudmouthed Jews would be treated in a state that nearly elected Ku Klux Klansman David Duke as its governor, but as always, we had a foolproof plan. We decided to avoid potential problems by making a few alterations to our names. After all, it did wonders for Geraldo. And thus, instead of Waldstein and Silverman, we planned to spend the next five weeks traveling as Bob Winston and Phil Silvers.

While our feeble attempts at checking our own transmission fluid must have attracted some suspicion, our cover was completely blown during our first Baton Rouge radio appearance. One of the listeners invited us to his tailgate, the culinary centerpiece of which was to be brisket. We offered to bring the rye bread, Russian dressing and kosher dills. After this slip-up, we abandoned our charade. Not that it mattered. The only time religion ever became an issue was when we decided to limit our daily pork consumption to only two servings for the entire week of the Jewish high holidays. Besides, those crackers were to busy recycling old Civil War jokes to even notice our Hebraic ancestry. (Can you imagine how cocky they would be if they had actually won the war?)

*   *   *   *

In Louisiana, "lagniappe" is a term used to describe any unexpected bonus. When the mailman accidentally delivers someone else's compact discs to your house, that's lagniappe. When you watch a rerun of *M.A.S.H.* and Col. Flagg makes a guest appearance, that's lagniappe. But most of all, when you're treated to an endless barrage of complimentary Cajun feasts, that's serious lagniappe! Lagniappe is the word that best describes our entire LSU experience. We were praying not to be lynched. Instead, we were treated like kings by the Tiger faithful. We were hoping the limo wouldn't completely fall apart. Not only didn't it break down, but we got it detailed and gassed for free, courtesy of Hammond Aire Spa. After an overdose of Baton Rouge lagniappe, we knew that the completion of the trip was our manifest destiny.

In hindsight, it seems ironic that the place we feared the most turned out to be the single place we would most readily revisit. In fact, LSU wasn't even on our original schedule. Thank goodness for transplanted southern football fanatic Sam Drucker, who had told us about "The Night the Tigers Moved the Earth." In a 1988 game against highly rated Auburn, LSU trailed 6-0 late in the fourth quarter. But when Tommy Hodson connected with Eddie Fuller for the game-winning touchdown, the Tiger Stadium crowd of 79,431 erupted with such a thunderous explosion that the resulting tremor registered on a nearby seismograph. Needless to say, we quickly revised our plans so we could witness Auburn's first visit to Death Valley since the night they rocked the earth.

We should have realized that the southern swing was going to be eventful after our pilgrimage to Graceland. There's nothing like getting ripped off by a dead hillbilly. The "King of Rock and Roll" has posthumously become the "King of Merchandising." They even sell Elvis cookbooks, as if anyone really needed a recipe to deep-fry a peanut butter sandwich. Marge Simpson may have best summed up Graceland when she said: "I used to think I had the tallest head of hair in the world, then I visited Graceland."

*   *   *   *

During the entire 1,500 mile drive from Michigan to Louisiana, Bob bragged about being an expert in southern culture. Thankfully, Baton Rouge radio personality Buddy Songy quickly pointed out that two years of watching basketball at Duke (The University of New Jersey at Durham) in no way qualified him as a child of Dixie. Aptly named, Buddy made it his personal mission to ensure that our week in Baton Rouge was the highlight of our trip. Beside stuffing us with what amounted to a city-wide complimentary buffet line of Cajun cuisine, Buddy introduced us to some of the most interesting characters ever to park their butts in a stadium seat. He even risked a catastrophic ratings disaster by allowing us to babble away during his afternoon sports-talk shows.

Just hours after we arrived in Baton Rouge, Buddy put us on the air. After describing us as a couple of Yankees writing a book about the best venues for college football, he let his listeners spend the rest of the afternoon explaining why there is no better football atmosphere than "Saturday Night on the Bayou." They alternated between entertaining us with stories of LSU football glory and describing their favorite game-day rituals. We couldn't believe how many ingenious methods there were for sneaking alcohol into a stadium. The calls ranged from one guy describing his attempts to convince his lady friend of the day to "stuff a half-pint of Jim Beam down her bra" to one liverless guy transforming his colostomy bag into a whiskey pouch. Respectful of his duty to maintain at least the appearance of propriety over the air, Buddy warned his listeners, "There's no alcohol allowed in Tiger Stadium, but beware of funny-looking radios." Buddy also solicited about a dozen invitations to tailgate parties for us. As if he could read our minds, he also made sure the menu was up to par before accepting on our behalf.

Every afternoon, we would tune in to Buddy's show and occasionally make short cameo appearances. Beside allowing us to embarrass ourselves in front of a larger audience than we had ever thought possible, these dalliances with radio made our research infinitely easier. At Penn State and Michigan, we had to hunt out stories. At LSU, stories found us.

Given our warped system of priorities, Buddy could have given us a publishing contract with a $500,000 advance and we still would have considered his role as maitre'd at Baton Rouge's tastiest eating establishments to be his greatest contribution to our trip. Every afternoon, Buddy took us to one of his sponsors' restaurants and stuffed us with everything on the menu. By the end of each day's feast, severe gastric distress would force us to retreat to our motel room. Then, two hours later, we would tune in Buddy's show only to hear him cackle, "You wouldn't believe what those Yankees ate today..."

The first stop on Buddy's caloric cavalcade was Cafe Louisiana. As an introduction to Cajun cuisine, Buddy started us off gently with some Cajun shrimp and crawfish, complete with pinching and sucking. This segued into fried catfish, Mama Jama's blackened snapper, stuffed jalapenos, red beans and rice, and jambalaya all topped off with Viola's famous bread pudding.

As tasty as the lunch was, Bill "Chico" Moore was the highlight. Chico provided our indoctrination into the cult-like mentality of the southern football fanatic. No, cult is not the right word. It doesn't quite do justice to the all-encompassing nature of these fans' support.

Like many of the other football fanatics we encountered, Chico could be compared to Sunny the Cuckoo Bird. Except for watching gladiator movies with Toucan Sam, Sunny is a seemingly normal cartoon bird. But put a bowl of Cocoa Puffs in front of him and Sunny goes completely cuckoo. Likewise, Chico is a well-respected Baton Rouge businessman with a lovely family and a beautiful home. But Chico goes absolutely cuckoo for LSU football. One look at his purple-and-gold limousine, with the words "LSU Fighting Tigers" painted on the side, made the comparison seem that much clearer. As we checked out his Tigermobile more closely, we found the words "Geaux Tigers" reversed into the front grill (so it reads perfectly in another car's rearview mirror). It became apparent that maybe Chico is a lot more closely related to Sonny the Cuckoo Bird than even he would like to admit.

Chico has gone to incredible extremes to show his LSU pride. For years, he attended every game feted in a purple-and-gold tuxedo, complete with matching cowboy boots and top hat. Chico admitted that the top hat might have been unnecessary, but he pointed out it blended nicely with his purple-and-gold afro wig. On a particularly cold day, Chico could be seen sporting his custom-made purple mink coat. Not one to hoard the LSU-wear, Chico bought his wife the perfect football gift: an LSU cheerleader outfit that, oddly enough, never made it out of the house. Sadly though, Chico's ensemble has been mothballed at the request of his mortified teenage daughter.

Chico's daughter was the only chink in his purple-and-gold armor. It was her birth that kept Chico from the only LSU game, home or away, that he has missed during the past 17 seasons. Not even his own sister could do this. (He skipped her wedding to attend a road game at Kentucky.)

Chico has even converted his living room into a shrine to Tigerdom. As we entered his personal mosque, Chico proudly proclaimed, "Everything has a personal connection." Not one for subtlety, Phil asked, "What's this chunk of garbage on the wall?" Pointing at a small red hat that had apparently been singed by flames, Chico explained: "That hat was thrown at me by an irate Alabama fan after we snapped an 11-game losing streak against them in 1982. After the flame burned out, I picked it up, wrote the score of the game on it and hung it here." One man's refuse can be another man's Picasso. (Would this also justify the empty pizza boxes that littered the back seat of our limo?)

Other items scattered across Chico's living room/shrine included: a plethora of shirts and helmets, a videotape of Shaquille O'Neal missing 19 consecutive shots at a birthday party for Chico's son, Gavin Grey's Heisman Trophy from the movie *Everybody's All-American*, the hunk of sod kicked up by Gary James as he scored the game-winning touchdown against

75

Notre Dame in 1985, a national championship ring and various other knickknacks. Each item provided insight into LSU's gridiron history — and the passions of one of its most devoted fans. As Chico described the history of each memento, a detailed story of his life emerged — sort of like a three-dimensional scrapbook. Maybe this sounds like an exaggeration, but it's a story common to those who have spent just about every fall weekend of their lives religiously following college football.

Everybody's All-American chronicled the rise and fall of fictitious football hero Gavin Grey. Because the movie was shot on LSU's campus, there was speculation that it was inspired by Billy Cannon's 1983 incarceration for counterfeiting. As a youth, Cannon possessed such an incredible combination of strength and speed that there was debate about whether he was the strongest sprinter or the fastest shot putter in track-and-field history. Beside being the first true southerner to win the Heisman Trophy, Cannon led LSU to the 1958 national championship. Dr. Cannon is now an orthodontist who, despite his legal predicaments, remains immensely popular in Baton Rouge. Of Cannon's run-in with the law, Chico said: "He got involved with the wrong people. He admits he made a mistake. He paid the price for it, and we forgave him." We guess disposable heroes aren't a part of southern culture.

---

* * * *

One of the most distinguishing characteristics of the South is the unique kinship that exists between politics and football. For example, it took a threatened act of the state legislature to get Alabama and Auburn to resume their rivalry after a 31-year hiatus. The football/politics connection was never stronger than during the reign of Governor Huey Long. When he wasn't running the Kingdom of Louisiana, the Kingfish was sure to be with his Fighting Tiger football team. Before games, he delivered inspirational pep talks. During the games, he paced the sidelines, arguing with referees and urging the coaches to run the plays he diagrammed. After an emotional loss to heavily favored Tulane, he granted the head coach a three-year contract extension, only to run him out of town the following season. (These moves had Phil scrambling for a copy of the Louisiana charter.)

Of all the Long stories (sometimes confused with tall tales) we heard, some give particular insight into the extent to which this infamous governor tipped the scales for his beloved Tigers. When advance ticket sales for a 1934 game against SMU were abysmally low because the circus was in town, Long resolved the situation with the same acumen he used to dispatch political rivals: He threatened to invoke an archaic ordinance that would have forced Barnum & Bailey to dunk each animal in cattle dip. (Does that taste anything like artichoke dip?) The circus was rescheduled, and game ticket sales soared. Spurred on by a thunderous crowd, LSU fought Rose Bowl-bound SMU to a tie.

In another Long shot, the governor wanted to increase Tiger support for a key road game against Vanderbilt by providing discounted travel to Nashville. When the railroads initially balked at his request, Long threatened to reassess the value of their land from $100,000 to $4,000,000. Naturally, the railroads drastically reduced their fares. When the train arrived in Tennessee, Long led a parade of 6,000 students and 125 band members down the streets of Nashville. Local headlines declared, "Huey Long Invades Tennessee." After quarterback Abe Mickal led the Bayou Bengals to the upset victory, Long tried to appoint him to the state senate, even though Mickal was an underage resident of Mississippi.

There were many other outrageous acts perpetrated by the Kingfish in the name of LSU football. He invited his favorite players to live with him in the governor's mansion, dispatched coaches on cross-country missions to bring home prized recruits and even co-wrote the band staple, *Touchdown for LSU*. And according to popular legend, as Long lay dying from an assassin's bullet, his final words were, "What's going to happen to my poor boys at LSU?"

*   *   *   *

The rest of the week was a continuous ride on the Buddy Express, with frequent stops at stations featuring Baton Rouge's most colorful characters. At Phil's Oyster Bar, we enjoyed some gumbo with proprietor Gus Piazza. Phil's has quite a reputation around town, in part due to Gus' Cajun magic and in part due to the clientele. On any given night, Phil's patron list reads like a veritable who's who in the world of sports. Having been a football manager during the early '70s, Gus had more than a few interesting stories to tell.

One of his favorite tales recounted LSU's 1972 victory over perennial rival Ole Miss. Led by Heisman Trophy candidate Bert Jones, LSU entered the game with a 6-0 record and legitimate national championship aspirations. However, Ole Miss was not intimidated and took a 16-10 lead late into the fourth quarter. With time running out, Jones drove his Tigers downfield for the potential game-winning score. With four seconds remaining, LSU lined up at the 12-yard-line for one final shot at victory. When the pass fell incomplete, the Ole Miss players euphorically celebrated their victory. But miraculously, there was still one second on the Tiger Stadium game clock. Given a second lease on life, Jones found Brad Davis in the end zone for the game-winning touchdown. With a sly Southern drawl, Gus admitted, "We got a little break there." After the controversial finish, a bitter Ole Miss fan left a sign at the Louisiana-Mississippi border reading: "Welcome to Louisiana. Turn your clocks back one second."

Gus also recalled the 1979 game against Southern Cal, when a rebuilding LSU squad came up against the defending national champion Trojans, a juggernaut that featured Heisman Trophy winner Charles White, future NFL Hall-of-Famers Ronnie Lott, Anthony Munoz and Marcus Allen, and the usual cast of collegiate standouts. On paper, the game appeared to be a rout. However, this contest was to be played at Tiger Stadium, and that alone gave LSU some hope.

Gus said the tone for the game had been set the previous summer when he was vacationing in Las Vegas and ran up against a gentleman who was heavily touting Southern Cal for the upcoming season. When the Trojan booster learned of Gus' occupation, he proclaimed, "We're gonna teach you something about how to play football."

Gus warned his overconfident adversary: "When you come to Baton Rouge, you better have your jock strap pulled up to your nose, 'cause we're gonna scare you!" Later, he learned that he had been talking with the longtime voice of the Trojans, Tom Kelly.

True to Gus' words, LSU played an inspired game, man-handling the much larger Trojans. If not for a controversial face mask penalty that extended USC's last drive, LSU would have pulled off the upset. After the game, the LSU fans cheered, "We're proud of you! We're proud of you!" Trojan coach John Robinson called Saturday night in Baton Rouge "the scariest place I've ever been." USC's All-American lineman Brad Budde later said, "Death Valley makes Notre Dame look like Romper Room." Even Tom Kelly was conciliatory, calling Gus after the game and admitting, "You kicked our butts; we just won the game."

No doubt a fair amount of credit for LSU's valiant perfor-mance could be attributed to the vocal support of the Tiger faithful, which probably accounted for the 150 cases of laryngitis reported to the university's infirmary the next day .

As much as we enjoyed Gus' stories, our most vivid memory of the afternoon (apart from Gus allowing us to lie down in his walk-in freezer and make snow angels) involved a nonde-script, denim-clad gentleman who joined us at Gus' table. When he introduced himself as Dr. Allen Copping, Phil leaned over to Bob and whispered, "Would it be in bad taste to ask this guy to cure my chronic flatulence?" (Of course, asking Bob about eti-quette is like asking Wilt Chamberlain about abstinence.)

After talking about college hoops with the doctor for close to half an hour, we were shocked to learn that he was actually the president of LSU. This experience explains a lot. Where else could two slobs enjoy a bowl of gumbo with a university presi-dent? Huey Long wasn't kidding when he declared, "In Louisiana, every man is king!" Proving that he was a much better administrator than judge of character, Dr. Copping even invited us to his house for pregame festivities.

*   *   *   *

On Friday, Buddy trucked us over to the Jones Creek Cafe. When they institute the death penalty for poor career deci-sions, we want our final meals at the Jones Creek Cafe. We started with a couple of huge bowls of shrimp bisque and enough oysters on the half shell to make us lust for Phyllis Diller. Semibloated, we thought we might get a short rest before the next course — course not. The waitress brought over a couple of soft-shell crab "po' boys," sandwiches big enough to make even Dagwood Bumstead envious.

If this lunch had been a prize fight, the referee would have stopped it midway through the po' boys. Instead, they may have inflicted permanent injury by feeding us a tray of boudin. Boudin is some sort of bizarre Cajun sausage. For our own good, Buddy wouldn't tell us what was in them. When one of the patrons explained, "They taste kind of like an uncircumcised penis, only better," we both made mental notes to never get incarcerated with him. We prefer to describe boudin as tasting of rice, spices and animal by-products too foul for ordinary sausage. We were instructed to cut off one end of the sausage and suck the meat out. (Phil's legal background made him particularly adept at sucking the meat out of things.) In hindsight, we're not sure whether this is truly the correct method of eating boudin, or whether we were on the receiving end of some sort of twisted Rebel vengeance prank. Bob claims he often wakes up in the middle of the night in a cold sweat, tormented by the faint memory of boudin.

Just as we were finishing our meat-sucking session, something unique happened. Into the restaurant walked LSU offensive coordinator, Lynn Amedee, along with several members of his staff. We suppose it's not unusual for a couple of guys to leave work a little early on a Friday afternoon and enjoy a few pops before the weekend. Heck, everyone needs to blow off a little steam. But to see a bunch of football coaches kickin' back the day before a game seemed weird to say the least. Shouldn't these guys be immersed in game films right up until kick-off? What were they doing drinking beers and making fairly specific references to their game plan with the other patrons in the bar, those same bozos who had been hootin' and hollerin' for us to suck more boudin? We were confused again.

The simple explanation is that LSU is just different. It seemed like everywhere we went, we were bumping into football coaches. That evening, we experienced the ultimate shock when we found head coach Curley Hallman mingling with the fans at the tailgates. According to the coach, "Tailgating with family, friends, and classmates is an essential part of the atmosphere of game day." Welcome to the Republic of Louisiana!

*   *   *   *

Nothing in our lives could have possibly prepared us for game weekend at Baton Rouge. As one fan warned us: "Saturday Night is LSU football. So is Saturday afternoon, Friday night, Friday afternoon..." Buddy maintained that the whole week in Louisiana builds to a crescendo of madness. He summed it up as, "You get six days of foreplay and one incredible bang on Saturday night."

The RVs start to line up Thursday afternoon, even though the tailgate doesn't begin in earnest until Friday night. Similar to the Olympic flame, the first flicker of barbecue fire signals the beginning of the festivities. The jambalaya (the consensus fan favorite, and Bob's adopted mantra) can be prepared on the morning of the game, but the meats need to begin slow cooking the night before. With giant spits for roasting the mammal du'jour (we think it was manatee) and witches' cauldrons big enough to bathe Chris Farley, the preparations for these dishes were so precise that even NASA could learn something from these people.

With Buddy serving as our guide and spiritual guru, we ran the gamut of Friday night hot-spots. Eventually, we were drawn to one particularly lively tailgate. This party stood out because of its two unique calling cards: a battle-scarred old camper ("The Party Box") and a rotating ceiling fan suspended from an old tree limb. The jubilant group enjoying the cool breeze of the fan told us that the Party Box was a broken-down conversion trailer that had been procured from the side of the road in exchange for some pocket change and cigarettes. Since that time, and with few refurbishments, the Party Box has become something of a legend in the annals of partydom Tigerstyle. For five years, the Box has served as the backdrop for everything from visits from Elvis impersonators to anniversary parties; it was also widely recognized as a favorite stop of former coach Curley Hallman. Once again, Buddy had led us to the promised land.

Editor's note....*Otey White, one of the owners of the Party Box, has used his public relations savvy to aggressively promote the "Party Box" to any media unfortunate enough to be within* *earshot. As Bob and Phil watched the denizens of the Box, I suspect that they had to have recognized a kindred spirit: talentless guys with a whacked out vehicle pursuing a little sports-driven public self-aggrandizement. When I brought this to their attention, they both shrugged, for their mouths were full.*

*　　　　*　　　　*　　　　*

Chico Moore in full regalia

Saturday morning, the parking lots filled with revelers. By noon, as far as the eye could see, parties erupted, partiers partied and party-hats festooned every Cajun noggin. LSU made the other tailgates seem like elementary school picnics in comparison, but tailgates are more than Bacchanalian orgies. These celebrations are focused on football sure, but football as it relates to family and friends.

Much to our delight, we were inundated with food (we grudgingly ate everything offered) and LSU football trivia, stories and lore. Fans told us one story more than all the others combined. It was sewn into their collective consciousness, like some Orwellian implant. It was the story of Billy Cannon's 1959 Midnight Run, but it might as well have been Paul Revere's Midnight Ride for the importance attached to it by the locals. Even people younger than the pizza burns on the roof of Phil's mouth could describe the eerie fog rolling in off the bayou and retrace Cannon's steps as he darted through defenders to return a punt 89 yards for the fourth-quarter touchdown that gave top-ranked LSU a 7-6 victory over third-ranked Ole Miss. The reality of the story was in itself exciting, but the embellishments added by the LSU fans make Cannon's Midnight Run one of the greatest stories ever told.

They told us that the fog was so thick that only the fans within a 10-yard swatch of the action could tell what was actually happening. Unfortunately, that accounted for a rather incongruous description. From all accounts, the story went like this: As Cannon fielded the punt deep in his own territory, he was beset by fog-spawned locusts. Undaunted, he darted in and out and through the locusts, would-be Ole Miss tacklers and even two 15-foot alligators that had happened to wander onto the field. Then, just as he was about to break the goal line with the game-winning touchdown, the marching band spontaneously combusted. Miraculously, he saved the entire brass section, resuscitated the tuba player, danced a jig in protest of the British occupation of Ireland and still had time to cross the goal line.

Beyond the collective memories, each fan had a personal story of exploits in support of their beloved Tigers. Jimee and Chip Simon told us how they were heartbroken when Chip's career forced them to move to St. Louis. Jimee can recall inviting people over who knew absolutely nothing about LSU football, and feeding them purple and gold pancakes before watching games. She also remembers serving 120 people gumbo before the 1983 Orange Bowl. At least those games were on television. When the networks weren't so kind, Chip lived in his car on Saturday nights, because it was the only place where he could pick up the LSU radio broadcast — as long as the sky was overcast, the car was parked at a certain angle on the uphill portion of the driveway and he was in the right position in his seat!

Even the Auburn fans were willing to put their two cents in. They overwhelmingly declared Baton Rouge to be their favorite SEC road trip. This sentiment seems to be echoed by virtually every red-blooded, 46-chromosomed, Saturday afternoon warrior who has ever experienced football on the bayou.

*   *   *   *

The tailgate that Buddy had set up with Chico attracted a wonderful, yet bizarre, menagerie of Tiger fanatics. In attendance was sports announcer and Louisiana native Tim Brando. When Bob later bragged to his mother about meeting Tim, she expressed relief that Mr. Brando had gotten over his legal difficulties, and mentioned how difficult it must have been to grow up in the shadow of such a famous father.

Also in attendance at the party was high school phenom Josh Booty, who was in the midst of an unofficial visit to LSU. Beside being rated by *Baseball America* as the single best high school prospect in the nation, Josh had been heralded by *USA Today* as the top quarterback in the country. After hearing his credentials, Bob pulled Josh aside and explained to him the advantages of playing Ivy League football. When Josh seemed unimpressed, Bob jokingly offered him $50,000 to quarterback the Pennsylvania Fighting Quakers. Before you could say, "recruiting violation," the entire Booty entourage was threatening us with bodily harm. The offer must have been insultingly low.

What a scene for an 18-year-old to witness. The electric atmosphere helped overshadow LSU's recent less-than-stellar performances. Apparently, a couple of strong recruiting classes had the fans believing that the program had rounded the corner to respectability. Furthermore, with the specter of darkness creeping over the bayou, the festivities were now in full swing. There was even a country band and hundreds of people doing the electric slide in front of the stadium. We weren't at all shocked when Josh signed a letter of intent to attend LSU. (Josh later broke the hearts of the Tiger faithful by signing a zillion-dollar baseball contract with the Florida Marlins that prohibited him from playing football.)

Shortly before kickoff, we followed a mass of fans over to a path being cleared from a road that led toward the stadium. It was here that the Golden Band from Tigerland and football players paraded by on their way into the stadium. We stood crunched together, like the devout at a papal procession, awaiting our newly adopted heroes. First the band and then the players filed by, eyes focused straight ahead, intent on the task at hand: defeating Auburn.

After the team passed, we entered Death Valley. Louder than a Who concert, and more closely packed than a coach flight to Hawaii, the physical conditions in the stadium can breed insanity. Tiger Stadium is one of America's most unique sporting venues. In 1928, the university wrestled with the dilemma of adding stadium capacity or building much-needed new dorms. Displaying the wisdom of Solomon, they built 1,500 dorm rooms within the stadium, while increasing seating capacity by 10,000. Similarly, not too long ago, a dispute arose about whether to allocate funds to expand the stadium or renovate the library. Some fans still refer to a certain section of the stands as "the library."

Much like the city of Baton Rouge, the pregame show was a gumbo of Southern spirit and Cajun fire with just a splash of New Orleans flair. It just may be the most spectacular floor show this side of Vegas. As much as we enjoyed the Golden Band from Tigerland and the dancing of the Golden Girls, the highlight was the rolling out of the live Bengal mascot, Mike the Tiger, with the cheerleaders dancing atop his cage.

Tradition says the Tigers will score a touchdown for each growl solicited from Mike. For years, Mike was prompted to growl by fans pounding on his cage, until some killjoys complained that pounding on a defenseless animal's cage was cruel and unusual. Recorded tiger growls are now played before and after big plays.

Earlier in the week, we had stopped by Mike's custom-designed pen, located in the shadows of Tiger Stadium. As a reflection of the hard-partying Tiger fans, we found the tiger mascot passed out next to a huge mound of manure and an empty beer keg. Perhaps it's been the marauding Tulane students that have driven Mike to drink. They've repeatedly kidnapped him, and once they even released him from his cage, freeing him to roam around the LSU campus.

*   *   *   *

Night football, played since 1931, has become as integral to the aura surrounding LSU as Mardi Gras is to New Orleans. Nothing like giving the fans eight hours of tailgating to get them primed for a game. A former Ole Miss coach once lamented, "The worst thing about night games at LSU was not being able to see the whiskey bottles being thrown at you." Accordingly, a recent coaches poll found Tiger Stadium to be the most dreaded place to play.

With game time quickly approaching, we assessed the prospects for wagering again. So far, our results had been abysmal. The failure of Penn State and Michigan to cover the spread left us down $220. But this time, we had an inside track. We had been infected with Lynn Amedee's contagious optimism regarding his team's prospects against Auburn. According to Coach Amedee, LSU was going to open up its offense. It would be a "coming out party" for two speedy young receivers, Germaine Sharp and Eddie Kennison. Unless Auburn had a spy at the Jones Creek Cafe, they would be totally unprepared for the offensive blitzkrieg that was about to be unleashed against them. Moreover, LSU was getting 3 1/2 points at home against an Auburn team that had been mediocre even before being hit with NCAA sanctions. With their program apparently on the rebound, LSU was expecting their largest crowd in years for a game being billed as "Rock the Earth II." Finally, Buddy had been pounding two things into our heads: 1) We should marry a girl from Louisiana, and 2) LSU was going to cream Auburn. We bet $200, double our normal bet. All signs pointed to LSU, or so we thought.

As the game began, we realized why Saturday night on the bayou has been called "a combination of Mardi Gras, the Coliseum during Rome's halcyon days, an early-day Fourth of July celebration, New Years Eve in Times Square and Saturn 3 blasting off." When LSU scored first against an obviously confused Auburn defense, the 74,000-strong erupted in a frenzy. Just as we began counting our money, the skies opened up and literally and figuratively rained on the parade. By the time the deluge ended, Auburn was well on their way to a convincing 34-13 victory. Auburn went on to finish the season as the nation's only undefeated big-time college football team.

After the drubbing, fans filing out of the stadium offered Buddy consolation as he contemplated a postgame beverage. In a procession vaguely reminiscent of a condolence call, the mourners silently met Buddy's eyes and acknowledged that the corner had not yet been rounded and the resurrection of the once-proud program was still off in the future. But if there's one thing that's certain in Baton Rouge, it's that none of the fans will stop waiting and hoping. For when LSU returns to prominence, no one wants to miss the party.

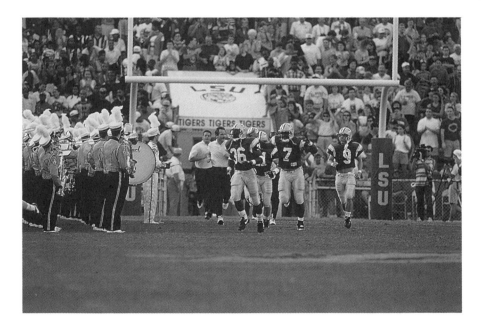

Clemson, South Carolina
Clemson vs. Georgia Tech

A Dinner at Frank's Place

After being wined and dined for an entire week in Baton Rouge, we needed to relax in a sleepy southern town like Clemson. So we left the food fest that was Louisiana and drove east. Unfortunately, our senses of smell had been forever burned out by a week of ragin' Cajun spices. Without nasal direction, we had to rely on guts and determination to find Clemson. "Guts and Determination" was a gas station in South Carolina run by Billy Ray Guts and Deter Mination; they gave us better directions than any map. Who would've imagined that the quickest way to Clemson was "bear left at da' ole Jamison place 'til ya reach da crick, den over an lef."

We entered the town of Clemson after an especially punishing twelve hours on the road. When we say punishing, we don't mean in the context of vehicular difficulty, as there was none (painting the radiator black must have done the trick). We mean ergonomically. You see, we had put on so much weight during our week in Baton Rouge that the seats of the limo no longer snugly caressed our bodies. After the grueling journey in the beast, we were both cramped and knotted up. This furthered our resolve to avoid camping in favor of the comfort of motel living. Fortunately, we came upon a Days Inn that had vacancies, and more importantly, a Jacuzzi.

Before we could even park the car, Bob had jumped out of the limo, ripped off all his clothes, and with the grace of a spherical Brian Boitano, triple-lutzed into the Jacuzzi. The resulting mini-tsunami sent lawn furniture cascading into the parking lot. But that was just the beginning of our problems. Before taking his naked plunge, Bob didn't notice the family wading in the adjacent swimming pool. While the Clemson police and reporters from the *Weekly World News* searched the area for an albino manatee, we checked into the Ramada Inn across the street.

*   *   *   *

Even though Clemson could easily pass for the laid-back small town where the "Bartles and James" commercials might have been filmed, there is an air of excitement that permeates the lazy atmosphere, and football is at the root of it. The 81,000 boisterous orange-clad fanatics that loyally arrive on game day transform Clemson's Memorial Stadium into South Carolina's second largest and worst dressed city.

Football has played a unique role in the development of Clemson University. Without football, Clemson may have just been another southern "cow college." But with football, and the extensive national exposure that accompanies it, Clemson has emerged as a top-flight educational institution. Perhaps the simplest evidence of this relationship is the doubling of applications that coincided with their 1981 national championship.

*   *   *   *

Clemson was founded in 1893 through the bequest of Thomas Green Clemson, who believed that training its citizens in scientific agriculture and engineering was the best way for South Carolina to recover from the catastrophic effects of the Civil War. Clemson was originally an all-male military school with the first coeds not arriving until 1955. In those early days, Clemson was such a bleak place that legendary coach/comic Frank Howard claimed that assistant coaches used to guard the train stations to prevent the love-starved players from skipping town.

The true transformation of Clemson began after an embarrassing loss to Wofford College in 1933. Having heard Coach Jess Neely claim that an extra $10,000 in the football budget would provide the talent necessary to produce a first class football team, Dr. Rupert Fike decided to raise the required funds $10 at a time. As a result, IPTAY (I Pay Ten A Year) was born. Considering the dominant role IPTAY now plays in Clemson athletics, its beginnings were rather humble. During the depression, Frank Howard remembers collecting stacks of bum checks, and many members often paid their dues with chickens. (While bartering is still an accepted from of payment at Clemson, the going tuition rate of 165 chickens per credit-hour is a bit more scratch than most students are willing to pay.)

Perhaps jealous of IPTAY's success in turning the school's football program around, Clemson's detractors claim that IPTAY stands for "I Plow Ten Acres Yearly" or "I Pay Ten Athletes Yearly," in reference to Clemson's numerous NCAA probations. Nonetheless, Clemson began to reap the benefits from IPTAY almost immediately. Aside from the less tangible benefits provided by an aroused community spirit, the quality of play improved. When IPTAY finally reached $10,000 in annual contributions, Jess Neely fulfilled his promise by leading Clemson to a 6-3 victory over Boston College in the 1940 Cotton Bowl.

Since then, IPTAY has become the most successful athletic fundraising organization in America. It has continued to fulfill its promise of providing athletic scholarships, and with annual dues now set at $100, its activities have expanded to providing funding for capital improvements and academic scholarships. It even provides money to send the Clemson band to all away games, a practice undertaken by few (if any) other schools. To show their appreciation, the names of all IPTAY members are duly noted on a commemorative plaque located on the facade of Memorial Stadium.

Nonetheless, when an organization as powerful as IPTAY emerges separately from the institution it supposedly supports, its activities are bound to arouse suspicion. Former South Carolina coach Warren Geise once commented, "Only God and Frank Howard know what goes on with IPTAY funds." It's not surprising that many people wonder who has the ultimate responsibility for the football team: IPTAY or the university administration. If that seems a bit overstated, keep in mind that it wasn't until 1984 that the university's fund raising efforts finally surpassed those of IPTAY. As further demonstration of their power, 56,000 of the 81,000 seats at Memorial Stadium are reserved for IPTAY members.

*   *   *   *

Undeterred by our little misunderstanding at the Days Inn, we headed over to the Esso Club. Located in the shadows of Memorial Stadium, the Esso Club is a converted gas station so down-homey that it once featured kudzu growing from its ceilings. Most of the time, it's a quiet country bar where locals (read: not students) can shoot pool, eat boiled peanuts and even enjoy a bowl of Brunswick stew. But on football Saturdays, the place becomes the mission control-like nerve center for all things Tigeresque, complete with live bands and hundreds of fans reveling in a huge Clemson blockparty.

We were welcomed into the Esso Club's "educational corner," so named according to "Professor" Jim, one of its agrarian inhabitants, because "if you hang out there long enough, you'll learn everything you need to know." The lesson of the day detailed Clemson's all-consuming hatred of their intrastate rival, the University of South Carolina. Professor Jim told us that even though Clemson was trailing the '92 contest by three touchdowns midway through the fourth quarter, his 83-year-old, partially disabled father refused to leave the game, reasoning "there's always the chance they might break that Gamecock quarterback's legs."

This story epitomizes the bitterness inherent in this rivalry. Until 1959, the Clemson/South Carolina game was always played at the State Fairgrounds in Columbia on the third Thursday in October. Although Clemson always wanted to make it a home-and-home series, the state legislature wanted to keep the game in Columbia. Because the legislature consisted mostly of lawyers, and most lawyers were graduates of South Carolina, the legislature had a decidedly anti-Clemson slant. Needless to say, the Cocks always seemed to receive the lion's share of the revenues, while the Clemson fans were stuck with the worst seats.

Given this shabby treatment, it's not surprising that most Clemsonites harbor deep resentment toward the Gamecocks, a resentment that has occasionally turned violent. After a controversial game at the turn-of-the-century, Clemson militiamen stormed the South Carolina campus with bayonets affixed. Still, common sense usually wins out and despite the heated rhetoric, the most the fans usually do is resort to an occasional practical joke. Even we were shocked by the bad taste of a stunt pulled off during the 1946 game. At half time, a couple of Clemson students stole the South Carolina gamecock mascot and choked the chicken in front of a stunned crowd.

Still, for pure audacity and originality, nothing quite matches the time when a South Carolina fraternity impersonated the Clemson football team before the 1961 game. South Carolina coach Marvin Bass provided the Sigma Nu fraternity with a full set of Clemson uniforms, and in order to be as convincing as possible, the Sigma Nus practiced their routine for an entire month. On game day, while the real Tigers were still in the locker room, the fakes took the field. They were convincing enough to elicit a standing ovation from the Clemson faithful, as well as a few bars of the *Tiger Rag* from the band. Borrowing equally from the Three Stooges, Keystone Cops and pre-Parcells New England Patriots, they put on a memorable pregame show. Even with the players falling all over each other, many fans weren't certain that it was a hoax until the players started dancing the Peppermint Twist. The Gamecock pranksters even planned to introduce a sickly old cow as the Clemson homecoming queen, but in the excitement, the cow dropped dead under the stands.

*   *   *   *

Proving they were far more insightful than their looks indicated, some of the faculty from the educational corner explained to us how there was much more to the Clemson-South Carolina rivalry than two neighboring schools battling for gridiron superiority of a football-crazed state. Football could be seen as a metaphor for Clemson's struggles for parity with their snobby rivals. After having this angle explained, we never watched college football the same way again.

Clemson could be seen as the agricultural school where the yeoman of society are trained to become farmers and engineers. South Carolina, on the other hand, is the capstone school where the sons and daughters of the establishment go to become doctors, lawyers and other members of the establishment.

Without even looking, we're willing to bet that South Carolina has the state's best medical school and Clemson has the leading veterinarian school. Being an Aggie (short for agricultural) isn't about money either. Even though a rancher may own thousands of head of cattle, those big-city white-collar snobs will still look down upon him as being from a lower social status. As demonstrated by the following article from Virginia's *University Journal*, the "Culture vs. Agriculture" theme is common to many other intrastate rivalries.

If you can't decide whether you would rather get a diploma or a head full of lice from your four years of college, here are some sure signs you belong at Virginia Tech:

1) Your parents shared the same womb before the same bed.
2) You think that you're better than your neighbor because he has only one pickup truck on cinderblocks in his front yard.
3) You can play the Star Spangled Banner with your armpits.
4) Your belt buckle is thicker than any book you've read.
5) Rats don't infest your house because they're afraid of what they might catch.

As Professor Jim said, "To understand the rivalry, you must first understand the animosity." The sociological implications surrounding college football are in no way restricted to the "Culture-Agriculture" rivalries. UNC-Duke features a southern state university battling a carpet-bagging wealthy private school. BYU-Utah has a holier-than-thou parochial school against a state school. Oregon-Oregon State could be seen as a politically liberal school clashing with their conservative rivals. Going back a few decades, there is nothing the Carlisle Indians relished more than defeating the oppressive white schools, and until recently, southern coaches often used the Civil War angle to pump up their players for games against northern foes.

*   *   *   *

As we were leaving the Esso Club, the faculty of the educational corner instructed us to seek out the legendary Frank Howard. Coach Howard has served Clemson University for more than six decades, including thirty seasons as head coach. He remains one of the winningest coaches in ACC history. Although he was a bit under the weather from recent back surgery, the opportunity to be entertained by him was one of the highlights of our journey. After spending the entire evening in stitches, we better understood why *Sports Illustrated's* Curry Kirkpatrick called him the only football coach "capable of turning Bob Hope into a straight man." How can you not enjoy listening to a man who once nicknamed a player "Dumb Dumb" because he was "too stupid for only one dumb name."

Although Coach Howard has mastered a disarming dumb hick routine, he is anything but dumb. Upon graduating from high school, Howard received five of the six academic awards given to seniors. Supposedly, the only award he didn't win was for best female scholar. In fact, he originally went to Alabama on an academic scholarship. Besides being a Phi Beta Kappa, Howard was the starting guard on Alabama's 1930 national championship team. In his spare time, he coached baseball at a local insane asylum, perhaps giving him his most useful experience in preparation for a career in collegiate athletics.

When Howard came to Clemson in 1931, he was paid the princely salary of $2,200 a year for services that can best be summed up under the phrase, "jack-of-all-trades." In addition to helping Jess Neely coach football, he served as director of ticket sales, trainer, and equipment room manager. In his spare time, he mowed the fields and lined the tennis courts. He even served as track coach, despite never having seen a track meet in his life. When one of his players asked him which javelin throwing method was better, the American or the Finnish, Frank sent him to the library to read the book *Track & Field.* Two years later, that kid set a new state javelin record, and Howard was proclaimed a coaching genius.

While Howard was performing his duties as team trainer, an injured player once asked him to rub his sore shoulder down with Absorbine Jr. When Coach Howard told him that they didn't have any, the player begged him to pick some up at the local drug store. Howard went down to the store, paid his dime and returned with a bottle of Absorbine Jr. (How heinous did Absorbine Sr. smell?) He pulled out the stopper and waved the bottle in front of the gullible player's nose, allowing him to get a strong whiff. Then, with a sleight-of-hand, Howard put the bottle aside and rubbed him down with hot water. The player sprang to his feet singing the praises of Absorbine Jr. Coach Howard later ventured back to the drug store, returned the bottle and got his dime back. Can you imagine Joe Paterno or Jackie giving one of their players a rub down?

Howard's lengthy tenure is truly incredible when compared to today's practice of hiring and firing football coaches at the drop of a hat. Frank Howard coached for 39 seasons, 30 of those as head coach, before serving as athletic director for several additional seasons. Until back surgery recently sidelined him, he could be found at his Clemson office virtually every day. Howard's dedication has provided the stability that serves as the backbone of the program, and not surprisingly, others have followed his example. Bob Bradley, Clemson's legendary Sports Information Director Emeritus, has been to 440 consecutive Clemson football games. Doc Hoover has joined the team in its traditional walk into Tiger Stadium for 175 games and plans to continue as long as he can walk. The late Herman McGee, longtime equipment room manager, was so devoted to the Tigers that he was buried in an orange casket.

Editor's Note... *I'm not sure, but I think I read the following in an old edition of Life magazine: Oddly enough, Coach Howard did not always harbor gridiron ambitions. As a young man, Frank thought an entertainment career with his cousins Moe, Shemp and Curly Howard was to be his lot in life. Unfortunately, Frank's shtick as the miming Stooge proved tremendously unpopular with fans spoiled on talkies. However, Frank's skills proved to be very useful in his coaching career. It's interesting to note in the old game films, his unique combination of berating a referee and the classic "walking-into-the-wind" routine.*

**Frank Howard carried off the field
after defeating Miami in the 1951 Orange Bowl**

Frank Howard retired from coaching in 1969 because of illness; he claimed the alumni were sick of him. It only seemed fitting that he was replaced with another Alabama man, and when that coach left, still another Bama man replaced him. In fact, Ken Hatfield was only the second coach since World War II without significant ties to the University of Alabama.

While all the subsequent boys from Bama have enjoyed success at Clemson, Danny Ford was undoubtedly the most popular of the lot. In fact, many fans are still fuming about his 1989 dismissal. In eleven seasons, Ford coached the Tigers to five ACC championships, one national championship and two probations. He molded Clemson into an intimidating physical machine that grinded opponents down with superior strength and power. Their blue-collar, take-no-prisoners approach to football appealed to Clemson's hard working fans. More importantly, Danny Ford was a tobacco-spitting, country boy just like Frank Howard.

In fact, there may be no bigger fan of Danny Ford than Frank Howard. Examining a copy of our itinerary, Coach Howard asked us to give Ford a message before the following week's Arkansas-Georgia game. We eagerly agreed and put a fresh tape into our dictaphone. We were expecting a simple salutation to an old coaching buddy. What we got was far better.

In a three-minute soliloquy, Frank told Danny how much he cared about him, and expressed his delight with Danny's success at Arkansas. By the time he had implored Arkansas to "whip those hairy dogs," there were tears in our eyes, and not just from the overpowering scent of tobacco juice in Howard's living room.

We left Howard's house amazed at the level of intimacy we had suddenly attained in the scheme of southern football. Our minds raced as we walked back to our hotel. We envisioned Danny Ford solemnly describing the deteriorating physical condition of one of college football's greatest coaching legends in a dimly lit locker room just minutes before kickoff. Then he would play the tape and the Razorbacks would be so inspired that they would play harder than they had ever played before. And none of this would have been possible without us. Once this fact reached the media, we would be welcomed with open arms into the coaching fraternity. Our trip would gain a new luster. We couldn't believe our luck.

At this point, a little background is needed. If you haven't already figured this out, neither of us possess a great deal of mechanical (or social) skill. Knowing this, Phil still borrowed a 35-millimeter camera to capture our journey on film. When we finally developed the pictures, we were disappointed that three of the five rolls didn't come out. Even worse, of the rolls that did came out, more than half of the photos captured the beauty and austerity of Phil's thumb. From that point on, we used disposable cameras. It was an interesting juxtaposition to see Phil with his cardboard camera standing next to the professional photographers with their 20-inch lenses. Obviously, they felt that they needed longer lenses to mask other inadequacies.

Keeping in mind our electronic shortcomings, you don't have to be a MENSA candidate to realize what happened when we tried to play back Coach Howard's touching message later that day. Realizing that Bob had hit the wrong button while recording, we sat there dazed. Suddenly, the open arms of the coaching fraternity changed their grip and had us in headlocks, while their helping hands gouged at our eyes. The luster of our media coup became a greasy smudge on the paparazzi lens. In an attempt to salvage a horrible situation, we transcribed Howard's message as accurately as we could and planned to deliver it to Ford at his hotel the night before the Georgia-Arkansas game.

*   *   *   *

Coping with the emotionally crushing blow of losing Coach Howard's message had one tangible effect: it made us hungrier. We descended upon the Ramada Inn lounge in search of the elusive chicken wing. Instead, we found Perry Tuttle (not quite as tasty as a properly seasoned wing, but with a splash of tobasco...), a former Clemson All-American cornerback who was in the midst of his weekly radio show. Even though we could have reached a larger audience by preaching at the local Pizza Hut, we eagerly agreed to be guests on his show. After all, the happy-hour food wasn't ready, and the show would keep us away from the video poker.

Perry entertained us with stories of Clemson lore and fan antics, while we shared our experiences from Penn State, Michigan and LSU. But when the waitress brought out a tray of happy-hour appetizers, we simultaneously threw down our head-phones and attacked the buffet. We're not sure who was more bummed out — Tuttle's producer who had to cope with seven seconds of dreaded dead air, or us, when we discovered that the happy-hour buffet consisted entirely of corn fritters.

*   *   *   *

While Howard might be the most sacred name on the Clemson campus (with ex-coach Danny Ford a close second), he isn't the most nationally recognized figure connected with Clemson football. That honor belongs to John Heisman, who coached Clemson from 1900-1903. Although more conventional football historians laud his outstanding coaching record and his innovations to the game (among other things, Heisman is credited with inventing the center snap, audibles, as well as the first scoreboard showing downs and yards), we were far more impressed with his ability to use trickery and deception to advance his team's cause and to cheat his neighbors out of their chickens and cows, which he would later turn into scholarships for his players.

Heisman originated the hidden ball trick. Possessed with the ability to suck his testicles up into his body, Heisman used to make his players watch as... whoops, sorry that was Phil's neighbor, Timmy Heintzman. Heisman's quarterbacks would tuck the ball under their shirts while their teammates scattered, with each pretending to have the ball. With the defense bamboozled and out of position, the real ball carrier would scamper downfield for a large gain.

The hidden ball trick was devious, but it pales in comparison with some of Heisman's other ploys. The evening before the 1903 Georgia Tech contest, Heisman sent a bogus team into Atlanta to whoop it up. When the locals saw this undersized motley crew face down in the gutter, they figured Georgia Tech would have an easy victory. Taking advantage of the inflated odds, Heisman bet heavily on his Tigers. Clemson easily whipped an overconfident Georgia Tech squad 74-0.

John Heisman and Timmy Heintzman

This wasn't the first time that Tech fell victim to Heisman's chicanery. A few years earlier, while Heisman was still coaching at Auburn, Georgia Tech traveled to Auburn for a football game. The evening before the game, scores of Auburn students covered the railroad tracks with pig grease. Those same students cheered wildly as the Georgia Tech train skidded right through the station, several miles down the track. The Georgia Tech players, exhausted from having to hike back to town under the searing Alabama sun, fell easy prey to Auburn. Sick of being on the butt end of Heisman's trickery, Georgia Tech hired Heisman away from Clemson after the 1903 season. For the next two decades, Heisman's Ramblin' Wreck dominated southern football.

> The greatest exhibition of Georgia Tech's dominance under Heisman occurred during their 222-0 rout of Cumberland College in 1916. The massacre was so one-sided that Heisman's players were only tackled 16 times as they scored 32 touchdowns. To prevent further embarrassment, the game was shortened by 15 minutes.

*   *   *   *

On football Saturday, Clemson transforms into Tigertown. As serene as Clemson was during the week, it absolutely erupts on game day. The acres of fields where students had been playing Frisbee and hitting golf balls just a few days before had become a vast sea of orange. Orange T-shirts aren't enough for the Clemson fans. We met people with orange pants, orange wigs, orange juice and orange cars.

After mingling with the tailgaters, we returned to the Esso Club. Fans packed the parking lot/outdoor bar, beer flowed from dozens of temporary taps, and country music blared from the band. Despite the game day commotion, the "professors" were still hanging out in the educational corner, perhaps unmoved since we spoke with them three days earlier. When we told them of our mishap with Frank Howard's message, they complained that Danny Ford never should have been fired. They called Ford's dismissal "the worst firing since Fort Sumpter." Many Clemsonites believe that Ford was the sacrificial lamb used to appease the NCAA when Clemson was investigated for improprieties during the late-'80s. As a testament to their devotion to Coach Ford, Arkansas T-shirts have become a hot item on Clemson's campus.

This lingering affection for Danny Ford didn't make life easy for his successor. When Ken Hatfield was introduced as the new coach, the "We want Danny" chants immediately started, and they never really stopped. Even after guiding the Tigers to 10-2 and 9-2-1 records his first two seasons, Hatfield remained an unpopular choice.

People didn't really question Hatfield's coaching ability, at least at first. Hatfield came to Clemson with an impeccable resume. Aside from winning 1983 national coach-of-the-year honors with Air Force, Hatfield was named Southwest Conference coach-of-the-decade after leading Arkansas to consecutive Cotton Bowl appearances. But whatever his coaching acumen may have been, the straight-laced Hatfield just wasn't the right coach for Clemson. While Danny Ford could be found eating greasy cheese burgers and talking football or farming with the folks down at Mac's Drive-in, Hatfield had an aloofness that was simply unacceptable at a place like Clemson. The fans couldn't forgive him for not moving his family from Arkansas to South Carolina. He just wasn't one of them.

If he wasn't accepted while leading Clemson to consecutive bowl games, you can just imagine the abuse he received following Clemson's 5-6 record in 1992, their first losing season since 1976. If the losing season had put one foot in the grave, an embarrassing 59-0 shutout loss to Florida State a few weeks before our arrival had put the other one on a banana peel. A popular sign at the tailgate parties summed up the attitude of the fans: "Arkansas got a good used Ford. We got a lemon."

*   *   *   *

At a school where the fans pride themselves on ostentatious displays of fanaticism, the tiger paw is the most easily observed demonstration of this fervor. Members of the Central Spirit Committee busily paint orange tiger paws on people's faces before all games. They even made it into the *Guinness Book of World Records* for adorning 43,000 fans with tiger paws before the 1985 Wake Forest game.

Tiger paws aren't just reserved for people's faces. The Sigma Phi Epsilon fraternity has gained notoriety for painting tiger paws on all the roads leading into Clemson. When Clemson played in the 1977 Gator Bowl, they lined the highway to Jacksonville with orange tiger paws. They lengthened their tiger paw path all the way to Miami for the 1982 Orange Bowl. Gamecock fans maintain that without the paws guiding them, the Clemsonites would have never made it back to their farms. Fearing a huge orange paw print on our limo, we avoided the Sig Eps.

Aside from painting paw prints, the Central Spirit Committee also runs Spirit Blitz. For one game each season, the Clemson faithful engage in a unique display of school spirit. Past Spirit Blitzes have included unfurling an 80-yard Tiger Paw flag and turning Death Valley into an 80,000-member kazoo band. The tradition began in 1983, when 363,729 helium balloons were released before a game. That stunt earned them another spot in the *Guinness Book*. We assume the choking deaths of 17,000 sea gulls later that day was also a record.

*   *   *   *

Overshadowing the countless tiger paws festooning Clemson proper, Tiger Stadium represents the manifestation of Tiger pride, loyalty and decibel production. If the stadium isn't the toughest place to play, it's a close second. Ironically, Coach

Jess Neely's final bit of advice to Frank Howard before leaving for Rice was not to get talked into building a large stadium. He figured 10,000 bleacher seats would be more than adequate. While Neely was somewhat prophetic in his prediction for what IPTAY could do for the program, his vision for the stadium was not so far-reaching. With virtually all of their 80,000 seats located on the sidelines, Clemson's Death Valley provides one of the most awesome home field advantages in all of sports.

The myths surrounding the stadium add to the aura of Death Valley. It received its nickname when an opposing coach said, "Going to play at Clemson is just like playing at Death Valley." Legend has it that when they were pouring the concrete for the stadium, Coach Howard blessed it by depositing plugs of Penn's Natural Leaf tobacco in the wet cement. But it's more than just the structure that makes this place special. Students pack section GG (Green Grass), a grassy knoll overlooking the east end zone. It's not all that uncommon for a fan who has had a few too many pregame libations to slip and fall, causing a domino effect with those standing below.

Aside from the chew plugs, 80,000 sideline seats and section GG, the crowning glory of the stadium is Howard's Rock. This prized pebble sits on a pedestal at the top of section GG. At first, we couldn't help but wonder what's so special about the rock. Fortunately, everyone at Clemson can (and upon request, will) recite the history of this memorable mineral. It seems that S.C. Jones, a 1919 Clemson graduate, brought Coach Howard a souvenir rock from Death Valley, California. After using the rock as a paper weight for a couple of years, Howard grew tired of it. Too lazy to carry it three feet to the wastebasket, he asked IPTAY Executive Secretary Gene Williamson to get rid of it. Instead, Williamson mounted the rock on a trophy stand. In one of Coach Howard's pregame pep talks, he told the team: "All of you who is going to give me 100 percent when you go into Death Valley today, you can rub my rock. It will give you good luck. Any of you who isn't going to give me 100 percent, keep your filthy hands off my rock."

The rock is now the centerpiece of a pregame ritual referred to as "The Most Exciting 25 Seconds in College Football." (The scramble for the auxiliary urinals at half time of the Arizona State games finished a close second.) We watched the team assemble at the top of section GG just minutes before kickoff. The band broke into the Tiger Rag and the team triumphantly charged down the hill, with each player rubbing the rock for good luck. As 70,000 fans screamed with approval, we now understood why former All-American defensive tackle Michael Dean Perry called running down the hill "the most emotional experience I've ever had." Needless to say, we no longer wonder why they rub a rock at Clemson.

*   *   *   *

In a less than inspired effort, Clemson beat Georgia Tech 14-13. Giving 3 1/2 points, we dropped another $110. After four weeks, the home team had yet to cover the spread. The low scoring game meant an easy afternoon for the Tiger mascot. After each score, the Tiger does a pushup for every point that Clemson has scored. During an 82-24 rout over Wake Forest, the mascot did 465 pushups. If the Clemson Tiger had been at Georgia Tech's 222-0 rout of Cumberland College, he would have done, or at least attempted, 3,600 pushups.

Clemson's one point victory over a mediocre Tech squad did little to placate Hatfield's detractors. The rest of Clemson's season, including a 21-0 shutout loss to North Carolina, was equally frustrating. As the season progressed, home attendance plummeted, inspiring the popular bumper sticker: "Memorial Stadium — Howard built it, Ford filled it and Hatfield emptied it." At the conclusion of the season, Hatfield was replaced by Tommy West, one of Danny Ford's former assistants.

Editor's note... *Shortly after being chased from Clemson, Ken Hatfield took over as coach of Rice University. In his first campaign, Hatfield led the long-suffering Owls to within one game of the Southwest Conference Championship. More importantly, he coached Rice to their first victory over Texas in three decades.*

*   *   *   *

As we walked from Memorial Stadium back to the Esso Club, our hearts were heavy with guilt. Not only had we botched Coach Howard's heart-felt message, we had also offended thousands of Clemson fans by using Howard's Rock to crack walnuts before we realized what it was. We took a little comfort in the fact that the limo hadn't broken down since LSU. Maybe it was really fixed? Yeah, and maybe Ken Hatfield will buy a condo in Clemson.

The Most Exciting 25 Seconds in College Football

Athens, Georgia
Georgia vs. Arkansas

Between the Hedges

While celebrating Clemson's victory at the Esso Club's Educational Corner, we debated our next destination. Phil wanted to witness the dotting of the "i" at Ohio State while Bob had his heart set on rafting down the Tennessee River and singing *Rocky Top* with 95,000 orange-clad Volunteer fanatics. Fearing that we might settle our differences with a game of Spin the Bottle, Professor Jim interceded, recommending a couple of interesting alternatives. After dismissing his suggestion that we "return to Boston and get real jobs," we listened to him sing the praises of Georgia and Georgia's rabid football fans. He even claimed that his cousin is such a diehard Bulldog fanatic that he always misses work the Monday following Georgia losses. What's more surprising is that these absences are somehow condoned as justifiable, much like a death in the family. Still, we knew we could find Saturday afternoon warriors wherever we went. But when Jim told us about the steak and seafood buffet at Charlie Williams' Pinecrest Lodge just outside of Athens, our mouths were watering and our minds were made up. We thanked him, grabbed one final handful of boiled peanuts and hit the road to Athens.

As we watched the tiger paws on the road leading to Clemson whiz by in the other lane, we were stricken by an overwhelming sense of self-assurance. Everything had gone smoothly with the car, too smoothly, so we needed to manufacture our weekly dose of strife, which we did. We made a couple of detours on our way to Athens. The first side trip, a demolition derby at the Anderson County Fair, was a no brainer. Being veterans of the Bangor, Maine State Fair, we couldn't even imagine what genetic mutations the state fairs of the deep south would hold. Anything short of a combination of *Deliverance*, *Texas Chainsaw Massacre* and *National Geographic* would be a major disappointment.

Upon arriving at the fair, our aspirations of entering the limo in the demolition derby were quickly dashed when we learned of the weight limit for the competition. The car was also too heavy, so we parked it in some lady's yard for $2 and entered the fair (a misnomer if ever there was one). As we approached the unruly crowd massed outside the sold-out derby grandstand, we quickly realized that few angry mobs can rival the furor raised by a group of South Carolinians denied their God-given right to watch cars slam into each other.

Displaying a potentially dangerous combination of resourcefulness and poor judgment, Bob slipped the shady fair employee $10 so we could watch the demolition derby while riding the Ferris Wheel for as long as we wanted. Remembering an old *60 Minutes* episode, Phil avoided the wheel of misfortune, instead opting to test his dexterity at some of the fair's other games of chance. To make a long story short, Bob puked up his corn dogs while watching bolts drop from the rickety Ferris Wheel, and Phil's Dartmouth education was no match for the toothless barkers who easily convinced him to empty his wallet on games that appeared to defy the laws of physics. And unless you think being propositioned by a 6-1/2-foot tall, hermaphroditic clown is cause for alarm, the fair wasn't nearly the freak show we were hoping to experience.

As we exited the fair, logic dictated that we drive 70 miles southwest to Athens. Bob dictated that we visit his alma mater, Duke, 275 miles to the northeast. But Phil had absolutely no desire to experience Duke, Duke's preseason basketball scrimmages, or Bob's favorite campus eateries. Because neither of us would budge, we needed a contest of skill to settle our differences. Phil refused to play Twister, claiming his achilles was still sore, so we opted for a game of Password.

There was just one problem. As every experienced player knows, Password requires four players. To circumvent this problem, we devised our own scoring system. For each clue given that resulted in a correct guess, the giver received 1/2 point, and for each correctly guessed word, the guesser received 1/2 point. After two hours and a score of 28-28, we realized that the score would be perpetually tied. Since the scoring system had been Phil's idea, he was deemed the loser and we motored toward Durham with Bob chanting, "Go to hell Carolina, go to hell," for the entire ride.

Upon arrival at Duke, we pitched a tent in front of Cameron Indoor Arena, unofficially opening up Krzyzewskiville, the basketball tent city inhabited by rabid Dukies during hoops season. Unfortunately, this was football season, so we were the sole inhabitants. As we waited for the afternoon scrimmages to begin, two campus cops demanded that we remove our tent. Summoning all of his legal expertise, Phil proclaimed our tent to be part of an anti-apartheid demonstration and warned that any further harassment would constitute a grave violation of our first amendment rights. When Phil saw them pondering the sincerity of his words, he started chanting at them in Hebrew. The officers either didn't know what to make of such a bizarre combination of defenses or grew uninterested, so they left. The immortal Coach K even paid us a visit. While Bob groveled at the feet of his basketball overlord, Krzyzewski made it quite clear that a) we should never ever again park our limo in two of his parking spots, and b) he probably spent too much time with the foul-mouthed Bobby Knight.

After four hours of camping through intermittent rain showers, we ventured into Cameron Indoor Arena to watch the Dukies scrimmage. While an unimpressed Phil napped in the stands, Bob screamed like a lovesick schoolgirl with every Hurley assist and Grant Hill jam. When the scrimmage ended, we packed up our tent, picked up a sandwich at Porky's Pig Palace and set out for Georgia.

*   *   *   *

Our first stop in Athens was the sports museum, where we were introduced to Bill Hartman, Georgia's kicking coach. Having been associated with Georgia football since winning All-American honors as a running back in 1937, this member of the College Football Hall-of-Fame served as an extraordinary tour guide. Beside serenading us with the legends of Georgia football, he futilely attempted to explain to us the nuances of the single wingback offense. (He'd have had more luck explaining Einstein's Theory of Relativity to Forrest Gump.) While immersing us in Georgia's football history, he pointed to a commemorative plaque and told us that if not for the Von Gammons, football might have been banned in the state of Georgia.

Georgia without football? It would be like Miami without beaches, a Big Mac without special sauce, or an autumn without a World Series — oops, guess that one doesn't apply anymore. But it almost happened.

In 1897, Georgia's Richard Von Gammon died from injuries sustained during a particularly brutal game against Virginia. His tragic death sparked the existing sentiment that football was much too violent. In response to this outcry, schools across the South canceled their remaining schedules, and the Georgia Legislature overwhelmingly passed a bill banning football at all Georgia colleges. But just as Governor W.Y. Atkinson was prepared to sign the bill, a letter arrived from Von Gammon's mother imploring him not to let her son's death "defeat the most cherished object of his life." On her urging, Atkinson vetoed the bill. The letter was reprinted in newspapers across the South, causing the anti-football sentiment to ebb. Southern football was saved, and the rest is history.

The Van Gammon incident was symptomatic of the harsh nature of early football. It was so violent, in fact, that after watching the 1893 Chicago-Purdue game, the district attorney tried to indict each and every player for assault and battery.

Despite the game's rough nature, football was very much like sex during the era: the participants seldom showered and wore very little protection. Instead of helmets, these warriors relied on long hair to ward off head injuries. Even when they were issued equipment, it was often used as a weapon rather than for protection. Harvard's Percy Haughton used to equip his team with skin-tight, hard-leather gloves that had much the same effect as brass knuckles. His players also wore horsehair jackets that ripped the fingernails from would be tacklers. The early Harvard-Yale games were so violent that one newspaper printed a postgame injury report instead of a game summary.

Editor's note... *Harvard probably won by a couple of swelled heads.*

During the first half-decade of the 20th century, 71 players died and countless others were maimed from football related injuries. As the injuries mounted, so did the critics. In 1905, President Teddy Roosevelt, whose second cousin suffered multiple fractures during the 1902 Rose Bowl, threatened to ban football unless the game was cleaned up.

In response to Roosevelt's ultimatum, a committee of representatives from 62 colleges met to cure football's ills. Spearheaded by Walter Camp and John Heisman, this caucus established the Intercollegiate Football Rules Committee, the forerunner of the NCAA. Among the sweeping reforms adopted by the IFRC were the legalization of the forward pass, creation of the neutral zone, and football's first rules against fighting. Not since Camp instituted the concept of possession in 1880 had football undergone such revolutionary changes. Heisman called the legalization of the forward pass "the dividing line between early and modern football."

Even after the legalization of passing, teams were slow to incorporate it into their offenses. For one thing, primitive footballs were especially difficult to throw. With a 27-inch diameter (as opposed to the modern-day 21-inch), only a giant could grip the ball. Furthermore, the soft leather ball sopped up moisture like a warm dinner roll, creating a ten-pound projectile that was impossible to control, let alone catch. To make passing even less attractive, several rules restrictions rendered it a high-risk maneuver. For example, passes that were touched but not caught by the offensive team were treated as fumbles.

Despite these restrictions, many schools dabbled with aerial attacks, but few had as much success as Alex Cunningham's Georgia teams. Through his deceptions, the Bulldogs were able to execute some of football's most memorable trick plays. To fake the opposition out of position, Cunningham hid ends out on the sidelines, only to have them sprint downfield at the snap of the ball. In his infamous "helmet play," the quarterback would throw his leather helmet to a receiver who took off with the bogus ball while the quarterback ran for long yardage. But for pure, unmitigated gall, nothing could match the "waterboy play" he pulled off against Alabama in 1912, a full season before Notre Dame supposedly invented the forward pass. During the first half, one of Cunningham's ends roamed the sidelines wearing civilian clothing and carrying a water bucket. With Georgia in need of a big play, the waterboy dropped his bucket and sprinted downfield for a long pass. In the ensuing melee, the Alabama athletic director flattened his Georgia counterpart.

*   *   *   *

While the entire Athens campus erupts with tremors of excitement on game weekends, the epicenter of the festivities is the Ramada Inn. Owned and operated by former letterman Leroy Dukes, the Ramada is more than a hotel; it's a football timeshare. Patrons stay in the same rooms, game after game, season after season. There's no need to check in. They just arrive on Friday, leave on Sunday and eventually settle up their bills. Their room keys are kept on the same key chains as their house keys, and rooms are so valued that patrons have even attempted to bequeath them to their descendants.

Even with an entire hotel packed with rabid fans, Brandon "Bugar" Seeley stuck out because of his fervent Bulldog obsession. While he's been part of the Ramada family since the late '70s, he claims to have been "a Bulldog from birth." Having attended over 350 Georgia football games, Bugar knows Georgia football, or so he told us. (As long as we bought him beer, he would have told us he was from the moon and spent the better part of his life following little green men.)

When we asked Bugar to name the greatest player in Georgia history, he thought for a few moments before responding: "Frank Sinkwich and Herschel Walker may have won the Heismans, but Charley Trippi was the best. Besides being a triple threat back, he was a monster on defense." Bugar also called Quinton Lumpkin the toughest person ever to don the red and black. We called Quinton the toughest person ever to be named Lumpkin. According to Bugar, Lumpkin supported himself by wrestling bears at carnivals.

On the subject of rivals, Bugar told us: "It's no contest. Every Dawg hates Florida." Every season since 1933, Georgia and Florida have clashed at the Gator Bowl in Jacksonville. Because of the exuberance of the fans, this game has been dubbed "The World's Largest Cocktail Party." When Phil asked Bugar if this was because they made the biggest cocktails or because of the number of people involved, the Bugmeister ignored the question. He ranked the 1980 Cocktail Party as being the greatest game in Georgia history, or was it that the 1980 game was the greatest cocktail party in Georgia history?

Behind the running of Herschel Walker and the stingy Junkyard Dog defense, the undefeated Bulldogs entered the Florida game as the second ranked team in the nation. But with a little over a minute remaining, things looked bleak. Trailing 21-20, Georgia faced fourth and eleven from their own 7-yard-line. They needed a miracle; they got a guy named Lindsey. Under heavy pressure, a scrambling Buck Belue hit Lindsay Scott with a crossing pass over the middle for a moderate gain, but Scott somehow juked by several defenders and outran the entire Gator defense into the end zone for the decisive touchdown. In the echo of announcer Larry Munson's now legendary call of "Run Lindsey Run," Georgia went on to capture the 1980 national championship.

Bugar recalled the Florida state troopers being in an especially foul mood following Scott's miracle run: "They were pulling over every vehicle with Georgia plates." One even had the nerve to write Brandon a citation for public urination. When the cop claimed to have spotted the alleged tinkling from a distant bridge, the resourceful Bugar warned him that if he was arrested, he would "bring all the press I could muster into the courtroom, pull out my pecker and challenge anyone to identify it from forty feet, never mind a quarter mile away." Realizing he was no match for Bugar, the officer tore up the citation. Score another victory for Georgia.

*   *   *   *

Beside serving as headquarters for Georgia's most rabid fans, the Ramada also houses most visiting teams. On weekends, its lobby becomes a melting pot of SEC athletics. What a scene. The Mississippi State volleyball players were mingling with their Georgia counterparts, kids were lined up waiting for autographs from their football heroes, and the Razorback boosters had filled the lobby with the Arkansas fight song (and the urinals with wads of chewing tobacco). But through the tumult and the shouting, Loran Smith was somehow able to broadcast his Georgia football show from the lobby. Despite the din, it was the most logical place from which to broadcast. Whenever he needed a guest, his producers simply yanked former players out of the lounge and put them on the air. Leroy Duke's Ramada was everything college football was supposed to be about: family, friends, sportsmanship, and most of all, fun.

As much as we enjoyed the atmosphere, we knew that we would, at some time, have to deliver and then explain the infamous Frank Howard message to Arkansas' Danny Ford. After screwing up the tape and transcribing Coach Howard's heartfelt greeting, we vowed not to let anything distract us from completing our mission. Having just missed Ford, we ventured into the lounge where we met a man who proclaimed himself to be the "Big Dawg" of Georgia football. After a couple of hours of trading stories and libations with this mountain of a man, he told us that he was having pancakes with Danny Ford the next morning. Perfect! Relieved to be lightened of this ponderous burden, we entrusted him with Coach Howard's message.

To summarize, an ailing coaching legend asked us to deliver an inspirational message to one of his favorite protégés, but through mechanical incompetence, we lost the recording. After diligently transcribing the message, we brought it to Coach Ford's hotel. But instead of leaving it with the desk clerk, we gave it to a canine impersonator who covers himself with red and silver makeup and barks at people during football games. Why? Because Coach Ford was going to have breakfast with Big Dawg just hours before an important conference game. Maybe not our stupidest decision, but certainly right up there near the top of the list.

Even though he took us for the college football neophytes that we were, we have nothing but the highest admiration for Big Dawg's commitment to Georgia and Georgia football. Along with his compatriot Super Dawg (thank goodness these guys aren't

South Carolina supporters), Big Dawg salutes the players before and after every game. And it's not just a quick salute either. They both stand at full attention saluting every player as they walk through the stadium's gates. One ex-player recalled returning to Athens following a tough loss only to find both Big Dawg and Super Dawg standing outside in the freezing rain loyally waiting for the team to arrive just so they could salute them.

While we were yapping with Big Dawg, Leroy Dukes attempted to introduce us to former defensive coordinator, Erk Russell. As much as we were impressed by Russell's resemblance to Jerry Tarkanian, we indignantly informed Dukes that since our book was from a fan's perspective, we didn't need to talk with any coaches. What a colossal mistake.

The next day, during the game's half-time celebration, the 1968 Sugar Bowl team was introduced to a healthy applause. When Vince Dooley, the winningest coach in Georgia history, was introduced, the applause grew even louder. But when Erk Russell was introduced, the stadium went dawg gone crazy. Dumbfounded by the thunderous ovation, we asked the student next to us what was the big deal. He looked at us like we had just spit in church and declared, "Erk Russell is the greatest man in the history of Georgia football!"

We later learned that Russell served as Georgia's defensive coordinator and spiritual leader for more seasons than most people could remember. If Dooley was the brains, then Russell was the heart and soul of Georgia football. He inspired his Junkyard Dog defenses by butting heads with them before and after important plays. By the end of most games, Russell's bald pate was completely covered with blood.

Erk was so beloved in Athens that when Vince Dooley was offered the Auburn job just months after leading Georgia to the 1980 national championship, there was strong sentiment for him to move on so that Erk could ascend to his rightful position at the top of the Dawg pile.

When Dooley decided to remain in Athens, Russell accepted the challenge of rebuilding Georgia Southern's football program. Through his energy and charisma, he brought three division 1-AA championships to a school that hadn't played football since World War II. Between 1984 and 1989, Georgia Southern won more football games than any team in America.

But Russell's impact extended far beyond the gridiron. When he arrived, enrollment was just 5,000 students. By the time he retired in 1989, enrollment had skyrocketed to 13,000 students. Coincidence? Maybe. Still, you can't underrate the far-reaching effects that football can have on a university.

As we left the Ramada in search of affordable lodging for the evening, it finally dawned on us that we had been slickered by the Big Dawg. Even worse, there was just no lodging to be found. As you can imagine, the evening took on a somber mood. We argued each other to sleep that night, hopeful that things would improve the next morning.

Erk Russell with blood trickling down his scalp

*   *   *   *

As the sun came up and woke us, we brushed away the leaves and sticks we had used for blankets, exited the cave and drove back to Athens. After a hearty pancake breakfast in honor of the Big Dawg, we took one final walk through Georgia's picturesque campus.

With its stately ante-bellum mansions and flowering magnolia trees, Georgia was one of the most scenic campuses we visited. While admiring the scenery (human and non-human alike), we noticed something strange, and we're not talking about the green-haired, pin-cushioned weirdoes who frequent Athens bustling music scene. We stood there dumbfounded, watching students going out of their way to avoid walking under an arch. We didn't know whether it was bad luck or what, so we stopped a student and asked. His name was Alexander Yaffee and he told us about the North Campus Arch. For generations, freshmen who dared walk under the historic arch were subjected to harsh retribution from the upperclassman. Even though hazing had been abolished, or at least sent underground, most frosh still refuse to walk under the arch. When we asked why they still adhered to such a seemingly meaningless tradition, Alexander explained: "It's a southern thing. You wouldn't understand."

There seemed to be a lot of "southern things" surrounding Georgia football. The Confederate flag flies over Sanford Stadium as well as countless tailgates, and the school song is sung to the tune of the *Battle Hymn of the Republic*. Even more foreign to a couple of carpetbaggers like ourselves, the students dress up for each game. With their white oxford shirts, school ties and tan pants, the men all looked like clones of each other. Except for the occasional flask of bourbon concealed under their sun dresses, the women looked like extras from *Gone with the Wind*.

Still, the most blatantly "southern thing" we observed was the seemingly unnatural loyalty these fans possessed for their football team. Herschel Scott has attended an incredible 467 consecutive games. Bill Robertson occasionally misses a couple of games, but his devotion is just as remarkable. Because of an aversion to flight and a love of fast cars, Bill drives from Ontario, Canada to Athens for almost every Georgia home game. Bahamians Fred and Bonnie Hazlewood didn't even know where Georgia was until they met some hard-core Bulldog fanatics on a cruise. They became so caught up in the Dawgie euphoria that they adopted the school as their own. Both their children now attend the university and the Hazlewoods fly in from Nassau for all home games. They even donated an air-conditioned dog house so that Uga, Georgia's Bulldog mascot, could enjoy the football games in cool comfort.

As we continued our campus tour, we saw scores of fans lined up behind Sanford Stadium hoping to catch a glimpse of or grab a handshake from one of Georgia's greatest legends; no — not Fran Tarkenton or Herschel Walker — but Uga. But the way the faithful were bowing down to him, Uga might as well have been the Pope. He is so revered in Georgia that his drooling mug adorns the cover of the media guide, where he received a two page write-up, double the space allotted to Vince Dooley. While watching him lick himself (Uga, not Dooley), we wondered what made him so popular. It certainly couldn't be intelligence. Generations of inbreeding have rendered Uga a moron, especially in comparison with Texas A&M's Reveille and Yale's Handsome Dan. (If you ask Dan whether he'd rather go to Harvard or die, Dan rolls over and plays dead.)

Furthermore, Uga has never served Georgia particularly well on the field of battle. While Auburn's War Eagle once attacked Florida's Wes Chandler as he scored a touchdown, Uga's most aggressive act has been pooping on Vanderbilt's artificial turf. Still, the devotion that Georgians share for their mascot is well deserved because there may be no harder working dog in college football.

What other mascot makes occasional appearances on the floor of the Georgia House of Representatives? Uga has served as spokesdog for the March of Dimes, the Easter Seals and the Ringworm Society. He is the only live mascot to ever attend the Final Four, and when Herschel Walker won the Heisman, Uga donned a black tie and accompanied him to the awards presentation. No wonder the Clemson fans claim that Georgians can't open up a gas station without Uga pissing on the pumps.

Before taking our seats, we accompanied Sonny Seiler, the man who has provided Georgia with its bulldog mascots since 1956, to the graves of Ugas I-IV, located within the confines of Sanford Stadium. We watched an emotional Sonny lay roses on the gravestones of the departed mascots, each of which was, according to Sonny, "A damn good dog."

> No book on football would be complete without some mention of the origin of Auburn's War Eagle mascot. In the aftermath of a horribly bloody Civil War battle, a wounded rebel soldier found an injured baby eagle. The soldier nursed the eagle back to health and kept him as a living memorial to his fallen comrades. Three decades later, he brought the eagle to the inaugural Georgia-Auburn game. After the Auburn victory, that old eagle let out a few tremendous squawks and flew a victory lap around the field before collapsing to its death. The Auburn faithful have been screaming "War-r-r Eagle!" ever since.

As for the game itself, Arkansas tore through Georgia's mangy-dog defense. Lucky for us that Danny Ford's boys didn't need Coach Howard's words of wisdom, otherwise we may have been hunted down by some tiger paw-wearin' thugs. Yet, even in the face of defeat, the Georgia fans displayed an unbridled enthusiasm for their team and the game itself. During the kickoff that followed a futilely late Georgia touchdown, we even saw one elderly women down on all fours barking for her Dawgs: "Goooo Dawgs! Sick 'em! Woof! Woof! Woof! Woof!" If it had be a professional game, the home fans would have already left or passed out from intoxication.

Some people claim that the lack of professional sports is what makes southerners so rabid about their college football. Bullshit! The devotion that many southerners harbor toward their schools can't be tempered by the presence of professional athletics. Case in point: While we were in Athens, the Atlanta Braves were in the final weekend of an incredibly tight pennant race. With an 0-3 conference record, Georgia was off to its worst start ever. Nevertheless, 80,000 Saturday afternoon warriors jammed Sanford Stadium to support their beloved Dawgs, while at the same time, the Braves were beginning a crucial three game series with the first-place Giants.

After Georgia's shocking 20-10 defeat, we were enjoying a few postgame libations with the Hazlewoods when we noticed their youngest daughter in tears, mourning Georgia's dismal performance. Being the tactful individuals that we were, we reminded her that Georgia was simply a horrible team that had been completely shellacked by a less than mediocre Arkansas squad. She grabbed our tape recorder and started wailing into it: "I love the University of Georgia! I love Georgia!" When you love something that much, every loss hurts.   With that thought in mind, we left Athens and eagerly motored toward Tallahassee for the following week's "Game of the Century" between Florida State and Miami.

Ten Notable Upsets

1911: Carlisle 18, Harvard 15
While Pop Warner's Carlisle Indians relished any opportunity to beat the white man, knocking off the undefeated defending national champions must have been especially gratifying. Jim Thorpe was a one man wrecking crew, scoring all 18 of Carlisle's points.

1913: Notre Dame 35, Army 12
Behind a barrage of forward passes, itty bitty Notre Dame defeated big bad Army. In one fell swoop, Notre Dame gained national football prominence, while legitimizing the forward pass. If Notre Dame lore were the Old Testament, this game would be right at the beginning of Genesis.

1928: Notre Dame 13, Army 7
In the most storied upset since David slew Goliath, Notre Dame "won one for the Gipper."

1921: Centre College 6, Harvard 0
On name recognition alone, this may be the most shocking upset in the history of the game. The Praying Colonels from tiny (300 students) Centre College of Danville, Kentucky used an end-around to hand Harvard their first defeat in five seasons.

1942: Holy Cross 55, Boston College 12
The lightly regarded Purple Crusaders shocked the gridiron world by thrashing their arch-rival, the top-ranked Eagles. However, Boston College's humiliating loss may have saved their lives. After the upset, Boston College canceled its Coconut Grove Club victory celebration. That night, 491 people perished in a tragic fire that consumed the famous night club.

1950: Navy 14, Army 2

This may have been the single greatest upset in a rivalry defined by incredible upsets. Riding a 29-game unbeaten streak, top-ranked Army was a four touchdown favorite over a Navy team that had won only two games all season. But the Middies dominated the game and eliminated the Cadets from the national championship race. Just months later, 90 cadets were dismissed from West Point in the worst cheating scandal ever to rock the Academy. Fielding a squad stocked with underclassman, Army struggled through a two-win 1951 campaign. Army football has never been the same.

1963: College All-Stars 20, Green Bay Packers 17

So what if it was only an exhibition game. How could Lombardi let his NFL champion Green Bay Packers lose to a bunch of college kids? This was the last college all-star game won by the collegians. The series was suspended after Pittsburgh's Steel Curtain ripped the collegians 24-0 in 1976.

1971: Alabama 17, Southern Cal 10

After consecutive five-loss seasons in '69 and '70, many dismissed Bear Bryant as a coaching relic whose drill-sergeant mentality left him ill-equipped for the modern game. Particularly embarrassing was the 42-21 defeat to a physically superior Southern Cal team in 1970. In that game, African-American Sam Cunningham ripped through Alabama's all-white defense for over 200 yards. For their rematch to open the '71 season, Southern Cal was the prohibitive favorite. But Bryant had a few tricks up his sleeve. Besides integrating his team, the Bear had secretly taught them Darrell Royal's vaunted wishbone offense. The new offense was such a closely guarded secret that Bryant placed assistants in the radio booths to ensure that the announcers wouldn't tip off the Trojans. Completely ill-prepared to defend the wishbone, Southern Cal was upset 17-10. With an integrated team running the wishbone, Alabama captured three national championships during the '70s.

1984: Miami 31, Nebraska 30

With Turner Gill, Heisman Trophy winner Mike Rozier, and Irving Fryar running behind an offensive line that had been compared to "seven refrigerators rolling down a hill," Nebraska was being billed as the greatest college football team of all-time. Conversely, Miami was a traditional lightweight that had been blown out 28-3 by Florida, their only ranked opponent. Accordingly, Nebraska was a double-digit favorite heading into their Orange Bowl showdown. In what may have been the greatest game ever played, Nebraska fought back from a 31-17 fourth quarter deficit and scored a touchdown to pull themselves within a point with less than a minute remaining. Coach Osborne could have simply kicked the conversion, settled for the tie and walked away with his first national championship. Instead, he went for two and the title of "Team of the Century." But his wings of wax melted and Miami began their "decade of dominance."

1993: Alabama 34, Miami 13

The end of Miami's "decade of dominance." The pundits dismissed the Tide as being too slow and one-dimensional to challenge the defending national champion Hurricanes in the Sugar Bowl. The Miami players were too busy running victory laps to participate in pregame handshakes. The ABC telecast was so geared to a Miami coronation party that their sideline reporters didn't even bother visiting the Alabama bench until the second half. But the good folks of Alabama got the last laugh, as their one-dimensional team ran right through the cocksure Canes.

Tallahassee, Florida
Florida State vs. Miami

Their Fifteen Minutes Were up a Half Hour Ago

Our next stop was the Sunshine State for what has become an annual classic: the Florida State-Miami game. What makes Miami-Florida State college football's hottest rivalry? In terms of pageantry, it pales in comparison with Army-Navy. If you're looking for unbridled animosity, the Hurricanes and Seminoles seem to detest Florida far more than each other. And as wild as Tallahassee can be on gameday, it's a tea party compared with Texas and Oklahoma's annual border war at the State Fair in Dallas. With over 700 drunkards being arrested before one game, sportswriter Dan Jenkins declared that rivalry to be the equivalent of "a prison riot with coeds." Along those same lines, Florida State-Miami can't compare with Stanford-Cal in terms of creative energy or Alabama-Auburn for underlying social conflict. But in terms of football, Miami-Florida State blows them all away. Quite simply, Miami-Florida State is college football's most exciting rivalry, featuring the most talented collegians competing for the national championship.

123

Despite their recent success, Miami and Florida State are college football neophytes. The City of Miami hadn't even been founded when Michigan and Notre Dame began playing football. And by the time Florida State admitted their first male students, Michigan and Notre Dame had already amassed a combined seven national championships. During the '70s, Miami and Florida State's gridiron fortunes had sunk so low that both schools seriously considered dropping football altogether. But how things have changed. With Florida State's seven consecutive top four finishes and Miami's quartet of national championships, these two schools now dominate the game.

And it goes beyond just being good. They have revolutionized the game. No longer is football the exclusive realm of the big and strong children of rural coal miners and farmers. Florida State and Miami have proven that you can dominate with quick and aggressive inner-city kids. When coaches talk about recruiting speed to compete on the highest level, they're talking about competing against Miami and Florida State. Even Notre Dame and Michigan have radically altered their football philosophies after being continually outrun by these Floridian superpowers. With Florida State ranked atop both polls as we rolled into Tallahassee, this promised to be a great week. We didn't realize it at the time, but our week in the Sunshine State would turn out to be the high point of our journey.

*   *   *   *

Our Florida experience started inauspiciously. As we drove south over the Georgia-Florida border, the airwaves were abuzz with the horrific news that a British tourist had been murdered at a Florida Turnpike rest area. From that point on, our only permitted roadside stops became Stuckey's and the Waffle House.

When we arrived in Tallahassee, something happened that almost changed Bob's life forever. Surprisingly, it had nothing to do with *Melrose Place* or the ongoing Three Stooges inheritance squabble. While flipping through the *Tallahassee Democrat* searching for two-for-one meatloaf coupons, we stumbled upon an article detailing Florida State's worldwide search for a new university president. We're not sure whether it was a desire to produce tomorrow's leaders or the prospects of unemployment after the trip, but Bob decided to apply for the job.

With the rallying cry of "a chicken wing in every pot," Bob's candidacy rested on the merits of his revolutionary "four point plan" to revitalize each student's educational experience. His "global vision" translated into serving Asian food in all campus cafeterias. The "integration of multimedia into the educational process" focused on the installation of cable television in every dorm room, with not one, but both ESPN channels. The final two points involved 24-hour bowling and guaranteed football tickets for all students.

We envisioned a grassroots movement, much like the "Pail & Shovel Party" that dominated the University of Wisconsin student government during the late-'70s. They once converted Wisconsin's entire student activities budget of $70,000 into pennies and dumped them on the steps of the library. The students were then given plastic pails and shovels to collect the coins. Bob was hoping to tap into this type of pocket of the lunatic fringe, and at a school as party-happy as Florida State, the pocket could be kangaroo sized.

Inspired by Bob's enthusiasm, Phil embarked on a similar quest, except he set his sights on becoming the general manager of the Boston Red Sox. Employing an equally prophetic platform, Phil promised to enhance the Red Sox home field advantage. Instead of loading up on right-handed power to take advantage of the Green Monster, Phil promised to deploy much more radical methods of delivering a title to the long-suffering Red Sox fans. Thus, bottled beer would once again be sold in the stands. High Intensity Flashlight Night, Pellet Gun Night, and the infamous Slingshot/D-Cell Battery Night would fill the seats while making Fenway Park the most dreaded visitors' venue in all of sport.

Phil never got a response from the Sox, but we were completely shocked when Bob received a letter from the Florida State Graduate Students United informing him that although he had not been nominated onto the short list of candidates, he had received the GSU's endorsement. Bob held his head high despite the failed candidacy. Much like the presidential bid of Ross Perot, he never expected to win. He just wanted to send a message to the Neolithic powers-that-be.

*   *   *   *

Possibly the best thing that came out of Bob's candidacy was a renewed commitment to learn about the university or at least about Florida State's football team. As a result, we now know a little more about how they attained their current lofty status.

The Florida State Women's College first admitted men in 1947 to meet the educational (and hormonal) demands of soldiers returning home from World War II. They fielded their first football team that same year. Unfortunately, their inaugural 0-5 season featured shutout losses to such featherweights as Jacksonville State and Cumberland College.

In those early days, Florida State's coaches seemed to have been good judges of thespian rather than football ability. Coach Tom Nugent out-recruited Miami for the services of Burt "Buddy" Reynolds. Although Buddy's career was cut short by injuries following his freshman season, Nugent loved him. But when one of his assistants presented Alex Karras to him, the Florida State coach ordered, "Get that fat slob out of here!" That fat slob is now enshrined in the Professional Football Hall of Fame. Then again, we'll take *The Longest Yard* and *Smoky and the Bandit* over *Webster* any day.

Although Bobby Bowden often gets exclusive credit for building the Seminole program, Florida State actually enjoyed a modicum of success during the '60s under Bill Peterson. With assistant coaches Bobby Bowden, Don James, Joe Gibbs and Bill Parcells, Peterson led the Seminoles to four bowl games and five consecutive victories over Miami.

The Cradle of Coaches

While Florida State's record for producing coaches is certainly exemplary, Miami of Ohio is the true "Cradle of Coaches," having been the birthin' room for many top-flight football minds.

Coach (year graduatcd)	Team
Earl Blaik '17	Army
Paul Brown '30	Cleveland Browns
Weeb Ewbank '30	NFL Colts, NY Jets
Ara Parseghian '47	Notre Dame
Paul Dietzel '48	LSU, South Carolina
Bill Arnspager '50	defensive genius
Bo Schembechler '51	Michigan
Carmen Cozza '52	Yale
John McVay '53	Tampa Bay Buccaneers
Gary Moeller '63	Michigan
John Mackovic '66	Kansas City Chiefs
Woody Hayes (Coach)	Ohio State

In a bizarre acknowledgment of the success of Miami of Ohio's coaching alumni, other schools have adopted similar names in hopes of copying the success. Unfortunately, Nome of Oklahoma, Omaha of Southern California and Grambling at Provo were never accredited, let alone able to field a Division I football team.

Despite the success of the Peterson years, the program fell into such disarray during the early-'70s that Florida State seriously considered dropping football altogether. The school became a laughingstock in the wake of the "Chicken Wire Scandal," in which Coach Larry Jones had tried to toughen up his players by making them wrestle under chicken wire. The national media had a field day with stories about bloodied and exhausted players beating each other senseless as sadistic coaches egged them on. A quarter of the team quit in protest, leaving the rest to finish an

0-11 season. The school was placed on probation, and Coach Jones was promptly canned.

Jones' replacement, Darrell Mudra, was unable to resuscitate Florida State's battered program. Mudra's insistence on coaching from the press box and going fishing on gamedays didn't exactly instill confidence in his players. He was dismissed after amassing a dismal two year 4-18 record.

As our country celebrated its Bicentennial, Florida State's program was in complete shambles. Fan interest was so minimal that the Marching Chief halftime show was outdrawing the football games. Worst of all, severe debt had forced them to schedule dozens of games against college football's most powerful heavyweights — all on the road. Florida State football had been reduced to preferred-opponent status. As the designated homecoming foe, they were repeatedly whipped in exchange for a nice paycheck.

Given FSU's abject situation, it seems surprising that they were able to coax the highly respected Bobby Bowden away from West Virginia, where his Mountaineers were the defending Peach Bowl champions. Although Bowden quips that his decision was governed by his "slipping on the ice one too many times," his true motivation reveals part of college football's darker side. Apparently, the fickle West Virginia fans turned against Bowden during his disappointing 4-7, 1974 campaign. After enduring a season of finding "For Sale" signs posted on his lawn and dummies hung in effigy from his trees, he jumped at the first opportunity to find a friendlier environment.

Bowden joked that at West Virginia, the bumper stickers read "Beat Pitt," at Florida State they read, "Beat Anybody." With Bowden at the helm, the Seminoles did that and more, beating not only the anybodies of the NCAA, but the somebodies too, regardless of where they played; the armies of Julius Caesar should have only been so successful on the road. Florida State went 2-0 at Ohio State, 5-1 at LSU's Death Valley, 2-0 at Clemson's Death Valley, 1-0 at Notre Dame, and, unbelievably, won twice at Nebraska. Besides earning Bowden the moniker "King of the Road," his ability to ruin so many homecomings helped him garner quite a few trophies for the so-called Sod Cemetery.

The Sod Cemetery stands as a tribute to Florida State's greatest road triumphs. Before each season, several road contests are designated as "Sod Games." These include bowl games, games at Miami or Florida, and any other road games in which they're expected to be underdogs. After winning a Sod Game, a piece of turf is cut from the stadium and interred back in the Sod Cemetery. Each piece is given its own tombstone, engraved with the score and the date of the conquest. When they beat Auburn in the 1987 Sugar Bowl, the euphoric players even cut a swatch of astroturf right out of the Superdome.

*   *   *   *

As you can imagine, tickets to this game were a hot commodity. With buyers seemingly outnumbering sellers 10-1, prime tickets were reportedly being scalped for $350 apiece. But according to Florida law, it's illegal to sell tickets for more than $1 above their face value. Undeterred, scalpers had devised ingenious methods for circumventing this legal snafu. We saw one guy selling a $450 T-shirt, which coincidentally, had a pair of free tickets stuffed in the pocket. Another hawker offered two free tickets with the purchase of a $400 parking space.

Meanwhile, thousands of students had been camped out for days waiting for tickets. Amidst the piles of empty pizza boxes, beer cans, discarded newspapers and ratty furniture, there were some highly agitated students. Apparently, the university had only allocated 18,000 tickets for 22,500 students, even though they had charged each student a hefty athletic fee as part of their tuition, with the promise that each student would be guaranteed a ticket to all football games. When the supply ran out, hundreds of students were livid.

Neither of us are activists in any sense of the word. We'd much rather lick John Madden's armpits after one of his vigorous aerobic workouts than stick our neck out for some crazy cause. But like any good Americans, we do have certain philosophical principles that we will fight to maintain: sports should be played on natural grass, pork is the noblest of the white meats and students have an inalienable right to attend their school's football games. More importantly, and despite our noble posturing, we simply wanted to cause some trouble.

To call attention to the ticket crisis, angered students staged a huge rally outside the administration building. Having nothing better to do, we spent the night before the rally plastering handbills around the campus outlining our own not so subtle and not so poetic opinion on the ticket issue:

> *Things seemed mighty rosy*
> *For this Seminole that day.*
> *Tickets were set to go on sale*
> *For the Miami game they'll play.*

> *I got up pretty early*
> *with my coupon and ID.*
> *I'd paid to see the ball game*
> *Through that stiff Athletic Fee.*

> *At noon, the ticket office said*
> *"Too Late. There's no more room."*
> *I'd have had no chance, if I'd lined up*
> *While in my mother's womb.*

> *Oh somewhere students will watch us win,*
> *And at the Canes they'll shout.*
> *But there is no joy for this student;*
> *The administration has struck out.*

*　　　　　*　　　　　*　　　　　*

From the standpoint of pivotal regular-season games, this one may be the most important. (***Editor's note...*** *Except for every Nebraska game.)* The winner automatically gains a leg up in the national championship race, while the loser can only hope that the winner falters later on. With Miami having been the decade's most dominant team and Florida State finishing a distant second, it's no understatement to say that the road to the national championship leads through Miami and Tallahassee.

The Hurricanes have captured four national championships during the past decade. More amazingly, they were just a Ty Detmer touchdown pass (BYU-1990), a last-second, touchdown-saving Pete Giftopoulos interception (Penn State-1986) and a missed two-point conversion (Notre Dame-1988) from having won an unprecedented seven national championships during the decade.

Florida State has been no slouch either. Aside from not having lost a bowl game since *Welcome Back Kotter* ruled the airwaves, Florida State had won 75 of its past 85 games going into the '93 Miami showdown. Unfortunately for the Seminoles, five of those losses were to Miami. The Red Sox had the Yankees, Colonel Klink had Hogan and Florida State has Miami. For eight of the past ten seasons, Florida State has led Miami going into the fourth quarter, only to come away with just two victories. These frustrating collapses have caused the Hurricanes to dismiss the Noles as "the best three-quarters team in the country," and Bowden to quip that when he dies, they'll inscribe "He played Miami" on his tombstone.

Like so many times before, Florida State was favored going into the '93 game, but the excruciating history of this rivalry has tempered Seminole expectations. FSU's agony began impacting college football on a national scale when Miami won the 1983 contest with a last-second field goal. If Miami had missed the field goal, they never would have had the opportunity to win their first national championship by upsetting Nebraska in the Orange Bowl. Four seasons later, Florida State blew a 19-3 second-half lead, only to close to within a point by scoring a touchdown with 42 seconds remaining. Foregoing an almost certain tie, Bowden elected to go for the two-point conversion. It failed. Miami went on to win their second national championship, while Florida State had to settle for being #2.

In 1988, the Seminole players were so impressed with their preseason number-one ranking that they recorded their own rap video before playing a single game. But after being blown out by Miami 31-0 on opening day, the *Seminole Rap* received even less air-time than the excruciatingly painful, yet strangely haunting *Love Songs of Bobcat Goldthwait*. When Florida State finally beat Miami in 1989, the Canes still had the last laugh, as they were awarded their third national championship at the end of the season.

Florida State's frustrations reached their peak with the 1991 and 1992 contests. Going into the 1991 game, the top-ranked Seminoles were being tabbed as the greatest team of all time, while Miami was supposedly rebuilding. But it was the

Seminole fans who watched in horror as a 16-7, fourth quarter lead evaporated into 17-16 deficit. Undaunted, Casey Weldon drove the Seminoles into position for a seemingly easy game-winning field goal. But Florida State's championship aspirations were dashed as Gerry Thomas' 34-yard field goal sailed off the mark. The victorious Canes celebrated at midfield, mockingly ripping up the turf in front of 72,000 despondent Florida State fans. In reference to the missed field goal, the next day's *Tallahassee Democrat* headline wailed, "Wide Right."

The 1992 contest was as Yogi Berra would have said, "Deja Vu all over again." Except this time, the goat was kicker Dan Mowrey and the *Tallahassee Democrat's* headline read, "Wider Right."

*   *   *   *

By midweek, the atmosphere on campus was electric in anticipation of the game and we could almost feel our hearts beating faster in response. Then we realized it wasn't our hearts at all. It was the revival of the Seminole drum beating tradition, in which students continuously beat a huge 12-foot drum for the 72 hours preceding the Miami game. However, not everybody was thrilled about the revival of this tradition, as the deafening beat was giving migraines to the workers at the nearby administrative offices, and productivity had been brought to a screeching halt.

Unfortunately, some overzealous (read: drunk) fraternity brothers unintentionally (read: unconsciously) smashed a hole in the drum. Despite this minor setback, they didn't miss a beat. While a replacement was being flown in, students continued the War Chant while beating on a nearby brick wall. In response to this concerted motivational effort, we retreated back to our hotel and watched television, well assured of college football's power to captivate a community.

At this point in the trip, bizarre events started happening at an accelerated pace. After a difficult day of eating and digesting, we turned on the television and learned that Michael Jordan had retired from the NBA. We were dumbfounded, dumberfounded than usual. To imagine how an athlete at the height of his career could so suddenly call it quits, we tried to put ourselves in his shoes. On our feet, however, his shoes would have been merely wearing out the carpet to and from buffet tables. More than that, could we have endured the pressure of displaying our prodigious eating habits day-in and day-out? Well, yes, because we were already doing it, but could we have done it everyday under the scrutiny of the media? Probably, yes again, but there was no way in hell we could have also carried Pippen, Cartwright, Armstrong and Grant the way he did, and still eaten as much as we wanted. In that light, we saw what Michael was up against and could relate to his decision. Still, we were despondent, and thus decided to engage in the distraction of Tallahassee's night life.

At Bullwinkle's, a lively college pub featuring a moose and squirrel motif, we joined a couple of coeds in a campus tradition known as the Tennessee Waltz. We danced with them for hours on end, all the while brushing up against their... whoops, wrong Tennessee Waltz. In this Tennessee Waltz, inebriated birthday celebrants stumble in and out of the bars along Tennessee Street, receiving a free birthday pitcher of beer from each place. Then, at the end of the line, or the night (which ever comes first), the birthday child is ceremoniously dunked into the Westcott Fountain. Squeaky clean from our fountain plunge, we called it a night.

While the Canes may have won the gridiron battles, Florida State outpolled Miami for party potential. In a recent survey, *Inside Edge* named Florida State as America's most fun school.

Inside Edge's Funnest Schools

1. Florida State	6. Syracuse
2. Cal Santa Barbara	7. Alabama
3. Vermont	8. Penn State
4. Rice	9. Connecticut
5. Georgetown	10.Tulane
14. Miami	291. Yale

Students at virtually every school we visited boasted of being one of *Playboy's* top party schools. Being longtime fans of *Playboy's* sardonic wit and perspicacious political commentary, we couldn't remember any such survey. It turns out that *Playboy* last rated the schools during Reagan's first term. In order, their top five were; Cal State Chico, Miami, San Diego State, Vermont and Slippery Rock. In their single greatest editorial blunder since printing naked pictures of Sandra Bernhardt, *Playboy* rated LSU #37 and left FSU unrated.

*   *   *   *

We arose the next morning, bought four different newspapers and settled in for what turned out to be a three-hour breakfast. One paper reported a rumor that a psychotically twisted Seminole fan was plotting to poison Miami's food supply (nothing life-threatening, just enough laxatives to keep them squirting for four quarters). Even Miami coach Dennis Erickson laughed away the rumor, proclaiming that his son Bryce, a freshman quarterback, had been elevated to the team's official food-taster. Erickson quipped, "What do you think that scholarship was for anyway?"

The papers also reported that Burt Reynolds would be attending the game. Reynolds is one of Florida State's most ardent boosters. The football team lives in the palatial Burt

Reynolds Hall and plays in the uniforms that he donated. Reynolds even invited Bobby Bowden to make a guest appearance on his television show, *Evening Shade.*

There were rumors that Miami's most high profile booster, 2 Live Crew's Luther Campbell, would also be at the game. Campbell's contributions to Miami football include setting up trash-talking phone calls between Miami and Florida State players and offering bounties to Miami players for touchdowns and bone-crushing hits.

After breakfast, we ambled over to the athletic department to send a few faxes and make some more photocopies of our butts. As we eyed an isolated copy machine, we were blindsided by Bobby Bowden himself. He seemed to appear out of nowhere, as if he possessed the speed of one of his defensive backs. He shook our hands and drawled, "Hey boys, how's it going?" He even seemed genuinely interested in our travels. Just 48 hours away from a monumental game against a team that has tormented him for two decades, and he was courteous enough to listen to us ramble on about happy-hour buffets and leaky radiator hoses.

Bobby Bowden is essentially the Roy Rogers of the coaching world. Additionally, his impact on the university extends far beyond the football field. It is no coincidence that Florida State's emergence as a top-flight educational and research institution has mirrored their emergence as a gridiron power. Football has provided Florida State the opportunity to showcase itself in front of millions of prospective students. To leverage this exposure, Bowden's wide-open, gambling offenses and defenses, which utilize a variety of trick plays, convey an image of university-wide vibrancy and innovation. Furthermore, Coach Bowden's gregariousness transcends football, making him the perfect goodwill ambassador for the university-at-large.

*   *   *   *

The campus was bracing for Miami's arrival. A popular sign read, "You can't spell SCUM without UM." Miami has that impact on fans. They are an outlaw program at a time when society is scrutinizing the way in which schools should balance big time athletics with their educational missions. The *Chicago Tribune* once described Miami as being "as far from the college ideal as a tire iron is from an ear swab." Yet, it is this outlaw mentality that stokes the Miami recruiting fires. A scholarship from the University of Miami ensures image and visibility, two important attributes for many modern-day athletes.

Yet, Miami football hasn't always had such a notorious reputation. Although the Hurricanes enjoyed decent success during the '50s and '60s, they slipped into the abyss of second-fiddlism when Miami was granted a professional franchise in the late-'60s. By the time the Dolphins had won back-to-back Super Bowls during the mid-'70s, Hurricane home attendance had plummeted below 16,000 fans per game. Like Florida State, Miami seriously considered dropping football altogether.

Instead, in 1977, just one season after Florida State hired Bowden, Miami entrusted their program to the highly respected Lou Sabin. Although he only lasted two seasons before moving on to Army, he laid the groundwork for the Hurricane dynasty. Realizing that Miami's success depended on their ability to recruit local athletes, Sabin spent an entire summer barnstorming talent-rich South Florida and selling his program to high school coaches. These efforts established the relationships that have helped Miami dominate South Florida recruiting for the past two decades.

Sabin's replacement, Howard Schnellenberger, continued to recruit the "State of Miami," while making Miami even more attractive by installing a pro-style offense and defense, similar to those he used as the Miami Dolphins offensive coordinator. Other programs could sell their recruits tradition; Miami could offer to prepare them for the NFL.

Buoyed by several seasons of solid recruiting, Miami had emerged as a respected program. In 1980, they were invited to the Peach Bowl, their first postseason appearance in decades. The following year, the Canes rallied behind freshmen quarterback Jim Kelly for a regular season upset over top-ranked Penn State.

But even these substantial strides couldn't have prepared anyone for what happened in 1983. After the Canes were shellacked 28-3 by Florida in their opener, local fans turned their attention to Dan Marino's rookie campaign with the Dolphins. With few people paying attention, and against dubious competition, Miami earned an Orange Bowl showdown against seemingly invincible Nebraska. When Texas and Illinois lost on New Year's Day, the fourth-ranked Canes suddenly found themselves playing for a national championship. In one of the most exciting games ever played, Miami shocked Nebraska 31-30, capturing their first national championship.

After Schnellenberger jumped to the USFL, Jimmy Johnson continued to build upon Miami's growing reputation. While Schnellenberger had stressed speed, Johnson made it an obsession. Safeties became linebackers, and linebackers became defensive linemen. On defense, Miami became a team of guided missiles that exploded on their slower opposition. Combined with a quick-strike offense, featuring too much speed on the outside for conventional defenses to handle, Miami emerged as the premier team in college football.

The program didn't miss a beat when Johnson left for the Dallas Cowboys in 1988. Miami captured their third national championship in Dennis Erickson's first season as coach, and two seasons later, they brought home their fourth championship of the decade. While other teams have enjoyed comparable runs of success, none have accomplished the feat in the face of so many distractions. Miami has somehow maintained their level of play through four different coaches, scores of arrests, and a *Sports Illustrated* cover declaring, "Miami should drop football."

If Notre Dame exemplifies historic football greatness, Miami represents the modern football machine. As much as their pro-set offenses and attacking defenses have revolutionized the strategy of the game, their nasty attitude has altered the entire way sports are played on both the collegiate and sandlot level. Although they certainly didn't invent trash-talking, they turned it into a science. Where else do players scour the opponents' media guides for family information so they can customize their trash-talking for optimum effect?

At times, Miami's intimidation tactics have gone beyond mere talk and bordered on being felonious. Before the 1991 Cotton Bowl, they confronted the Texas Longhorns in the tunnel leading to the field. Despite being outnumbered and outweighed on a man-to-man basis, the Canes taunted and jostled the Longhorns. On the opening kickoff, Miami's Robert Bailey knocked the Texas return man cold and danced over his motionless body. The rest of the game was a mere formality. Before the

46-3 demolition was over, Miami had amassed 202 yards in penalties — 135 of them for personal fouls and unsportsmanlike conduct. It's no wonder people in Tallahassee were practically boarding up their homes in anticipation of the Hurricane arrival.

*   *   *   *

On Friday morning, all hell broke loose. Phil woke up early and sped off to the local gym for a workout (assuming you define a workout as sitting on a stationary bike sipping coffee while watching hard-bodied coeds climb the stairmaster). But on this particular morning, Phil was on the receiving end of the gawking stares. He was confused until he opened up the *USA Today*. There it was: on the second page of the sports section, under the caption, "Road Warriors Take Trek to Tallahassee," Phil saw God. Well, that's the way he described it. What he was really looking at was a picture of us standing in front of the limo and a story detailing our wild ride.

Andy Warhol claimed that everybody gets "fifteen minutes of fame." These were obviously ours. When we called our answering machine back home, we listened to message after message from newspapers, radio stations and bill collectors — all wanting a moment of our time. We couldn't even drive down the streets of Tallahassee without people stopping us for autographs and pictures. We're still not sure why they kept calling us Mr. Farley and Mr. Candy, but we were happy to oblige. Considering that the closest either of us had ever come to any sort of publicity was an article in our camp newspaper debating whether it was Bob's immense girth or shaggy body hair that caused him to become wedged in the middle of a 200-foot water slide, this undeserved attention was unreal. Who would have ever guessed it? Peace in the Mideast, the end of the Cold War and people were accosting us for autographs.

Even more incredibly, one of the phone messages was from ESPN. In the world of the sportsaholic, ESPN signals the crowning achievement. ESPN's Steve Cyphers told us how well our insane journey fit in with the offbeat image that ESPN2 was attempting to foster, and invited us to appear on ESPN2's *Sportsnite*. He even mentioned that we could possibly become a weekly feature on "The Deuce." For a couple of class clowns, this was a dream come true.

During the rest of the afternoon, we kept Steve Cyphers in stitches with stories about two clueless slobs wandering through the South in search of the perfect tailgate. A live interview was scheduled for that evening. Given our one shot at the big time, we put forth the worst opening night performance since the Titanic. When the producer signaled us to begin the interview, Bob was off heeding nature's call. Arriving back in front of the camera with barely enough time to zip his pants, Bob was visibly shaken. Despite seldom being at a loss for words, all he could muster up were nervous salutations to two dozen of his relatives in an excruciating thirty-second soliloquy.

On the other hand, Phil wasted his chance at stardom doing repeated imitations of Popeye the Sailor. Well, they had allz they could standz, and they couldn't standz no more. We were cut off 45 seconds into a five-minute interview. To make matters worse, we were constantly reminded by our friends that when they switched back to the studio, the host disapprovingly shook his head and declared that our "fifteen minutes were up a half hour ago." From that point on, we avoided live TV. Perhaps more accurately, live TV avoided us. To put an exclamation point on the entire fiasco, Bob's father left the following cryptic message on our answering machine: "If I were Japanese, family honor would compel me to stick a samurai sword through my stomach."

Nevertheless, some people appreciated our distinctive lack of talent. Peter Rudman arranged for camera crews to meet us at each campus we visited. We contend that his reassignment to scholastic soccer had nothing to do with the inclusion of that footage in his nationally syndicated *College Bowl Preview Show*.

*   *   *   *

On gameday, the stadium parking lot was transformed into a frenzied sea of garnet and gold with scattered patches of orange and green. Most fans were ecstatic about being a part of the spectacle. As one fan explained, "If you can't get up for this game, you might as well go to college for the education." Others were even more enthusiastic, including one fan who identified himself as Chief Wahoo. He stood before us, adorned with a headdress, war paint and a ceremonial outfit that his wife made from the upholstery of an abandoned sofa. Had he not been at the game, we would have mistaken him for an Elton John roadie. But we were at the game, and the teepee affixed to the top of Chief Wahoo's car reinforced this fact. He let out a few high-pitched war cries and declared: "The Noles are on the war path! We're gonna scalp those nasty Canes!" Gee, we wonder why Native Americans find these displays demeaning.

As confident as some of the Seminole fans were, most were cautiously skeptical, if not downright nervous about the impending game. According to the *Tallahassee Democrat*, another loss to Miami could trigger massive attacks of anxiety and depression. In order to mitigate this potential disaster, the paper offered recommendations from several psychologists detailing the best methods of dealing with this sort of traumatic loss. The only remedy that caught our eyes consisted of holding a can of creamed corn between the knees while singing the Seminole War Chant until passing out.

To continue our wagering ways (albeit wasteful wagering ways), we searched the papers for a story telling us who to bet on. While both schools entered the game undefeated, Florida State was already being anointed as the "Team of the Century." They had absolutely dominated their opposition, outscoring those teams, three of which had been ranked in the top twenty, 228-14. Accordingly, Vegas installed them as a two-touchdown favorite. But we knew better. As a team that thrives on an us-versus-them mentality, the underdog role merely inspires the Hurricanes. They had won an unprecedented eight consecutive games against top-ranked teams. While we were looking forward to rooting for the Noles, there was no way that we were giving 13 points to the third-ranked Canes. We decided not to bet.

         *   *   *   *

Although it was 78 degrees and sunny outside, inside the stadium it was rain-forest muggy. We could almost see a cloud of condensed perspiration hovering overhead. Of course, this was to be expected when 75,000 screaming fans cram into a stadium that should hold only 60,000. The fans in our section stood the entire game. With no room to sit, they had no choice. The tension flowing between the throngs of sweaty bodies amplified the already awesome crowd noise, giving us a firsthand demonstration of why Doak Campbell Stadium provides such a formidable home-field advantage.

Moments before the kickoff, we experienced one of college football's most inspiring rituals. The field was cleared and the crowd noise reached an apex as Chief Osceola astride the noble Renegade galloped to midfield. As Renegade reared up on his hind legs, Chief Osceola thrusted his flaming spear into the field. The crowd went berserk and the Marching Chiefs broke into the Florida State Fight Song. The running of Ralphie at Colorado and the rubbing of Frank Howard's Rock at Clemson were both electric, but the planting of Chief Osceola's spear was the best pregame ritual we witnessed.

In stark contrast to the noble, but somewhat humorless Chief Osceola, Miami's mascot is the whimsical and fiendish Sebastian the Ibis. Supposedly, the ibis is the last bird to flee before a hurricane. Although Sebastian looks like a cross between Donald Duck and the Reverend Jim from *Taxi,* his toughness is legendary among the mascoting fraternity. Not even a stray bullet to the cheek received while strolling down Bourbon Street before the 1990 Sugar Bowl could put Sebastian out of action.

On more than one occasion, Chief Osceola has been the butt of Sebastian's biting humor. When Osceola planted his burning spear at midfield before the 1989 game, Sebastian ran onto the field, equipped with a fireman's hat, slicker and fire extinguisher. But Chief Osceola got the last laugh as the ibis was immediately swarmed upon by Tallahassee's finest and slammed up against a fence. Replays of this display of police brutality sparked outrage among the ibis community, as a badly beaten Sebastian pleaded, "Can't we all just get along?"

It's not enough for this sun-baked school to have the most exciting football team and wildest campus, they also have one of the best cheers in all of sports. The War Chant is both fun and effective. If a couple of bad breaks should silence the crowd, it only takes five notes from the Marching Chiefs to get the War Chant going, elevating the crowd noise back to rocket pad levels. Furthermore, the War Chant's rhythmic arm-chopping movement has the dual effect of firing up the Seminoles and airing out the sweaty fans' armpits. Perhaps it is this double function that has led many clubs, professional and collegiate alike, to adopt the cheer as their own.

*   *   *   *

The Seminoles must have been riding the same high that we were that day, as Charlie Ward led them to a cathartic 28-10 victory. They snapped the Miami jinx while moving one step closer to their first national championship. The engravers could finally etch Charlie Ward's name into the Heisman and the fans exacted some measure of revenge on Miami by chanting "wide left" after a Miami field goal attempt missed its mark. After the game, fans celebrated in the stands while the jubilant players hugged each other at midfield. As we made our way back to the limo, a half-naked fan ran by us screaming, "Ding dong the witch is dead!"

Slightly disgusted by this sight, we nevertheless decided to break our trip-long norm of immediately leaving after the game. We joined in the frenzied celebration, in part because of a shared Seminole happiness and in part due to our own good fortunes. Six weeks earlier, we were two underachievers vainly wallowing in self-pity, but now, we were two underachievers wallowing in a sea of fame, food and football... and loving every minute of it.

Tuscaloosa, Alabama
Alabama vs. Tennessee

Football Now, Football Tomorrow, Football Forever

Having been raised in Boston's western suburbs, our support of sports teams had always been seasonal and strictly reserved for the professionals ranks: the steadfast grit of the Bruins warmed our hearts during the cruel East Coast winters. The Red Sox quest for redemption captured the springtime dreamer in us while their inevitable swoon helped cool the sweltering New England summers. Finally, the pride and glory of the Celtics historically justified the over-hyped passion surrounding the pre-Parcells Patriots. The periodic Boston sports scene was a major part of our "coming of age."

After only one week in Tuscaloosa, it was obvious that the intersection of sports with our lives paled in comparison to that of Alabamans and college football. Quite simply, Alabama is the most football-crazed state in the most football-crazed region of the world. While our allegiances may shift with the seasons, Alabamans perennially support their football teams. There are only two sports that really matter in Alabama: football and spring football. And when they're not talking football, they're usually talking football recruiting.

In Alabama, football isn't a matter of life or death, it's far more important. Legend has it that when some warped fanatic shot his wife for switching channels during the Alabama-Auburn game, the judge dismissed the case as justifiable homicide. Former Crimson Tide coach Bill Curry understands this mentality. He had just completed a 10-2 season when he was accosted by an irate fan demanding to know "when are we gonna have a good team?"

       *   *   *   *

As we drove through rural Alabama, we continued to reflect upon our new-found celebrity status and how it would influence the rest of the trip. We even decided to pursue an off-price beer endorsement, reasoning that our journey would probably appeal to unmotivated, unemployed, sports fanatics — the exact market segment that swills the most cheap beer. But for some reason, the beer companies seemed wary of our services. A representative from Miller informed us that breweries try to "avoid sponsoring drunken road trips." Boy do we miss the '80s.

Not that it mattered, of course. It turns out that our celebrity status was short-lived. Like the cast of *F-Troop*, we quickly slipped into obscurity. After leaving Tallahassee, the closest we ever came to giving an autograph was signing the Motel 6 register. Occasionally, people would ask us if we were the knuckleheads following college football while shaking their heads and giving us a "get-a-life" stare. Still, it was fun while it lasted.

       *   *   *   *

We arrived in Tuscaloosa on a Sunday morning, when as every myopic Yankee knows, all southerners are in church. Accordingly, we descended on our altar of worship — television. Unable to find any good informercials, we took in some professional wrestling.

Enthralled by the spectacle, we watched in amazement as through pure inspiration and determination, a wiry and athletic wrestler known as the "1-2-3 Kid" held his own, and occasionally even gained an upper hand over a sluggish behemoth known as Bam Bam Bigelow. But after some high-risk maneuvers backfired on the Kid, the match was, for all intents and purposes, over. The next few minutes seemed like an eternity as Bam Bam inflicted tremendous and possibly permanent injury upon his weary adversary. Even after the battered 1-2-3 Kid finally submitted, the onslaught continued. Bigelow's manager, the Million Dollar Man, entered the ring and verbally and physically assaulted the fallen Kid. We could only speculate about the lasting effects this beating would have on the 1-2-3 Kid's psyche.

Likewise, it's impossible to measure the devastating effects the Civil War had on the South. Hundreds of thousands died, countless others were maimed, and property values plummeted to one-tenth their ante-bellum levels. Even more devastating, the war and its aftermath inflicted a horrible mental toll that reverberated throughout the South for decades.

That was the backdrop for George Denny when he became president of the University of Alabama in 1912. The visionary Denny decided to restore Alabama pride by building a winning football tradition. He took his mission so seriously that he helped prepare the team for its big games by serving as a human tackling dummy. (Think about how much you would have liked to tackle the president of your college during the early fall, just after you had been closed out of the one class you needed to maintain your tenuous graduation path.)

It didn't take long for Denny's vision to materialize. In 1922, Alabama traveled north to take on mighty Pennsylvania, a school where the grandchildren of Union soldiers still sang "Hang Jeff Davis from a Sour Apple Tree" after every touchdown. Because eastern football was considered far superior to anything played in the South, Penn was a prohibitive favorite. Like the socialites that lined the battlefields of Manassas, the Penn fans expected an easy victory over the undermanned and ill-equipped Alabama football regiment, but the Tide prevailed 9-7. At the Tuscaloosa train station, thousands of delirious fans welcomed home their conquering heroes. One student told us, "As much as we love beating up on the SEC, there's nothing like going north of the Mason-Dixon line and showing you Yankees how football is supposed to be played."

When the Great Depression delivered a forearm smash to an already crippled Alabama economy, football provided Alabamans with a beacon of hope. The ability to vicariously share in the victories of their championship football teams somehow made their daily struggles for survival seem bearable.

More than just a common source of pride, Alabama football offered many young men the opportunity to escape the toil of rural poverty for a chance at a better life. Paul "Bear" Bryant was one of these young men.

In terms of combined victories and national championships, Paul W. Bryant was the most successful coach in the history of college football. He won a record 323 games and six national championships during a coaching career that spanned four schools and eight presidential administrations. Still, the victories and accolades don't even start to explain the Bear Bryant phenomena in Alabama. Images of the Bear are everywhere, from posters to billboards to T-shirts depicting him walking on water. Football is played in Bryant-Denny Stadium, located on Paul W. Bryant Drive, only a short walk from the venerable Bear shrine known as the Paul Bryant Museum.

Quite simply, Alabamans love Bear Bryant. In the book *Alabama Showdown*, Geoffrey Norman compared the passionate reverence that Alabamans have for Bryant to the affection that many southerners felt for Robert E. Lee: "They believed in their leader with a devotion that was both touching and frightening." NFL Hall-of-Famer George Blanda once said, "When Coach Bryant walked into the room, I always had the urge to stand up and cheer." After John Wayne died, Alabamans wondered who could possibly portray Bryant in a movie of his life. No wonder people told us, "In Alabama, an atheist is someone who doesn't believe in Bear Bryant."

*   *   *   *

We couldn't spend a week in Tuscaloosa without talking to someone who actually knew the Bear, and Jim Goostree was the perfect person. We ran across his name when Phil insisted that the South was infamous for surnames combining plant and avian life. He maintained that his semester with Janice Fernpecker had taught him this. Fortunately for us, Goostree served as Alabama's trainer from 1957 until 1993. Jim, as he told us to call him (although we couldn't help but refer to him occasionally as Mr. Ganderbush), held his position throughout Bryant's Alabama coaching career and then some. In part due to his lengthy tenure and in part due to his wry sense of humor, Coach Goostree has become a folk-hero in Tuscaloosa. We sat there mesmerized for an entire afternoon as he spun tales of Bear Bryant and Alabama football lore. Having spent the previous day in the Bryant museum, we were fascinated by Jim's personal spin on so many of the famous stories we had discovered just the day before.

Jim began by telling us that Coach Bryant had confided in him after Bear told Joe Namath's mother that her son had been suspended for the year for disciplinary reasons. Having the Bear tell him personally, "That was the hardest thing I ever had to do," left an indelible mark on Jim's 'Bama experience. Coach Goostree also told us about how he could physically feel the fear emanating from those around him when Bryant would descend the stairs of his practice-field observation tower: "You knew he was coming down with a purpose... and it was always a thrill when someone else got it and not you."

With Coach Goostree's insight, we realized we weren't merely hearing about a legend of football. In the eyes of Alabamans, Bryant is the personification of the American success story: a rags-to-riches tale, hailing the virtues of hard work, determination and devotion.

It all began in Moro Bottom, Arkansas. Even if the twelve-year-old Bryant had never wrestled that bear for $5 at the local carnival, he probably would have earned the "Bear" nickname anyway. He looked like a bear, growled like one and some say, with his soft, rumbling voice, he even sounded like a bear. Bryant stood a powerful 6'4" tall, and the deep lines etched into his sun-baked face told the story of his painful climb to prosperity. George Blanda's first impression of Bryant was "This is what God must look like." (Actually, according to the *Weekly World News*, God bears far more resemblance to Don Knotts.)

One of twelve kids born to a sickly father, Bryant escaped the poverty of Moro Bottom when he received a scholarship to Alabama. Alabama football was the catalyst that transformed him from a dirt-poor farmer into one of the most revered figures in southern history.

As a player, Bryant was the "other end" on the championship teams that featured the legendary passing combination of Dixie Howell to Don Hutson. Nonetheless, he earned second team all-conference honors and gained a well-deserved reputation for his toughness. He once played a game with a broken leg because, in his words, "There was only one bone broke."

As a coach, Bryant demanded the same dedication from his players. With rural poverty often their only other alternative, they usually gave Bryant what he wanted. After serving his nation during World War II, Bryant became head coach at Maryland in 1945. In his first season at College Park, Bryant transformed a wretched 1-7-1 squad into a solid 6-2 team, only to abruptly quit after the university president reinstated a player whom Bryant had suspended.

At Bryant's next stop, he used fear and discipline to mold a 2-8 Kentucky team into a 7-3 contender in his first season. At Kentucky, he coached future hall-of-fame quarterbacks Babe Parilli and George Blanda. The story goes that Parilli was once recuperating after knee surgery when Bryant marched into his hospital room and dropped a stack of new plays on his bed. The new plays ran out of the shotgun, a formation which allowed the immobile Parilli to throw the ball with minimal movement. Parilli told *Time* magazine: "I thought he was crazy. I could barely move. But I did what I was told." Kentucky won 14-0, and Parilli never got touched.

Bryant's success at Kentucky reached its pinnacle when his Wildcats capped off an 11-1 season by knocking off the "crowned" national champion Oklahoma Sooners in the 1951 Orange Bowl. Still, Bryant realized that as long as Adolph Rupp was coaching basketball, he would remain Kentucky's "other coach." Bryant claimed he "knew it was time to leave when they gave Adolph a Cadillac and me a cigarette lighter." To this day, Kentucky fans are still waiting for another conference championship.

UNCROWNED CHAMPIONS

In a move akin to awarding World Series rings in September, the wire services used to select their national champions before the bowl games. This practice wasn't completely abandoned until the early '70s. As a result, the following schools culminated their "championship" seasons with a bowl loss:

Year	Poll Champion	Bowl Result	"Uncrowned" Champions
1950	Oklahoma	Kentucky 13, Oklahoma 7	Kentucky
1951	Tennessee	Maryland 28, Tennessee 13	Mich St.
1953	Maryland	Oklahoma 7, Maryland 0	Notre Dame
1960	Minnesota	Washington 17, Minnesota 7	Ole Miss
1964	Alabama	Texas 24, Alabama 17	Arkansas
1970	Texas	Notre Dame 24, Texas 11	Nebraska
1973	Alabama	Notre Dame 24, Alabama 23	Notre Dame

Paul "Bear" Bryant, Football's Greatest Coach

After leaving Kentucky, the restless Bryant transformed Texas A&M into a juggernaut while cementing his reputation as a football tyrant. Before coaching his first game, Bryant bussed his 96 players about 200 miles west to a small town in the desolate Texas plains known as Junction City. There, he conducted three grueling practices each day, with the first beginning promptly at 5 a.m. All practices were in full pads, and despite the 110-degree heat, the players were denied water because, as Junction City-survivor Jack Pardee explained, "If you had to have water, it meant that you didn't have any discipline."

On the first day of practice, Bryant booted an all-conference center off the team for what seemed to be a minor infraction. When five other players pleaded their teammate's case, Bryant sent them packing too. After ten days of this torture, only 27 players remained. Bryant canceled the final four days of training camp out of fear that he wouldn't have enough players left to field a team. Later in life, Bear looked back on his Junction City methods and conceded, "I might have quit too."

The undermanned Aggies finished the season with a dismal 1-9 record, Bear's only losing campaign as a head coach. Still, the shared adversity of Junction City and Bryant's methods served to bond the players, and within two seasons, they were undefeated Cotton Bowl champions.

At this point, we interrupted Coach Goostree, confused about how such an obviously brutal bully could have attained cult status. Goostree explained that if you did your job, there was no one more loyal than Paul Bryant. He seemed to spend as much time helping his former players as he did coaching football. He even loaned them money, never expecting to be repaid a single dime. According to Goostree, Bear's players weren't motivated as much by Bryant driving them as they were by the fear of disappointing their beloved coach.

While Bryant was transforming the hapless Aggies into a national power, Alabama had amassed a pathetic 4-24-2 record from 1955-57. To make matters worse, during this same period, Shug Jordan had transformed arch-rival Auburn into a juggernaut that outscored 'Bama 100-7 in the three so-called Iron Bowls played. The Alabama faithful were anxious for a messiah to bring them back to the gridiron promised land. And even more importantly, we assume they were embarrassed about continuously losing to a guy named Shug.

The 1957 Texas Aggies were undefeated and in national championship contention when Bryant announced that he would be returning home to Alabama at the season's conclusion. Subsequently, the demoralized Aggies lost their final four games, and Bryant was criticized for not showing his players the same commitment and loyalty that he demanded from them. In response to these criticisms, Bear simply responded, "Momma called." (Unfortunately, this excuse didn't work for us when we tried to leave the Crimson Wok without paying our dining bill.)

Despite jokes that he would "win them a championship in two years and have them on probation in three," Bryant was welcomed home to Tuscaloosa as a savior. Jim Goostree recalled his first meeting with the new coach. Bryant called him into his office and said, "If you like me and I like you after spring practice, you've got a job here forever." Goostree turned and headed out the door, chuckling, "I got 50 percent of that licked already, so I better go and work on the other 50 percent." That was the only contract Jim Goostree ever had (or needed) at Alabama.

Bryant believed that there are three kinds of players: "First, there are those that are winners and know they're winners. There are those who are losers and know they're losers. Then there are those who are not winners but don't know it. They're the ones for me. They never quit trying. They're the soul of the game." Fortunately for the Bear, he never met the fourth group of players, of which we are proudly a part. This groups consists of those losers who are so comfortable in their loserdom that winning seems like a frivolous waste of energy.

Bryant's teams of the '60s were stocked with his third groupers: undersized but aggressive kids that seemed to win by sheer determination. Their ability to beat bigger, stronger (and in some cases, racially integrated) teams gave them tremendous appeal to Alabamans.

Although his legend was firmly entrenched in Alabama and the South, Bryant was perceived as a tyrannical outlaw by much of the nation. In 1962, the *Saturday Evening Post* accused Bryant of conspiring with Georgia's Wally Butts to fix a football game. Shocked that Coach Bryant was labeled a Butts' boy, outraged Alabamans saw these baseless accusations as yet another example of the Yankee press libeling one of their heroes. The courts agreed. Bryant's subsequent lawsuit against the Post resulted in a half-million dollar settlement.

As the social upheavals of the '60s reached their height, Alabama was thrust into the public limelight. The images raised by Rosa Parks' arrest, the Selma March, and George Wallace defiantly blocking African-American students from entering the University of Alabama turned the nation against the people of Alabama. Their isolation even extended onto the gridiron. Before the 1963 Orange Bowl, President Kennedy visited the Oklahoma locker room and wished Bud Wilkinson's Sooners good luck, but he snubbed Alabama. Nevertheless, Alabama won 17-0 behind the passing of a little known sophomore named Joe Willie Namath.

Bryant's teams of the early '60s were one of football's great dynasties. His '61 squad captured the national championship while allowing only 25 points the entire season. His '64 and '65 teams brought back-to-back national championships home to Tuscaloosa. Bryant called the '66 team his greatest ever. They culminated their perfect season with a 34-7 thrashing of a Nebraska team that outweighed them by 35 pounds per man, only to finish the season ranked third (behind the Michigan State and Notre Dame teams that played each other to a tie). To Alabamans, this was just another slap in the face from the hostile media.

By the late '60s, the gridiron victories for the segregated Crimson Tide became few and far between, as they slipped into mediocrity. The program reached a turning point in 1970 after USC's Sam "Bam" Cunningham, an African-American, tore through 'Bama's once vaunted defense for over 200 yards during a Southern Cal blowout. Coach Goostree repeated the famous joke: "Sam Cunningham did more for integration in two hours than Martin Luther King did in ten years." Alabama football integrated the following season.

The Southeastern Conference was so backward that they didn't even allow their schools to compete against racially integrated teams until the mid-'60s. Just a year after losing the 1966 NCAA basketball championship to a Texas Western team that featured an all-black starting line-up, Kentucky became the first conference school to integrate their football team. Tragically, Greg Page, Kentucky's first African-American player, suffered a broken neck when he was gang-tackled by his own teammates during practice. He died a few weeks later.

The 1971 season marked the beginning of Bear's second era of success at Alabama. Aside from winning three national championships, Alabama became the first team ever to win one-hundred games during one decade. Instead of little quick kids, these teams consisted of big quick kids. While Bryant certainly appreciated the conditioning and discipline necessary for one-platoon football, no other coach took better advantage of this new era of specialization. Coach Goostree boasted that Bryant's teams were so deep that their second and third stringers could have placed and showed in the SEC. In fact, many letterman never even played, but as Bryant reasoned, as long as they were on his sidelines, they weren't in uniform against him.

As the victories and national championships continued to mount up, Bryant's legend grew to mythological proportions. He retired after the 1982 season as the winningest coach in college football history. During the twilight of his career, Bear often joked that he would "croak in a week" if he ever quit coaching. He actually lasted five weeks. It might not be an exaggeration to say that Bryant coached his heart out. Over a half million mourners viewed his funeral procession as it made its way from Tuscaloosa to Birmingham. A popular sign along the route read, "God just got himself an offensive coordinator."

After sharing that final Bear fact, Jim bid us his leave. Except for the spit ball war we had with the kids at the next table, our time with Coach Goostree was the longest serious interview we did on the entire trip. It had to be that way because Bear Bryant is a serious subject in Alabama.

153

*   *   *   *

Toward the end of his career, Bear Bryant was asked to name the player whom he thought would make the greatest impact on society. Without hesitation, he answered, "John Croyle." When Bryant left the field after coaching his final game, a fan offered to donate $1,000 to Bryant's favorite charity in exchange for an autograph. After signing his name, Bryant instructed the man to mail his check to John Croyle's Big Oak Ranch, a home for abused and neglected children.

John Croyle was an All-American defensive end on Alabama's 1973 national championship team who turned down lucrative offers from the NFL in order to pursue a calling he considered to be far more rewarding. Since its opening in 1974, over a thousand children have called the Big Oak Ranch home. Several residents of the ranch told us that if not for John Croyle, they'd be in jail or dead. Instead, using a combination of tough love, fundamental religion and hard work, the Big Oak Ranch offers its kids a solid foundation upon which to grow.

Justly so, the Big Oak Ranch has become Alabama's favorite charity. With benefactors such as Auburn's Terry Bowden and Alabama's Gene Stallings, the Big Oak Ranch is one of the few things on which fans of these football rivals can agree. After hearing countless people sing the praises of John Croyle, we felt compelled to visit the ranch. Perhaps sensing that he may have two more souls to save, John Croyle agreed to meet us for breakfast at a local diner, after which he gave us a tour of the ranch.

Editor's note...*At this point, I thought to myself, "What the hell were two agnostic Jews doing at a fundamentalist ranch?" There they were, two vagrant football fanatics who shirked responsibility and took off in a limousine, meeting with one devout Christian who existed on the opposite extreme of the responsibility continuum. He was probably the single person, aside from their parents, who would be least amused by their incoherent ramblings. Thankfully, they claim to have been on their best behavior. Furthermore, they maintain that visiting the Big Oak Ranch was one of the most rewarding experiences of the trip. Just as I was beginning to think that there may be a more sensitive and mature* *side to these two, they started belching the "Green Acres" theme song.*

Several weeks after visiting the ranch, we took refuge from a Boulder, Colorado snowstorm in the warmth of an ABC production truck. In exchange for some coffee, donuts and sweatpants, we entertained them with stories from the road. We were completely shocked when the employees from the same network that brought us *Three's Company* and *Fantasy Island* were more interested with John Croyle's efforts at nurturing children than our ability to empty buffet tables and talk our way into places where we shouldn't have been. They were so impressed with the Big Oak Ranch that they made a few phone calls to the head honchos in New York, and within days, ABC had a camera crew in Alabama filming a half-time feature that was broadcast nationally during their Thanksgiving Day games. From that time on, our mothers could rest easily, knowing that at least something useful had come out of this debacle of a trip.

*　　　　*　　　　*　　　　*

When we met ABC's Brent Musberger and Dick Vermeil at West Point later in the trip, we asked them to name their favorite campus eateries. Without hesitation, they simultaneously answered, "Dreamland!" That sentiment seems to be shared by virtually every red-blooded, pork-loving American who has ever visited this celebrated Tuscaloosa rib-shack.

Dreamland is located on a dusty access road, a half-mile and a world apart from the Jiffy Lubes and McDonalds that litter Tuscaloosa's McFarland Boulevard. With its Fred Sanford decor, Dreamland could be described as quaint, but as one of the patrons told us, "We don't use that word 'round here, son." The beauty of Dreamland lies in its simplicity. For a couple of guys who don't like to think and really don't like to make decisions, it's a slice of heaven. There are literally only three choices on the menu: ribs, white bread and sauce. But what a sauce it is! After causing more damage to the pig population than the tragic Porcine Plague of 1972, we split an entire loaf of bread just sopping up the heavenly nectar. Months later, we had a case of sauce shipped home to Boston.

*　　　　*　　　　*　　　　*

Imagine trying to fill Bear's shoes. Now, imagine trying to fill Bear's shoes with cream cheese. An Alabama radio announcer once postulated that the only way to please the fans would be to drop football altogether: "Every Saturday they could go to the stadium and watch old game films. 'Bama would always win and more importantly, the Bear would always be coaching." The Chinese will kick the rice habit before Alabama drops football.

When Ray Perkins was chosen as Bryant's successor, he was initially a popular choice. He was a respected NFL coach, and more importantly, he had been an All-American receiver on Bear's championship teams of the '60s. Perkins and Alabama seemed like a perfect post-Bear marriage. Unfortunately, the union was never consummated.

While his teams were mediocre by Alabama standards (no SEC titles) and his surliness ruffled quite a few feathers, his biggest mistake may have been trying to remove all vestiges of the Bear. He fired Bear's assistants, scrapped Bryant's wishbone offense and removed Bryant's signature coaching tower from the practice field. He supposedly even discouraged the mentioning of former coaches around the football office.

When Perkins returned to the NFL, a place where winning three of every four games earns you a million-dollar bonus instead of the title "Perk the Jerk," he was replaced by Bill Curry. As evidenced by the death threats Curry received upon his appointment, his tenure was doomed from the start.

Curry's only connection to Alabama or the Bear was playing and coaching for arch-rival Georgia Tech. The Tech rivalry was so heated that Bryant used to wear a hard hat whenever his team ventured to Atlanta. Furthermore, there was the perception that Curry, a leading voice of academic reform, was brought in to graduate players rather than churn out football victories. When he lost his first three Iron Bowls to Auburn, his fate was sealed. After winning the Southeastern Conference title in 1989, Curry couldn't take the pressure anymore and bolted for the more genteel fans of Kentucky.

As the '80s came to a close, Alabama had slipped from college football's elite. While they may have dominated the SEC during the '60s and '70s, they had won only one conference championship during the post-Bryant Era. Like the disgruntled boosters of fellow fallen powers Ohio State, Texas and Southern

Cal, 'Bama fans could only scratch their heads and wonder whether they would ever regain their past glory.

In 1990, Gene Stallings was picked to be the man who followed the man who followed the man who followed the legend. Despite having only one winning season in eleven years of coaching at Texas A&M and the NFL Cardinals, Stallings was welcomed with open arms. His status as one of the 27 survivors of Junction City earned him instant credibility with the 'Bama fans. He was so respected by Bryant that when his Texas Aggies beat Alabama in the '68 Cotton Bowl, Bear actually helped carry Stallings off the field. Many insiders insist that Stallings was Bryant's selection to replace him when he retired, but Bear refused to sit on the selection committee, reasoning that he had too many favorite sons.

Although no one will ever replace Bryant, Stallings does comes close. He looks a little like Bear, sounds like Bear, played for Bear, coached under Bear and in many respects, coaches like Bear. He's a no-frills coach who believes teams "win with defense and entertain with offense." While his predecessors squirmed in Bryant's shadow, Stallings relishes it. Pictures of Bryant hang in his office. He even resurrected Bryant's old coaching tower.

Still, taking the 'Bama helm was no cakewalk for Stallings. When his first team dropped five games, Alabama's fickle fans questioned the logic of hiring a coach with such a dismal track record. But that all changed in 1992.

Alabama's 1992 national championship was another example of the Tide proving their critics wrong. All season long, the pollsters debated about the relative merits of Miami and Washington. Unlike the defending co-champion Huskies and Hurricanes, the Crimson Tide didn't rack up large margins of victories. Heck, they barely got by Louisiana Tech. With a dominating defensive front and conservative offense, Stallings' team was a throwback to a bygone era.

However, when Alabama squeaked by Florida in the inaugural SEC championship game, they earned a national championship showdown against Miami. Despite Alabama's perfect record, few pundits believed they had a chance against the Miami juggernaut. ABC's entire Sugar Bowl telecast seemed geared toward a Miami coronation party. In fact, their sideline reporters didn't even bother visiting Alabama's bench until the second half.

Like Miami's 1987 Fiesta Bowl fiasco against Penn State, the Hurricane players showed little respect for their opposition. They griped that Alabama, with their one-dimensional offense, should be playing some Big Eight patsy in the Weed-Whacker Bowl. When Alabama took the field for the pregame introductions, the Miami players turned their backs in disgust. Alabama, however, had the last laugh, as their players dominated the line of scrimmage, and their fans dominated the war of decibels. As the 34-13 Alabama victory concluded, fans were seen addressing the heavens with shouts of "Thank You Bear."

*   *   *   *

After six weeks on the road, stress finally got the best of Bob. Emerging from the shower on a humid afternoon, Bob was dismayed to find there were no clean towels. For almost five minutes, he stood there motionless, looking like a wet Yeti. Then he snapped like a dried out pretzel stick and sloshed out of the room wearing nothing but a strategically placed washcloth and a menacing scowl. To no one in particular, he began screaming about towels, government conspiracies and Billy Buckner's inability to field ground balls.

Bob exploded into the front desk area, loudly demanding his God-given right to clean towels. From the small room behind the front desk, a disembodied voice attempted to make it clear that the front office did not store the towels. In response, Bob changed tactics. Adopting a position similar to that taken by the North during the Civil War, Bob knew that time was on his side. He yelled back to the voice that he would stand in the lobby until she finished whatever she was doing. Clearly, the clerk had had enough of this loudmouth. The sound of her footsteps made their way out to the lobby, followed by a booming voice announcing: "I thought I told you that the front office doesn't have..." She stopped in mid-sentence. Something about the sight before her convinced her to immediately accommodate Bob's request. She was back in a minute with a towel the size of a small state, a bit more respectful and a bit wiser for the world. In the end, the good folks at the Motel 6 got the last laugh as Bob carelessly forgot to pack his clothes when we checked out.

*   *   *   *

"Alabama vs. Tennessee is the quintessential college series. There's no place I'd rather be on the third Saturday in October than Knoxville, Tennessee, or Birmingham, Alabama."
—Keith Jackson

We were fortunate to be witnessing such a great rivalry, even if in recent years, Alabama has dominated Tennessee. The series has been so lopsided, in fact, that a seemingly outrageous prediction (made by the Bear years before to a sad little nine-year-old Tennessee fan) was becoming a self-fulfilling prophecy. After a heartbreaking Volunteer loss to the Crimson Tide, the little girl tearfully asked Bear if Tennessee would ever beat Alabama again. The compassionate Bryant consoled the small child: "Tennessee will beat Alabama... Maybe not in your lifetime, but eventually they will beat Alabama."

While the Bear once amassed a ten-game winning streak against the Vols, Stallings' teams were in the midst of a seven-game streak. At least Bryant's teams were always better than Tennessee. Five of Alabama's seven wins during the current streak could be classified as upsets.

In many ways, the 1990 contest best represents Tennessee's frustrations. Playing in Knoxville, third-ranked Tennessee was a prohibitive favorite over unranked Alabama. But as Tide fanatic Butch Gurton explained: "We're Alabama, they're Tennessee. That alone gave us a distinct advantage." Despite self-destructing all afternoon, the Volunteers seemed destined to eek out a victory as they drove down field in the waning moments of a tie game. But with just over a minute remaining, 'Bama blocked Tennessee's potential game-winning field goal and recovered the ball on the Tennessee 37-yard-line. Three plays later, Philip Doyle kicked the decisive field goal, giving the Tide an improbable 9-6 victory.

Aside from leading to the demise of former head coach Johnny Majors, the recent 'Bama domination has led to quite a few derisive jokes. A fan came up to us with his right arm chopping the air and asking, "What's this?" After observing our dumbfounded looks, he continued, "In Atlanta, it's the Tomahawk Chop; in Tallahassee, it's the War Chant; but, in Knoxville, it means First Down Al-Aah-Bama!" Either confidence is running high in Alabama, or this is just one of those rivalries where the opposing fans really enjoy antagonizing each other; it's probably a combination of both. A *Tide Sports Weekly* poll revealed that 33 percent of the Crimson Tiders found Tennessee to have the most obnoxious fans in the Southeastern Conference. (Auburn finished second with 25 percent, followed by Florida at 19 percent. Georgia Tech received a couple of votes retroactive to when they were members of the SEC.)

*   *   *   *

This year's game promised to be a classic. Led by Heisman Trophy candidate Heath Shuler, the Vols were considered to be one of the most talented teams in the country. Gameday morning, we got up early, drove from Tuscaloosa to Birmingham and set off to see the whole spectacle of devout 'Bama fans and their version of the pregame tailgate. There we were, two would-be journalists surrounded by acres upon acres of rabid football fans in a city that prides itself on being the "Football Capital of the South." So, what do we do? Do we search out Dick Coffee, who has been to 528 consecutive games, or Jeff Coleman, who has attended 43 of Alabama's 45 bowl games? Do we find Alf Van Hoose, the 86-year-old retired editor of the *Birmingham News*, who may be the world's foremost authority on Alabama football? Or, do we chat with fans whose personal anecdotes could fill an entire book?

How about not doing any of it? As luck would have it, the very first tailgate we visited was catered by Dreamland. Just as the hypnotic song of the Sirens distracted the sailors of Greek mythology, the aroma from those succulent ribs made us completely forget about why we had come to Alabama. Wary of suffering sauce-induced gastritis, we attempted to moderate our intake — not of the ribs, but of the air in between mouthfuls. We figured that if we were going to get stomach aches, we might as well get it over as quickly as possible. Luckily, an early kickoff prevented us from doing further damage to ourselves.

Apart from failing to purchase a few slabs of ribs for the ride north to South Bend, our biggest regret was not meeting Jerry Bogle and Troy Ferguson, Alabama's two most recognizable fans. Standing 6'5" with a combined weight over 600 pounds, they're known by various names ranging from the Roll Tide Guys to the Big Dogs. Even if they were pencil-necks, you'd have to be colorblind to miss them in their crimson pants, garish suspenders and oversized Alabama ties. Before during and after games, they wield their signature pieces, clubs with a box of Tide and an attached roll of toilet paper (get it, *roll tide*). They've become so entrenched in Alabama lore that their original Tide boxes (autographed by the Bear) are enshrined in the Paul Bryant Museum. It has become a tradition among those visiting the museum to rub the Bear's autograph for luck. So many have rubbed the Tide box that the autograph has completely worn out. We rubbed it anyway

Roll Tide!

*   *   *   *

Sitting right behind Jim Goostree, we watched the game from the press box. Because of the restrictions against cheering, there is no worse place from which to watch a game. Completely cut off from the fans, we restlessly roamed the press box in search of amusement and immediately stumbled upon a shameless Tennessee Sports Information Department promotion. To advance Heath Shuler's Heisman campaign, they had left informational folders for every member of the media. To leave a sweet memento, each folder contained a Heath Bar.

One of the biggest fallacies with the Heisman race is that it often boils down to a contest of gimmicks rather than performance. To promote Ty Detmer for the Heisman, Brigham Young sent ties to the media. Notre Dame's Joe Theisman actually changed the pronunciation of his name as part of an unsuccessful Heisman bid. (His name used to rhyme with the last two syllables of the phrase "Lawrence Taylor snapped my knees, man!") Hopefully, it was Charlie Ward's offensive leadership and not us swiping the Heath Bars out of every folder that cost Shuler the Heisman. Regardless, we did filch enough candy to last until the end of our trip, or so we thought. Actually, we finished the last of the three dozen candy bars three days later.

*   *   *   *

Suffering no ill effects of our rib feast, we watched Alabama write another chapter in Tennessee's frustrating attempts to turn the Tide. With 104 seconds and no time-outs remaining, Alabama trailed 17-9 with the ball on their own 18. *Rocky Top* was blaring as the Tennessee fans began celebrating their impending victory. The Volunteer faithful then watched in amazement and disgust as Jay Barker engineered an incredible last minute touchdown drive. Still down by two points, Alabama's David Palmer scrambled across the goal line to tie the game. Amid the game-ending hysteria that even permeated the press box, an elated Jim Goostree turned to us and said, "That's what it's all about!"

Coach Goostree's succinct summation would have been a fitting ending to this chapter, but prior to our departure from the last school on our southern swing, we caught another sight that moved us. While patiently waiting in line in the bathroom, we spotted two guys standing side-by-side at the urinals. One was dressed in crimson and the other in the ugliest shade of orange this side of Danny Bonaduce's hair. There wasn't a natural fiber between them. They were both obviously disappointed at the sister-kissing tie they had just witnessed. The Tennessee fan commented, "Well I guess this way both sides have something to bitch about." The 'Bama fan responded "You guys played one heck of a game." Then in a gesture that exemplifies the sportsmanship that college football is supposed to be about, each one removed his hand from where it had been only a few moments before and exchanged what must have been a very warm hand-shake.

On that note, we made our way back to the limo, bid the South adieu, a few pounds heavier and a wealth of information richer, and set out for the college football promised land: Notre Dame.

Alabama's elephant mascot prepares to enjoy some Dreamland ribs.

SATURDAY AFTERNOON MADNESS
FOOTBALL HALL OF FAME

A few years ago, ESPN named its all-time college football team. The team was selected by a panel of former college players, coaches and media representatives.

OFFENSE	DEFENSE
QB Roger Staubach, Navy 1964	L Lucious Selmon, Oklahoma 1975
QB Sammy Baugh, TCU 1938	L Hugh Green, Pitt 1980
QB John Elway, Stanford 1982	L Bob Lilly, TCU 1960
HB Red Grange, Illinois 1924	L Alex Karras, Iowa 1957
HB O.J. Simpson, USC 1968	LB Lee Roy Jordan, Alabama 1962
HB Jim Thorpe, Carlisle 1912	LB Dick Butkus, Illinois 1964
HB Herschel Walker, Georgia 1982	LB Tommy Nobis, Texas 1965
WR Don Hutson, Alabama 1934	LB Chuck Bednarik, Penn 1948
WR Johnny Rodgers, Nebraska 1972	DB Ronnie Lott, USC 1979
WR Lynn Swann, USC 1973	DB Kenny Easley, UCLA 1978
L John Hannah, Alabama 1972	DB Mel Renfro, Oregon 1963
L Leo Nomellini, Minnesota 1948	DB Jack Tatum, Ohio State 1968
L George Connor, Notre Dame 1947	P Ray Guy, Southern Miss 1972
L Ron Yary, USC 1967	P Russell Erxleben, Texas 1977
L Anthony Munoz, USC 1978	
C Dave Remington, Nebraska 1983	Coach Paul Bryant, Alabama 1982

While there is no arguing the merits of these outstanding players, we would like to salute some of college football's more intriguing personalities:

Pete Tinsley, Georgia: When this All-SEC guard of the late-'30s was questioned about his toughness, he demonstrated his manhood by cutting a slit through his cheek and smoking a cigar through it.

Bob Khayat, Mississippi: This Ole Miss place-kicker of the early sixties dated Barbara Sue Jansen and Mandy Pepperidge, back-to-back Miss Americas. Although Ole Miss quarterback Archie Manning was never one to kiss-and-tell, he supposedly surpassed Khayat's accomplishments.

Tommy Lewis, Alabama: With Alabama trailing Rice 7-6 midway through the second quarter of the 1954 Cotton Bowl, Owl halfback Dickie Moegel broke free and scampered down the Alabama sideline headed for an apparent touchdown. Just when all hope seemed lost for the Tide, fullback Tommy Lewis raced off the bench and made an astonishing open field tackle. Despite Lewis' heroics, the stunned officials awarded Rice the touchdown. An apologetic Lewis later explained that he was "just too full of 'Bama."

Roy "Wrong Way" Riegels, California: This All-American center's accomplishments have been eclipsed by his infamous wrong way run in the 1927 Rose Bowl. With the Bears trailing Georgia Tech 6-0, Riegels snatched up a Tech fumble and made a mad dash toward the end zone. But after absorbing a couple of hits at midfield, the dazed and confused Riegels started running in the wrong direction. 70,000 spectators watched in bewilderment as Riegels raced toward his own end zone with his frantic teammates in close pursuit. After Riegels was tackled at the 3-yard-line, Cal elected to punt on the next play. The punt was blocked, resulting in the safety that proved to be the margin of defeat in Cal's heartbreaking 8-7 loss. For the rest of his life, "Wrong Way" Riegels lived with the ignominy of committing the biggest boner in the history of college football. Lehigh's Snookie Dowd pulled a similar *faux pas,* but upon crossing his own end line, he realized his error, circled the goal posts and ran the length of the field, culminating the longest touchdown run in football history.

Denny Clark, Michigan: Entering their 1905 contest with Chicago, Fielding "Hurry Up" Yost's Michigan's teams hadn't lost in five seasons. With no score, Denny Clark fielded a punt in his own end zone. Instead of downing it for the touchback, Clark attempted to advance the ball and was flattened by the Chicago defenders. The resultant safety proved to be the game's only score. Headlines read, "Clark 2, Michigan 0." Within a weak, a distraught Clark dropped out of school and became a hermit in Northern Michigan.

Clarence Herschberger, Chicago: This halfback, who was the Midwest's first All-American, was the originator of the spiral punting style. For years, spiral punts were often referred to as "Herschbergers." However, we were more impressed with his feats of gluttony. He once suffered such severe gastric distress after downing 13 soft-boiled eggs that he missed an important game against Wisconsin. After Chicago's defeat, legendary coach Amos Alonzo Stagg remarked, "We weren't beaten by 12 Badgers, but by 13 eggs."

Jim Thorpe, Carlisle: As a football player, there was no one comparable. With an inhuman combination of strength and speed, he was just as comfortable faking out would-be tacklers as he was plowing right through them. On defense, he used cross-body blocks to completely flatten the opposing ball carriers. He could also punt the ball the length of the football field. But his talents extended far beyond the gridiron. In addition to playing professional baseball for the New York Giants, he was a champion boxer, swimmer and professional wrestler. After he won both the decathlon and pentathlon at the Stockholm Olympics in 1912, Sweden's King Gustav declared him to be "the greatest athlete in the world." He won't get any arguments here.

Byron "Whizzer" White, Colorado: With a combination of speed, strength and intelligence, Whizzer White earned All-American honors and a Rhodes Scholarship while leading the nation in scoring and total offense in 1939. He was also an All-American in basketball. With the Detroit Lions, he led the NFL in rushing, while simultaneously earning a law degree from Yale. As a World War II intelligence officer, Whizzer was awarded two bronze stars. Years later, President Kennedy appointed White to the Supreme Court, where Justice White presided until 1990.

Tommy "The Toe" Walker, Southern Cal: Besides originating the "da da da dut da duh, charge!" cheer, this USC drum major of the mid-'50s also kicked field goals for the Trojans. He wore no pads, and at the end of the second quarter, he would quickly slip into his drum major uniform and lead the band's half-time show

Amos Alonzo Stagg, Chicago: "Football's Grand Old Man" may be the most noble figure in the history of American sports. After earning All-American honors for Walter Camp at Yale, Stagg embarked on an illustrious coaching career that spanned three quarters of a century. When Knute Rockne commented, "All football comes from Stagg," he wasn't exaggerating. Among his innovations, Stagg is credited with originating the center snap, backfield shifts, the numbering of players and wind sprints. But his contributions to sports and education extend far beyond the gridiron. Beside pioneering baseball's first head first slide and the indoor batting cage, Stagg is credited with introducing baseball to Japan. At Springfield College, he was a close associate of Dr. James Naismith when the game of basketball was being invented. In track, he served on the Olympic committee for almost three decades and coached the first sprinter ever to break 10 seconds in the 100 meter dash. He even presided over a folk dancing society. As a football coach, Stagg's longevity records may never be equaled. After being forced into mandatory retirement from Chicago following his 70th birthday, he went on to coach at Pacific for fourteen more seasons. For six subsequent seasons, he helped his son coach at Susquehanna. In fact, Stagg remained active in the game until the ripe old age of 98. Although he retired as college football's all-time winningest coach, Stagg is remembered as the sport's ultimate gentleman. Not only did this former divinity student never drink, smoke or swear, he was so honest that he once asked the referee to call back a Chicago touchdown because he thought his team had committed a penalty on the play.

South Bend, Indiana
Notre Dame vs. Southern Cal

Gin One for the Gipper

After a five-week trek through the heartland of southern football, we were both ready for a change. Notre Dame was next and offered us a welcome break from the overabundance of southern hospitality and food. Don't get us wrong, we loved the South and everything associated with it. But, if we had dedicated the whole season to covering southern football, we would probably have weighed 300 pounds by the time the bowl games rolled around. It was time to move on, and what better place to go than the collective soul of college football: Notre Dame.

Notre Dame has the most ballyhooed history of any football school. In fact, it may have been a Golden Domer who coined the term "ballyhooed." To say Notre Dame is ingrained in American culture is an understatement. Its *Victory March* is America's fourth most recognizable song,[1] and the institution of Mother's Day was the brainchild of Frank Hering, a former Notre Dame coach. Notre Dame's impact on the American psyche is so pervasive that it even played a role in Ronald Reagan's election to the presidency. Reagan's spin doctors used his Notre Dame

---

1 In terms of recognizability, the *Victory March* trails only the *Star Spangled Banner, God Bless America,* and *White Christmas.* Wild Cherry's *Play That Funky Music White Boy* rounds out the top five.

connection to bolster his image, nicknaming him the Gipper in honor of the heroic Notre Dame player whom Reagan portrayed in *Knute Rockne: All American.* To celebrate Reagan's landslide election victories, Notre Dame's *Victory March* blared out at his inaugurations. No matter what people thought of his policies, how could you doubt anyone who made such a heartfelt deathbed request?

Much like our 40th president, Notre Dame evokes an emotional response in all fans. You either love them or hate them. Lou Holtz once said: "Only an atheist doesn't care whether Notre Dame wins or loses." Former Notre Dame coach Dan Devine maintained: "There are two kinds of people in the world: Notre Dame lovers and Notre Dame haters. And quite frankly, they're both a pain in the ass."

With legions of fans vicariously sharing their victories and defeats alike, Notre Dame is undeniably college football's marquee team. While the mystiques surrounding the Yankees and Celtics have dissipated with their descents into mediocrity, the public's fascination with Notre Dame remains. No matter where they finish in the polls, Notre Dame is always the national champion in fan interest.

Quite frankly, Notre Dame sells. Whether it be on TV, in the movies or in the bookstores, there is an insatiable thirst for Notre Dame. During our football trip alone, three books and one Hollywood movie about Notre Dame football received national attention.

*   *   *   *

As we left Ann Arbor, our vermin-hating friends, Scott and Paul, warned us not to be lulled by the aura of the Golden Dome, not to be driven like lemmings into the Irish sea, not to be attracted like birds to bees and, most of all, not to be lured like herring to the pickling barrel of Notre Dame lore. Having always possessed an antipathy towards Notre Dame, we assured them we were more likely to become vegetarians than Notre Dame zealots.

Had Scott or Paul been with us as our 10,000-pound black scrap-metal collection motored toward South Bend, they would have puked. In anticipation of visiting college football's most historic campus, our hunger for Notre Dame knowledge grew and grew — possibly compounded by the fact that we hadn't eaten in nearly two hours. Unbelievable as it may seem, our hunger vanished as we crested the final hill leading toward Notre Dame because suddenly, right before us, rose the Golden Dome. We were lulled, driven, attracted and pickled.

For two decidedly non-Catholics, the feelings we felt as the Mecca of college football appeared before us can only be described as baptismal. Suddenly, Scott and Paul's words became mere clatter in our ears. We were sucked in by the seductive call of Notre Dame like a lo mein noodle. Spielberg, Capra, Craven and Kubrick couldn't hope to capture the emotion of our first sight of the fabled Golden Dome.

Mesmerized by the Midas-like opulence, Phil barely noticed the car rising again. Yet he was vaguely aware that we were not driving on a hill. We were levitating, the pull of the sweet Irish *Victory March* drew our physical beings higher and higher and...

"I'm hungry, Let's pick up a sack of cheeseburgers." Bob's voice shattered the image. He rescued Phil from his MSG flash-back in time to see he was pulling into a service station. Even though food was often present, we had come to loathe gas stations. Each stop reminded us that we were traveling in the economic leper of the industry. Forty-two dollars and three zagnuts later, we were back on the road. If only we could find a Holiday Inn with an all-you-can-fuel gas bar to compliment what had become our standard dinner fare: the happy-hour buffet.

Back on the road, we passed through the none-too-sleepy burg of South Bend just itchin' to jump into the Irish hype. Suddenly, Bob executed a driving maneuver that, until that point in time, had only been performed by Buddy Joe Hooker in the painfully vehicular *Smokey and the Bandit* series. Bob managed to combine a 180-degree turn at 35 mph with parallel parking. The resulting screech only barely covered the sound of shrieking coeds as our 20-foot-long black wave slid into a parking spot. Phil looked over at Bob, who said in his best Bill Murray voice, "Gunga, galunga." Phil acknowledged Bob's insight with a slight nod and we dove into the sea of Domers.

*   *   *   *

The Fighting Irish have carved a unique niche in the American sports psyche through a careful blend of myth and reality. While other schools have stories, Notre Dame has lore. Having both seen *Knute Rockne: All-American* at an early age, we knew a little of the folklore. Now, as wiser, wider, and more mature consumers of propaganda, we wanted a little more depth.

Answers weren't hard to find. They were only as far away as the next group of Irish coeds, or the nearest South Bend bar stool. Over the course of five days, we heard enough aggrandizing Irish lore to make us seriously consider conversion. (We eventually decided that guiltless pork consumption didn't justify further alienating ourselves from our families.)

The first legend we sought out was that of the Gipper. To Golden Domers, the mere mention of the word "Gipper" creates chills, similar to the feeling we get when somebody sneaks up behind us and whispers, "free chicken wings."

According to Notre Dame lore, George Gipp, one of the greatest all-around players in college football history, contracted strep throat while leading the Irish to victory over mighty Northwestern in 1920. As he lay dying, he was baptized into the Catholic church. Moments later, the heroic Gipp died in Rockne's arms, but not before uttering this immortal last request:

> I've got to go, Rock. It's all right. I'm not afraid. Some time, Rock, when the team is up against it, when things are wrong and the breaks are beating the boys, tell them to go out there with all they got and win one for the Gipper. I don't know where I'll be then, but I'll know about it, and I'll be happy.

Knute Rockne waited eight years to grant Gipp his final request. An injury-riddled Notre Dame squad was given little chance against the undefeated Army juggernaut in 1928. When Rockne told his team of Gipp's death-bed request, there wasn't a dry eye in the locker room. In what some have called the greatest display of inspirational football ever played, Notre Dame upset Army 12-6.

Just how inspiring was Rockne's "Win one for the Gipper speech?" When Pat O'Brien delivered it to his players while filming *Knute Rockne: All American*, the actors were driven to tears. Before O'Brien could finish, one of the players jumped to his feet and screamed, "Let's Go!" The actors literally tore apart the set while charging out of the locker room. Filming was delayed several hours while the set was rebuilt.

Much like his presidential portrayer, historical revision has not always been kind to George Gipp. There's no denying the magnitude of his athletic accomplishments. Walter Camp named him college football's most outstanding player in 1920 and Knute Rockne compared him favorably to both Red Grange and Jim Thorpe. Beside leading the Irish in passing and rushing for three straight seasons, Gipp could drop-kick a ball 70 yards. His name still peppers the Notre Dame record book and his career rushing record wasn't eclipsed until the late '70s. Even more amazing, football was his second sport. Gipp was so skilled at baseball that he planned to play for the Chicago Cubs after his Notre Dame eligibility expired.

Despite his authenticated athletic talents, revisionists now focus on his off-field exploits as indicative of the time and the man. Apparently, Gipp was a drunk and a womanizer who favored the local pool halls and saloons over the classroom. Boasting that he was the finest gambler ever to attend Notre Dame, Gipp's gambling income allowed him to reside in South Bend's luxurious Oliver hotel. He also used to bet on Notre Dame football games, often feigning illness and hangovers to swing the betting odds against his own team. Like *Animal House's* Daniel Simpson Day, his academic transcript was completely blank. In an era where athletes, especially athletes playing for Rockne, were allowed tremendous leniency, Gipp was actually expelled from Notre Dame. Only after Rockne pulled a few strings was he readmitted.

There is even considerable doubt as to whether Gipp ever made his famous dying request, or whether Rockne was in any position to hear it. But what kind of depraved individual would make up such a story? Just remember, Rockne once claimed his son was dying just to give his team an added emotional edge against Georgia Tech.

While there's no doubting the Gipper Speech did inspire his team and Notre Dame did beat a supposedly superior Army squad, it may not have been the most important ingredient in Notre Dame's 12-6 victory. That distinction probably belongs to Rockne and his dedicated band of crony-officials. With Army inside the Notre Dame 1-yard-line, Rockne's ringers declared the game to be over. Nevertheless, the phrase "Win one for the Gipper" has become ingrained into American culture as a rallying cry against seemingly insurmountable odds.

*   *   *   *

Legend has it that the Gipp's ghost still haunts Washington Hall. One story explains that a drunken Gipp contracted his fatal strep throat while sleeping on its steps, so there he remains. Another tale claims that Gipp's specter is drawn there by the pool table. However, we felt the most logical explanation was the one offered to us by student Shamus McAnus. He told us the villainous Captain Parmenter concocted the ghost rumor to scare the students away while he searched for Chief Wild Eagle's treasure in the basement. Would have succeeded too, if not for those meddling kids!

We attempted to contact the legendary spirit. Since neither of us had ever been to a seance, we weren't sure how to communicate with the dead. Per an old episode of Gilligan's Island, a Ouija board would have helped. Unfortunately, we only had a Monopoly board. Nevertheless, we descended upon Washington Hall and in tribute to Gipp's presidential portrayer, we sprinkled jellybeans throughout the basement.

All-American George Gipp

Editor's embellishment...Unfortunately, the jelly bean selection doomed their ceremony. In some sort of bizarre transference, a shimmering, iridescent ape appeared and began pelting them with their own jelly beans. Welts erupted on their faces and hands. They surely would have perished, or received a lot more welts anyway, if Bob had not been able to scream, "Away Bonzo!" Upon hearing the sound of his own name, the transparent ape vanished. Humbled and shaken, they left Washington Hall, but not before toasting the legendary Gippster with a shot of gin and chanting the following incantation in his honor.

We decided to take a journey,
A college football tour,
To search the football history,
The legends, myths and lore.

And the story that we needed
to complete our football trip
is a name that lives at Notre Dame,
The legendary Gipp

They say you were like no one else
for a run or pass or kick.
And no one less than Reagan
could have played you in that flick.

Revisionists have questioned you
and called your legend fraud.
They say you caught pneumonia
from to much brew and broad.

But we now wish to honor you
in your final resting home.
Your head should be anointed.
Yours was not a tarnished dome.

So, if you now are hearing us
We leave you with this thought:
If you were into booze and broads
we drink to you a shot.

As you look down upon your team,
we raise a toast to thee:
A "gin one for the Gipper"
and bad luck to USC.

      *   *   *   *

Notre Dame football is a unique synthesis of religion and athletics. If Alabama earned its glory from the brawny drudgery of sheer hard work, Notre Dame's fortunes have emanated from deep within the soul. Catholic ritual has become so ingrained in football that even non-Catholic players have been known to take pregame communion and light candles in the Grotto — as if a team stacked with all those prep All-Americans actually needed divine intervention. To further underscore their belief that they are the very antithesis of evil, Notre Dame deems all games against Miami as "Catholics vs. Convicts." Even the players themselves have helped perpetrate the gridiron Holy Trinity (God, Notre Dame, Football). With names like Jerome Heavens, Sonny Church and Norb Christman, how could the school not promote this angel, er angle? Only Notre Dame could win a championship with a coach named Devine and sink to the unspeakable depths of mediocrity under the leadership of Faust.

As we walked through the picturesque campus, we couldn't help but notice that landmarks amplify this football-religion connection. Nowhere is this integration better illustrated than the 132-foot mosaic of Jesus on the facing of the Hesburgh Library. Because Jesus has His arms extended like a referee signaling a touchdown, fans have christened Him as "Touchdown Jesus." With the top of the mural looming ominously over the stadium, Touchdown Jesus serves as Notre Dame's spiritual twelfth man.

Although Touchdown Jesus has become a fixed component of the mystique surrounding Notre Dame football, many Catholics consider this trivialization of a devout religious symbol to be nothing short of blasphemy. One purple-haired lady harshly lectured us for almost ten minutes for referring to the mosaic as Touchdown Jesus. (Bob's sneeze into her artichoke dip may have also contributed to her fury.) She explained how the mural depicts Jesus coming off the cross, one of the most sacred events of her religion. We apologized for our insensitivity and promised never again to debase her religious symbols with football-related nicknames.

So from that point on, we referred to the mosaic as "I Caught A Fish This Big Jesus." Just a few yards from the mosaic stands a statue of Moses with his right hand and index finger extended heavenward declaring, "There is only one God." While blasphemous football fans have dubbed the statue, "We're #1 Moses," we alternated between the less offensive "Turn Your Head And Cough Moses" and "Show Us A Booger Moses." Continuing our purge of football-related nicknames, we dubbed the statue of "Fair Catch Corby" as "Who Wants Seconds On Last Night's Meatloaf Corby."

I Caught A Fish This Big Jesus

Turn Your Head and Cough Moses

*   *   *   *

Notre Dame was founded by Father Edward Sorin in 1842 to educate the frontier dwellers. Unlike more established schools, Notre Dame never turned down a student for lack of funds or previous education. Indigent students could work off their tuition by performing odd jobs around the campus. Notre Dame even served as a secondary school to bring substandard students up to speed.

Because Sorin was a Frenchman who, supposedly, was never very fond of the Irish because of a perceived lack of obedience, we're not exactly sure why Notre Dame is referred to as the "Fighting Irish." Perhaps the "Non-bathing Frenchmen" nickname was too hard to accurately depict on a helmet.

Despite moderate success during their first quarter-century of football, the Notre Dame legend wasn't truly established until their monumental upset over Army in 1913. When easterners saw Army's 1913 football schedule, they asked, "Notre who?" Knowledgeable fans knew that Notre Dame was a decent western team that had lost only once during the past three seasons while feasting on such cupcakes as St. Viator and Morris Harvey (two schools slated to appear on Nebraska's forthcoming schedule). Nevertheless, when Army agreed to pay Notre Dame

$1,000 to come east, they anticipated little more than a warm-up for the following week's Navy game. This assessment, however, turned out to be the biggest military miscalculation since General Custer concluded that Geronimo was only bringing his tribe to Little Big Horn to build a casino.

As this dialogue between quarterback Gus Dorais and end Knute Rockne from the film *Knute Rockne: All-American* indicates, Notre Dame had a little surprise for the Black Knights of the Hudson:

> **Dorais:** Army will outweigh us twenty pounds to the man. We couldn't lick them if we took a shotgun along.
> **Rockne:** All right — We'll take a shotgun... We're going to pass the Army... pass 'em dizzy!
> **Dorais:** Rock — if that works, it'll make history!

Although the forward pass had been legalized in 1906, it remained, for the most part, an untapped weapon. Mainstream schools considered it a risky tactic, only to be used as a last resort. As luck would have it, several rules changes (most notably the reduction of the football circumference by almost four inches) were adopted after the 1912 season, thus further liberalizing the passing game. After Gus Dorais and Knute Rockne spent the entire summer perfecting their pass patterns, the forward pass was inserted into the Notre Dame offense.

Even with this offensive surprise, no Notre Dame fable is complete without the use of Irish cunning and guile to pull the whole thing off, and the 1913 Army game was no different. When Army sent scouts to Notre Dame's game against Alma College, the Irish concealed their aerial abilities by running into the line, the standard conservative offensive tactic of the era. Accordingly, Army prepared themselves for Notre Dame's ground attack.

Many bodies of literature share recurring themes. For example, the plot lines of the Greek New Comedies featured a deceptive and witty slave outwitting his idiotic master. Every episode of *Columbo* involved the humble but brilliant Inspector Columbo outmaneuvering his wealthy but morally corrupt adversary. Likewise, Notre Dame lore contains a similar populist theme. Despite great odds, the Irish always "win over all" through determination, emotion, intelligence, deception, and divine luck.

On November 12, 1913, 18 Notre Dame players and 14 pairs of cleats arrived in New York City after an arduous cross-country train journey. The gamesmanship started right from the opening kickoff. To lull his opponent into a false sense of security, Rockne played possum. (No, he didn't root around in garbage cans before getting run over at night.) He pretended to have an injured leg, but when the time was right, Rockne broke out of his limp and into a full sprint. Quarterback Gus Dorais hit a wide open Rockne and the game of football has never been the same. Behind a balanced attack of running and passing, Notre Dame coasted to a shocking 35-13 upset. In one fell swoop, Notre Dame had earned national prominence, while legitimizing the forward pass.

       *   *   *   *

Whatever his acumen as a player may have been, Knute Rockne truly established his legend as a coach. Rockne coached in an age of heroes. Baseball had the Babe, golf had Bobby Jones, boxing had Jack Dempsey and football had Knute Rockne and his Notre Dame Ramblers, as they were known back then. Under Rockne's tutelage, Notre Dame earned three national championships and enjoyed five undefeated seasons. Rock's .881 (105-12-5) lifetime winning percentage remains unsurpassed by any other collegiate or professional coach. Still, the importance of Rockne's Notre Dame teams cannot be measured by wins and losses.

Those Rockne-led Notre Dame teams seemed to embody the American Dream: no matter how humble your roots were, with hard work and a little luck you could succeed. Rockne molded the children of immigrants into a cohesive unit that barnstormed across the country, upsetting the bigger and stronger teams from the more established universities. Just as successful football teams helped rebuild the wounded psyches of southerners, Notre Dame football became a symbol of the triumph of Catholicism in America. In an era where NINA (No Irish Need Apply) signs were posted in shop windows and 30 percent of the white male population of Notre Dame's home state of Indiana belonged to the Ku Klux Klan, Irish Catholics could feel vindicated with every Notre Dame triumph. Yet, Notre Dame's appeal extended far beyond Irish Catholics. Notre Dame served as a bastion for all nationalities. For example, the backfield for their 1930 national championship team consisted of two Jews and two Italians (and four nagging mothers).

While Knute Rockne may not have been the chemistry prodigy that he was portrayed to be in the highly sanitized film *Knute Rockne: All American*, he was truly a brilliant and innovative football strategist. He designed his own uniforms that were both lighter and stronger than anything on the market. His "shock troops," a full team of second stringers that he deployed at the start of most games, were the predecessors of two-platoon football. Rockne is also credited with inventing the buttonhook, albeit accidentally. (During the 1913 Penn State game, he slipped while going out for a pass, but scrambled to his feet in time to catch the pass when the Penn State defender overran him.)

Knute Rockne

Still, Rockne's greatest innovations were his deceptive Notre Dame shifts. Inspired by the rhythmic precision of a chorus line, Rockne had all four backs in motion when the ball was snapped. The shift's reliance on speed rather than brawn is best illustrated by the fact that Elmer Layden, the largest of the legendary Four Horseman, weighed only 162 pounds, not much more than Lou Holtz. Rockne's shifts so dumbfounded the opposition that many of football's illegal motion penalties came about in an effort to limit the Rock's advantage.

Although it's fun to chuckle at his flair for melodrama, Rockne's fire-and-brimstone pep talks really did work. During half time of a 1927 game against Minnesota, the Golden Gophers sat silently in the locker room listening to Rockne's pep talk through the thin walls. When Rockne finished, the Minnesota coach jumped to his feet and screamed, "You heard what [Rockne] said. Now do that to them!" His players were so inspired that they tied Notre Dame 7-7.

      *   *   *   *

No discussion of Notre Dame during the Rockne era would be complete without some mention of the Four Horsemen. Notre Dame's 13-7 triumph over Army in 1924 inspired Grantland Rice to write the most famous column of his illustrious career. We even met several alumni who had committed Rice's words to memory. The column read:

> Outlined against a blue-gray October sky, The Four Horsemen rode again. In dramatic lore they are known as famine, pestilence, destruction and death. These are only aliases. Their real names are: Stuhldreyer, Miller, Crowley and Layden. They formed the crest of the South Bend cyclone before which another fighting Army team was swept over the precipice at the Polo Grounds this afternoon as 55,000 spectators peered down on the bewildered panorama spread out about the green plain below.

If we had been covering the game instead of Grantland Rice, Notre Dame's backfield would have long since slipped into obscurity, but the press box buffet would have been forever immortalized. Still, can you imagine what Rice would have written if Notre Dame had scored more than 13 points? When the wire services picked up a publicity photo of the four uniformed men atop horses, their legend was born. The Four Horsemen quickly became the most fabled quartet in sports history. Just how good were the Horsemen? Good enough to earn three of the four spots on various All-American teams, and if not for Red Grange, the Horsemen might have enjoyed a clean sweep.

Notre Dame only lost twice during the reign of the Four Horsemen. Both losses were at Lincoln, Nebraska. The bigger and slower Nebraska teams neutralized Notre Dame's speed by turning their field into a giant mud pit. While these football setbacks loom as insignificant tiles in the grand mosaic of Notre

Dame's gridiron history, what is significant is the harsh treatment Notre Dame received from the fervently anti-Catholic fans in Lincoln. According to Murray Sperber's opus, *Shake Down the Thunder,* local headlines read "Horrible Hibernians Invade Today," and mobs of bigoted fans taunted Notre Dame's Irish Catholic heritage. Incidentally, when Nebraska finally ventured to South Bend in 1924, The Four Horsemen shellacked them 34-6.

*   *   *   *

With their upset over Michigan during the second week of the 1993 season, Notre Dame was instantly transformed by the media from a punchless rebuilding squad into a bona fide championship contender. It seemed only fitting that the rancor surrounding *Under the Tarnished Dome* dissipated in favor of the Hollywood hype accompanying the release of the movie *Rudy.* Even though Rudy's detractors have written him off as a publicity-seeking buffoon (hey, that's what they said about us), we broke our long-standing boycott of all movies devoid of *Saturday Night Live* cast members to see *Rudy* in South Bend.

Rudy tells the inspirational tale of an underdog who triumphs through his indomitable will. Because of his dearth of intelligence and diminutive stature (5'6", 170 pounds), Daniel "Rudy" Ruetteger's lifelong goal of playing football for Notre Dame appeared to be unattainable. Nevertheless, Rudy pursued his dream. After finally being admitted to Notre Dame as a 26-year-old junior, Rudy toiled on the practice squad where his fearless demeanor and dogged determination earned him the respect of his teammates and coaches.

He was rewarded for his commitment and sacrifice by being allowed to dress for the final game of his senior season. As the game clock wound down on another Notre Dame victory, the fans started chanting "Rudy! Rudy!" When Coach Devine inserted him into the game, Rudy made the most of his opportunity. On the game's final play, he sacked the opposing quarterback, and to this day, he remains the last Irish player to be carried off the field (in a conscious state).

*   *   *   *

In many ways, Notre Dame's gridiron success stems from a culture of athleticism that has permeated the South Bend campus since the 19th century. In *Shake Down The Thunder*, Murray Sperber points out that "Notre Dame's ability to harness and focus the majority of its students into sports endeavors and... attract like-minded and athletically talented boys to campus" was absolutely integral to its transformation from a small parochial school into a national football obsession.

This culture of athleticism still thrives at Notre Dame. The school annually finishes near the top for overall athletic performance, and an overwhelming majority of their students lettered in high school. Still, nowhere is this athletic culture more evident than in intramural football. Notre Dame is one of only a handful of schools that still play intramural football in full pads. During the '20s, the inter-hall squads served as training grounds for the varsity, a place where players could, in effect, be red-shirted for several seasons without sacrificing eligibility. Today, dorm football at Notre Dame could rival some Division III programs. Some halls are even supported by makeshift bands and cheerleaders. Judging by their near-flawless execution as well as the plethora of trick plays in their offensive arsenals, it was obvious that these teams spent considerable time practicing. Decked out in hand-me-downs from the varsity, participants in dorm football reportedly take the game as seriously as those on the varsity. Then again, Lou Holtz's players probably wouldn't blow off a game's final moments to catch an episode of *Melrose Place.*

Inspired by *Rudy,* we contemplated joining a dorm team for just one play. Being intimidated by the size of the players, we decided to set our sights a little lower — or so we thought — and challenged the women of Badin Hall to a game of touch football. The women's flag football league is one of Notre Dame's most competitive and popular intramural sports. It's taken so seriously that the student paper, *The Observer*, publishes weekly power rankings of the teams.

With just enough common sense to recognize the potential for embarrassment (and injury), we knew we needed a couple of ringers to make us competitive. When Ron Powlus failed to return our phone calls, we recruited Andrea Ricker, reputed to be "the league's dirtiest player." Even with Andrea, we knew we needed a good quarterback to complement (read: off-set) our relative athletic inabilities. So we picked up Mary Beth Failla, the league's top passer. Mary Beth's brother, Paul, was slated as the starting quarterback for the varsity against USC that weekend. But this particular fall, Mary Beth was having a better season than her brother.

The game was uneventful, unless of course, you believe some dainty art history major beating Bob deep for a touchdown was of any consequence. We did, however, attempt a trick play that would have made Knute Rockne proud. Before the game, Phil started complaining that he couldn't play because he forgot his knee brace. After an Oscar award-winning argument, Phil reluctantly agreed to take the field. Early in the game, he feigned a minor knee injury and hobbled off, only to be goaded back moments later.

The stage was set. During our next possession, Phil lined up wide right and went into motion before the snap. As he was waddling across the backfield, he collapsed to the ground and let out a blood-curdling scream while clutching his injured knee. According to plan, the opposition would be so overwhelmed by their feminine compassion that they would come running to his aid. When they were sufficiently out of position, Mary Beth would snap the ball to herself and run in for an unmolested touchdown. Unless kicking dirt in Phil's face was their way of expressing compassion, they weren't fooled at all. The final score was 6-6. We're still waiting for our scholarship offers.

*   *   *   *

Notre Dame-USC is college football's greatest intersectional rivalry. With few exceptions, the Golden Domers we met agreed. It seems "there's nothing better than schooling surf-dudes with attitudes," as one coed put it. Except for a brief hiatus during World War II, these teams have met every season since 1926. Whether it's played on Thanksgiving in the Coliseum or on a fall afternoon in South Bend, it's invariably an epic struggle, pitting the fighting monotheists against the obviously pagan Roman rabble from the Left Coast.

Much of the impetus for the first game may have come from Bonnie Rockne's desire to escape the frigid cold of South Bend for a couple of weeks in sunny Southern California. When Notre Dame beat Howard Jones' Trojans 13-12 before 75,000 fans in 1926, the rivalry became an instant classic. The crowds of 120,000 and 113,000 that crammed Chicago's Soldier Field in '27 and '29 remain two of the three largest crowds in college football history. (The 1928 Notre Dame-Navy game drew 120,000 to Soldier Field.) These spectators were not disappointed, as three of the first four games were decided by a single point.

Of these early contests, the 1930 game is remembered as one of Rockne's greatest psych jobs ever. Even though the Irish were the undefeated defending national champions, Rockne was somehow able to manipulate the media into installing Southern Cal as a two-touchdown favorite. According to the Rock, there was no possible way that his emotionally and physically emaciated squad could rebound from the brutal Army game and compete against the greatest USC team of all time.

Rockne used the media circus surrounding a scheduled practice stop in Tucson to motivate his team while spreading misinformation to the Southern Cal coaching staff. By covertly locking the training room doors, Rockne caused his players to be late for practice. An incensed Rockne attacked his team's lack of commitment, asking them why he should be risking death by coaching with phlebitis when his team didn't even care enough to arrive punctually at practice. After what he termed to be a lackluster practice, Rockne lambasted them again, threatening to resign and return to South Bend. Only after his players pledged to beat USC did Rockne agree to stay.

That was just the beginning of the mind games. At that same practice, Rockne had various players switch jerseys, making the media pawns in his game of misinformation. He had one of his former assistants leak a story to the Los Angeles papers claiming Notre Dame was too fat and slow to compete against USC. Rockne's players were so hurt by their former coach's fabricated treachery that they swore to prove him wrong. On the eve of the game, Rockne even made an appearance at the Southern Cal pep rally, where he apologized for bringing such a mediocre team west and promised to give them a better game next year.

The *coup de grace* came just moments before kickoff. Rockne had the doctors bandage up his phlebitis-ravaged legs as his stunned players looked on in silence. No pep talk was necessary because every Irish player knew exactly what he needed to do that afternoon. They had won games for the Gipper and for Rockne's son, but this one would be for Rock.

An inspired Irish team completely overwhelmed the overconfident Trojans 27-0 giving Rockne his third national championship. Tragically, this triumph was Rockne's swan song, as he died in a plane crash that winter. These classic early games left an imprint on this series. Whether it was Leahy vs. Hill, Parseghian vs. McKay, or Holtz vs. Robinson, Notre Dame-USC has remained college football's most glamorous rivalry.

Despite its glorious tradition, the series has become incredibly one-sided during the last decade; the Trojans last won in 1982, John Robinson's final season as USC coach. But Trojan fans have a new reason for optimism. John Robinson has returned to Southern Cal vowing to rebuild the Trojan dynasty. Before becoming the winningest coach in Los Angeles Ram history, Robinson had led Southern Cal to three Rose Bowl victories and one national championship. More importantly, he was 6-1 against Notre Dame. One of Robinson's first official acts during his second reign at USC was to erect a billboard in downtown Los Angeles reading: "Be a Trojan: Beat ND."

*　　　　*　　　　*　　　　*

No one has seen more USC-Notre Dame games than Giles Pellerin. In fact, USC's 87-year-old king of superfans has attended every single USC-Notre Dame game. For that matter, he's witnessed every Southern Cal game, home and away, since 1926. (As we go to print, Pellerin has attended a world-record 751 consecutive games.) Maintaining the streak hasn't been easy. Shortly following an emergency appendectomy in 1949, Pellerin snuck out of a hospital bed to preserve his streak. After the '93 Penn State game, Pellerin suffered an aneurysm and was laid up for 12 days in a Pennsylvania hospital. Luckily, Southern Cal had an off-week, and Pellerin was released in time for the Washington State game.

The maroon and gold runs in the Pellerin family. Giles' 84-year-old brother, Oliver, hasn't missed a game since 1945. Baby brother Max is the black sheep of the family. He was forced to break his 300-game streak when he was sent to work overseas.

Giles Pellerin, College Football's Most Devoted Fan

Greatest Notre Dame-Southern Cal Games

We asked Giles to select the greatest USC-Notre Dame games of all-time. Not surprisingly, he chose three Trojan victories:

1931: Southern Cal 16, Notre Dame 14

With both teams competing for the national championship, Notre Dame took a 14-0 lead into the fourth quarter. Believing that victory was already in hand, Notre Dame coach Hunk Anderson inserted his entire second-string into the game. Playing against Notre Dame's scrubs, USC mounted an amazing comeback. Because of the archaic substitution rules, Anderson was unable to bring his first-teamers back into the game. 300,000 jubilant fans greeted the national champion Trojans when they arrived home in Los Angeles.

1974: Southern Cal 55, Notre Dame 24

With a half-time 24-0 lead, Notre Dame seemed to have derailed Southern Cal's championship aspirations. But five Anthony Davis touchdowns and 55 USC points later, Notre Dame was just another "W" in the Trojans' championship season. After the game, Davis was accosted by an elderly lady waving a cross at him screaming, "You can't be human!"

1978: Southern Cal 27, Notre Dame 25

Joe Montana rallied Notre Dame from an 18 point fourth quarter deficit and took a 25-24 lead with less than 30 seconds remaining. Somehow, USC was able to preserve their championship season with a miraculous last-minute drive culminated by a 37-yard field goal on the game's final play.

*   *   *   *

The evening before the game, we set out to experience two of Notre Dame's most enduring traditions; the painting of the helmets and the Friday night pep rally.

Before each home game, dozens of student volunteers meticulously buff and polish every football helmet. In tribute to the Golden Dome, the helmets then get a fresh coat of gold lacquer. To give them extra sparkle, real 24-karat gold dust is added to the paint. The painting of the helmets is a prime example of the student participation that makes Notre Dame football so special.

While the buffing, polishing, and painting of 120 helmets is an arduous task, the students seemed to be having a great time, with some of them spending more time painting each other than the helmets. Nevertheless, we were so impressed with their work that we asked them to spraypaint a gold "ND" on the limo. Although it was a nice conversation piece and seemed like a reasonable idea at the time, it absolutely destroyed the limo's resale value. At the conclusion of the trip, we were unable to convince any funeral directors that ND stood for "Now Dead."

While the students were painting the helmets, we wandered into the locker room. In the movie *Rudy*, Daniel Ruetteger was completely overwhelmed by emotion when he first entered the hallowed Notre Dame locker room. The sense of camaraderie and tradition that emanates from this room buckled the young Golden Domer's knees. Likewise, we were in awe of this legendary place. With light fixtures that date back to the days of Rockne, the locker room helps connect the current players with their glorious past.

As Rudy walked through the locker room, he was overcome by a deep desire to serve Notre Dame in any way possible. Conversely, we were overcome by an uncontrollable urge to pilfer souvenirs. If we had taken this trip a decade ago, the limo would have been filled with helmets, jerseys, footballs and anything else that wasn't nailed down. But with the maturity that college and graduate school brings, we merely opted to heist a box of rubber surgical gloves so we could make water balloons later in the trip.

Before leaving with our booty, we mimicked Notre Dame's traditional run from the locker room to the playing field. Joe Montana probably never tripped over his shoelaces while jumping up to slap the "Play Like a Champion" sign hung over the exit to the field.

Unfortunately, we can't describe the pep rally all that vividly. For on our way, we got sidetracked at the Holiday Inn's Gipper Lounge, where we each ate like a champion. By the time they ran out of those succulent pieces of deep fried chicken ligaments and skin, the pep rally was over and we were suffering from such severe wing-bloat that we were forced to find a hotel room and hibernate for the rest of the evening.

*   *   *   *

Because a letter from a bishop and a few "Hail Marys" are necessary to get a hotel room in South Bend for a football weekend, we were forced to leave South Bend in search of lodging. Much to our dismay, we ended up in Michigan City, well over an hour away. In retrospect, we probably should have kept driving, because at about 1:30 a.m., we were awakened from our chicken wing-induced comas by three members of a federal drug interdiction squad. Apparently, their dog smelled drugs in our car and they wanted to lock us up with a pair of mutant, inbred hicks. We were aghast. Drugs? No way! Chinese food? Sure. Stale sweat socks? Yes. Wayne Newton Fan Club newsletter? Maybe. Drugs? Not us. The only way we burned our brains out was by overdosing on Saturday morning cartoons.

Actually, we couldn't really blame the police. Any police officer who stumbles upon a six-door limousine sporting more than forty bumper stickers and a menagerie that included a big purple cow, a gator's head and several cockroaches snacking on leftover sandwiches, is compelled to investigate, because there must be drugs involved. Months later, Phil's research revealed that the purple cow alone constituted probable cause for a search.

After their dog found no illicit substances (he did find a couple of spare-rib bones that we judiciously decided not to wrestle from him), they decided to "rouse the owner of the purple Volkswagen mini bus." Although watching these storm troopers harass some harmless Deadhead would have been amusing, we knew we had a long day in front of us and went back to sleep.

*   *   *   *

In spite of the mystique and tradition that permeate the South Bend campus, Notre Dame Stadium is the single key ingredient that makes Notre Dame such a fabulous place to experience a football game. We had heard Notre Dame Stadium referred to as a smaller version of Michigan Stadium, but that comparison doesn't capture the essence of the place. We saw no other stadium where the fans were so close to the field. Three steps out of the end-zone puts you in the second row of the student section. And if the opposition isn't intimidated by the

Irish fans, as soon as they look heavenward and see Touchdown Jesus staring down at them from the north end-zone, they realize the odds are stacked against them.

Aside from creating an intimate setting, Notre Dame Stadium's minuscule capacity of 59,075 makes this the hardest ticket to get in all of football. Notre Dame has sold out all but one of their home games since 1964, second only to Nebraska's continuous sellout streak, which began in 1962. Because of the scarcity of tickets, most alumni can attend just one or two games each season, giving every game the feel of a homecoming. Like Christmas and New Year's Eve, Notre Dame football games are special occasions to be relished. One alum told us confidentially that his annual pilgrimage to South Bend is the "highlight of the year." To fully relive his Notre Dame experience, he provides the residents of his old dorm room with a hotel suite and meal money, and moves back in for the weekend.

The pregame pageantry associated with Notre Dame football takes on an almost religious tone. We must have witnessed at least a dozen tailgates surrounded by scantily clad children running around with cherubic and seraphic wings attached to their backs. Not only that, but we noticed no less than five full-sized harps included in the pregame festivities.

Of the real tailgates we visited, Christy Szarwark's party was one of the more memorable. Amidst the silver chafing dishes adorning her tailgate table sat a little tree stump with a pair of ratty football shoes hung over it. She proudly explained that her father had been in the Class of 1944, which actually graduated in the '50s because of the war. (Nowadays, this prolonged college career is called redshirting.) He lived in Sorin Hall with the owner of the shoes, Heisman Trophy winner Johnny Lujack. We're glad our mothers weren't there to see those dirty shoes sitting on the dinner table.

Another pregame activity of note pertains to Notre Dame's marching band, the oldest such group in the country, established in 1845. The band is led onto the field by its drum major and a group known as the Irish Guard. These gentlemen wear authentic kilts of blue and gold — the school's colors — with a little green mixed in for the Irish. On any other collegiate campus (except Princeton), men in plaid skirts marching around might be met with a little less enthusiasm, but in South Bend the honor is immense. With their head gear, they stand eight feet tall. Each member is chosen for the ability to march in a precision fashion, as well as for their ability to look stately in such a ridiculous get-up.

The Irish Guard

*   *   *   *

When Beano Cooke said, "There's never been a bad Humphrey Bogart movie, and there's never been a boring Notre Dame-USC game," he obviously wasn't thinking about this one, which turned out to be a thorough 31-13 Irish victory. The win extended Notre Dame's victory streak to fifteen, tying them with Florida State for the longest streak in the nation. Entrepreneurs were already making a killing on "Catholics vs. Creminoles" T-shirts in anticipation of their upcoming "Game of the Century" against top-ranked Florida State.

During the press conference following the Southern Cal game, Lou Holtz downplayed his team's chances against the Seminole juggernaut. The pundits seemed to agree, with Florida State being declared the overwhelming favorite, even though the game was to be played at South Bend and the Irish were significantly bigger on both sides of the ball. After learning about Notre

Dame's past success as an underdog and witnessing first-hand their humiliation of the heavily favored Wolverines at Ann Arbor, we expected the Irish to have a few tricks up their sleeves.

Three weeks after Notre Dame's massacre of the Trojans, the top-ranked Seminoles rolled into South Bend to battle the second-ranked Irish. Because of the astronomical television ratings (it was the highest-rated regular season game of the past two decades) and the unprecedented blitz of pregame hype surrounding this battle between college football's most storied program and its most potent team, we believe the 1993 "Catholics vs. Creminoles" showdown deserves to join the pantheon of games worthy of the title "Games of the Century."

GAMES OF THE CENTURY

1926: Army 21, Navy 21
A record crowd of 110,000 witnessed this epic battle between two of the best teams ever fielded by the service academies. Army was led by future hall-of-famers "Lighthorse Harry" Wilson and Chris Cagle. Navy boasted Tom Hamilton and Frank Wickhorst. In a game that featured more momentum shifts than a professional wrestling match, Navy intercepted an ill-advised Army pass late in the fourth quarter and drove down the field for the game-tying touchdown.

1946: Army 0, Notre Dame 0
Led by back-to-back Heisman Trophy winners Doc Blanchard and Glenn Davis, Army carried a 25-game winning streak into this game. West Point's teams of the war years were arguably the most dominant dynasty in the history of the sport. Playing other schools whose rosters were depleted by military commitments, Army captured two straight national titles. However, when the war ended, veterans flocked to the colleges, ushering in a golden era of football. With Frank Leahy coaching an all-star squad that featured George Connor, Emil Sitko and Johnny Lujack, Notre Dame sought to avenge the 48-0 and 59-0 shellackings they had received from the Army in their two previous meetings. Before a sell-out crowd at Yankee Stadium, these teams battled to "the most exciting scoreless tie in college football history."

1966: Notre Dame 10, Michigan State 10
Going into their mid-November showdown, Notre Dame and defending national champion Michigan State were the consensus choice as the two best teams in college football. With monstrous defensive players such as Alan Page and Bubba Smith playing in an era where 230-pound offensive linemen were still common, these two teams redefined college football. Justly so, this game was arguably the most hyped event in the history of collegiate athletics. With a minute remaining in a tie game, Notre Dame had the ball on their own 30-yard-line. In a decision tremendously unpopular with both the Irish and Spartan partisans, Coach Ara Parseghian ran the clock out and settled for the tie.

1969: Texas 15, Arkansas 14

Using Darrell Royal's revolutionary wishbone offense, top-ranked Texas had been unstoppable, scoring more than 40 points per game. Undefeated Arkansas was no slouch either. With the winner of their annual showdown having gone to seven of the past nine Cotton Bowls, this was the Southwest Conference's premier rivalry of the '60s. Before a sellout crowd in Fayetteville, Texas rallied from a 14-0 fourth quarter-deficit for a miraculous 15-14 victory. After the game, President Nixon presented Darrell Royal with a national championship plaque in the victorious Texas locker room.

1971: Nebraska 35, Oklahoma 31

Played before millions of viewers on Thanksgiving Day, second-ranked Oklahoma stormed back from a 28-17 deficit to take a 31-28 lead. But in the closing minutes, top-ranked Nebraska drove the ball 74 yards for the decisive touchdown. With 5 lead-changes and a combined 829 yards of total offense, this may have been the most exciting game ever played. As evidence of how much better these teams were than the rest of the nation, Nebraska later humiliated undefeated Alabama 38-6 in the Orange Bowl, and Oklahoma rolled over Auburn 40-22 in the Sugar Bowl.

1993: Notre Dame 31, Florida State 24

With prime tickets reportedly being scalped for over $1,000, this may have been the toughest ticket in the history of the game. Led by eventual Heisman Trophy winner Charlie Ward, top-ranked Florida State seemed invincible, rolling over its opponents by an average of 38 points per game. Conversely, Notre Dame had been solid but unspectacular while winning its first nine games. Even though the battle was waged in South Bend, most experts believed Notre Dame was too slow for the Seminoles' blitzkrieg attack. But Notre Dame controlled the game and upset Florida State 31-24. Still, Florida State got the last laugh as Notre Dame lost at home to Boston College the following week. Although both teams had similar records and Notre Dame won their head-to-head match-up, the pollsters still sent Florida State to the Orange Bowl for a national championship showdown against Nebraska.

Boulder, Colorado
Colorado vs. Nebraska

Buddhists, Buffets and Buffalo Chips

Upon leaving Notre Dame, we began assessing the limo's chances of making it through the Rockies. It wasn't too hard to imagine the brakes failing, the limo smashing through a guard rail and us plummeting to our deaths. The thought of never eating another Moo Goo Gai Pan was terrifying, but luckily, our fears were unfounded. The limo didn't even make it to Colorado, never mind through the Rockies, before popping yet another radiator hose, stranding us in the middle of a desolate Illinois cornfield. Compounding our difficulties, AAA (whose stock must have taken the Nestea plunge from the unexpected expense of having to continually bail us out of trouble) suddenly declared that their standard service excluded "commercial vehicles." "A limousine is a commercial vehicle," asserted the AAA operator whom Bob called.

Who did they think they were dealing with? A couple of uneducated morons? We're educated morons. With this in mind, Phil grabbed the car phone and started spouting random tenets of contract law from one of his law school exam outlines that somehow made it along for the trip. The AAA operator wasn't particularly impressed, obviously failing to grasp the difficulty of compiling an entire contract law course into a 10-page outline in limerick form. Perhaps out of pure pity or perhaps out of fear of being on the receiving end of a "decade of annoying crank calls," the AAA operator eventually dispatched a tow truck. To add insult to automotive injury, we racked up $20 in futile cellular phone charges. Apparently, Dominos also had an exclusion in their service contract regarding pizza delivery to cornfields.

Another couple of hundred bucks worth of repairs and two days later, we finally reached Boulder. The sheer splendor of the Rockies made every other place we had visited seem plain by comparison. As we stared at those stark peaks, we became overwhelmed by an almost religious feeling. We then realized that those feelings were hunger, induced by the eerie similarity between the flatirons and wedges of German-dark-chocolate cake. We decided to grab a sack of cheeseburgers, find a suitable hotel, and lounge away the rest of the afternoon in front of the comfortable fodder of tabloid TV.

Unfortunately, scaling the flatirons may have been easier than finding affordable lodging in Boulder. We had grown accustomed to the allure of Motel 6, its somewhat clean beds, ESPN, maid service, proximity to McDonalds, and $30 per night price tag. However, Boulder was a bit too upscale for Motel 6. Fortunately, the local Best Western's loss was our gain. Because of a broken hot-water heater, they were offering half-price rooms. While the absence of hot water was easily circumvented, we still have to wonder whether the Best Western workforce was ever able to get that nasty soap scum and razor stubble out of their Jacuzzi.

*   *   *   *

Nestled in the foothills of the Rockies, Boulder offers a seemingly incomprehensible combination of decadence and exercise. Even the heroin addicts looked fit. Its residents are so fitness-crazed that *Outdoor Magazine* named Boulder America's top outdoor-sports town. Conversely, the only outdoor athletics we attempted were beer-squats, wing-pulls and deep-fried cheese curls.

This atmosphere of athleticism goes hand-in-hand with the emergence of the football program. During the early '80s,

Colorado was a college football nobody, only receiving national attention when they were being blown out by either Nebraska or Oklahoma. But that all changed when Bill McCartney guided Colorado to national prominence during the late '80s. Today, Colorado is one of college football's elite programs.

Nobody would have predicted McCartney's eventual impact on Colorado after his disastrous 1984 season. When his team finished 1-10, fans were screaming for his butt to be sling-bound. If he had been at Clemson, McCartney would now be three coaches removed from the current regime. Instead, Athletic Director Bill Marolt, citing an unwavering faith in McCartney and a desire to develop a staff with a commitment to the long-term, granted McCartney a two year extension. (We could never substantiate the rumors that Marolt mistakenly thought the school had hired Paul McCartney, and this was the McCartney that had warranted the AD's commitment.) In any case, McCartney certainly justified Marolt's confidence. The following year, he guided Colorado to the Freedom Bowl, their first bowl appearance since 1977. A few years later, his Buffs were national champions. Before resigning in 1994, McCartney had become the winningest coach in Colorado history.

As consistent as McCartney's success was, his reign didn't lack controversy. His players seemed to get as much press on the police blotters as they did on ESPN. In 1987 alone, 17 players were arrested for charges ranging from simple assault to one unconfirmed report of implication in the Lindbergh kidnapping. McCartney was continually attacked for his fundamental Christian beliefs which he espoused at almost every opportunity. He was even censured by the university president for endorsing his religious and lifestyle views on Colorado stationery and wearing Colorado clothing to religious and political meetings.

Despite the criticism, his religious conviction must have helped guide him through the gut-wrenching 1989 season, a season during which his Buffs experienced both exhalting highs and catastrophic lows. The hardship began shortly before the start of spring practice when starting quarterback Sal Aunese was diagnosed with an inoperable stomach tumor. From day one of the '89 campaign, when a cancer-ravaged Aunese attended the team's first preseason workout with an oxygen mask strapped to his face, his tragic demise served as a catalyst for one of the most remarkable seasons in the history of the sport. By the season's start, Aunese was so ill that he was forced to watch the games from a private hospital box. After big, and not so big plays alike, his emotional teammates frequently pointed to his box, saluting their fallen leader.

Sal succumbed to cancer after the third game of the season. Heightening the emotion at the memorial service attended by over two-thousand mourners was McCartney's startling revelation that Aunese had fathered his grandson. During the eulogy, McCartney turned to his daughter and praised her courage for not having an abortion and rejoiced that everyone would have the opportunity to watch Sal's legacy grow up. The emotionally charged service concluded with the McCartney and Aunese families joining behind the casket for the singing of *I've Got Peace Like a River in My Soul.*

At a second memorial for the Colorado team, Sal's sister read a letter that provided them with a clear sense of purpose for the remainder of the season:

> "...Even though you can no longer see me in the flesh... I'll always be with you in spirit... hold me dear to your heart, as you know I do all of you... Strive only for victory each time we play... I love you all. Go get 'em and bring home the Orange Bowl. — Love, Sal."

The memorialization of Aunese straddled the border between pure reverence and the macabre. It might have been expected that his teammates would dedicate the season to him, and it's also not surprising that they enshrined his locker, but the homage went even further. Instead of taking 60 players on road games, Colorado brought 59, leaving a space for Sal. There was always an empty seat on the team bus and an empty place setting at team meals. They even left a hotel bed empty for Sal on all road trips.

The effect on the football team was astonishing. Sal's death helped mold a collection of talented but bickering players into a cohesive unit. As evidence of their newfound sense of purpose, Sal's teammates limited their social activities to Saturday nights, virtually eliminating the off-field problems that had previously plagued the program.

With Sal's teammates frequently breaking down in tears during games, Colorado played inspired football. Within a seven-day period, they beat Oklahoma in Norman for the first time since 1965 and Nebraska for only the second time since 1967. The victory over Nebraska granted Sal his final wish by earning the upstart Buffs an Orange Bowl bid. They finished the regular season 11-0, perched atop both polls with only defending national champion Notre Dame standing between them and immortality.

With the entire nation rooting them on, the Buffaloes completely dominated the Fighting Irish in the first half of the Orange Bowl. But Notre Dame also had a Twelfth Man watching over them. After Colorado failed to convert on three golden first-half scoring opportunities, Notre Dame dominated the second half and defeated Colorado 21-6.

Despite their Orange Bowl collapse, 1989 was a season to savor. It was a season in which Colorado ended Oklahoma and Nebraska's quarter-century stranglehold on the Big Eight. It was a season in which one of college football's traditional lightweights came within thirty minutes of an improbable national championship. More significantly, it was a season in which 300-pound linemen and a 49-year-old head coach frequently broke down in tears. College football had a new Gipper story, only this one was even better than the Hollywood-scripted version. This one was entirely real.

*   *   *   *

Football in Boulder isn't like football in Tuscaloosa or Happy Valley. If the University of Colorado ever dropped football, Boulder would still maintain its unique identity. The city doesn't really need football, even if football has proven to be a very worthy attraction. Boulder's scenic beauty is so enticing that locals now complain of Chief Natwak's Curse, named after the Arapaho Indian who helped the pioneers settle the area. According to the curse, when people visit the area, they fall in love with it, resulting in a current population explosion.

Apparently, liberals tend to be quite susceptible to Natwak's curse. Residents of nearby Colorado Springs, home of the Air Force Academy, refer to it as the "People's Republic of Boulder." Boulder's Bronson Hilliard countered that Colorado Springs was nothing more than "a better-dressed Nazi Germany." We naturally wanted to experience a little more of the counter-culture that had given rise to such attitudes toward Boulder. As luck would have it, the school itself was hosting the Rocky Mountain Men's Conference. Having an affinity for whiny, bearded men, we made the conference our first stop.

Of course, we had plenty of preconceptions as to what the Men's Conference would entail. Basically, our ideas fell into two groups: First, the whole thing could be like a scene out of the *Odd Couple* with a lot of older men sitting around playing cards, smoking cigars, belching, and swearing. Or, probably closer to the truth, the conference could play host to a bunch of men badly in need of reaffirming their virility. We could envision them stripped of the trappings of this gender-repressive existence. They would probably be clad in the manliest of manly apparel (leather loincloths or unitards), communing with nature as God had intended (rooting around for grubs or hunting harmless quadrupeds), and stopping to offer thanks to their maker by unleashing bestial howls of satisfaction. To top it all off, they would probably share in the glory that is men by removing all the doors and walls from their bathrooms, thereby allowing each to join in the unique aromatic glory that is the male of the species. Not a pretty picture, but one we felt compelled to see.

When we arrived at the conference, neither of our stereotyped predictions held true; it was worse. It was like a bad *Saturday Night Live* sketch: completely ridiculous but not humorous enough to hold our attention. A Niles Crane look-a-like was standing in front of a group of very unmanly men and earnestly asking, "Why don't men hug?" We looked at each other, then at each other's stomachs. We both shrugged. The physiological impediment to hugging was obvious. Still, you'll find Boris Yeltsin at an Alcoholics Anonymous meeting before you catch either of us group hugging, so we bid adieu. But on our way out, we stumbled upon their ceremonial drums. Having watched decades of *I Love Lucy*, we decided to salute the late-great Dezi Arnaz with some Samba rhythms. Two "babaloos" later, a livid Niles was threatening us with bodily harm. Alas, our sensitive sides may be forever scarred.

After being unfairly ostracized by our brothers at the Men's Conference, we sought spiritual redemption at the Naropa Institute, America's only accredited Buddhist College. When not studying abroad at affiliated institutions in Bali or Nepal, students choose from such courses as Body Cosmology and

Shaṁbhala Meditation. Environmental Studies are taught by Oak Thorne and Forrest Ketchin (we're not making that up) and Human Sexuality is taught by Haywood Jablowme (well, we might be making that one up).

They even play football, albeit an intramural variety only. Of course, there are probably a few rule modifications necessary for a game of this type. We hope that levitating across the goal line has been outlawed to give both novice and veteran Buddhists a level playing field. Also, there is the possibility of virtual scoring, that is, 3 points would be awarded for meditating to the point of visualizing the ball being kicked through the goal posts. Finally, there is the chance that the Buddhists could have salvaged one of Walter Camp's original rules, awarding 17 points for head-butting the referee in the groin. The reality is, though, that there is probably no physical aspect to the game; players just visualize what they think the game would look like, before gathering with each other to compare final scores. Maybe it happens this way, or maybe they play full-contact without pads as a release for pent-up, negative energy. We never found out which, but it's nice to imagine.

Except for the Keith Richards look-a-like who kept insisting that he was Gozer the Keymaster and that Phil was the Gatekeeper, these granola-crunching, tree-hugging students were very accommodating to a couple of guys who weren't exactly on the same self-awareness and inner peace plane. They even urged us to attend the Jack Kerouac School of Disembodied Poetics' annual summer program. At first, we balked at the idea of watching the Buddhists cut the stomachs, intestines and other major organs out of defenseless poets. Then we were told it was disembodied, not disemboweled.

We tried to convince the Buddhists that we were actually talented "beat poets" (we could "beat" anybody in a race to recite "There once was a man from Nantucket"), who had studied under the master, Alan Ginsberg. After a five-minute interrogation, Bob cracked, admitting that the only Alan Ginsberg he ever knew was an 8-year-old kid down the street whom he beat up in a fight over football cards. Unfortunately, Bob was 24 at the time.

After the Naropa Institute turned down our offer to guest lecture at their summer poetics program, we decided that if we were going to be rejected anyway, why not be rejected by the best.

Having always aspired to work for David Letterman, we knew that he could give our careers a colossal boost. Look what he did for Larry Bud Melman, a.k.a. Calvert Deforest. Granted, we didn't possess the cunning or guile of Larry Bud, but perhaps Dave's show would provide the proper venue to showcase our unique lack of talent. Besides, we already had Late Nite experience, of sorts. At camp, Phil put on the weekly *Late Nite with Phil Silverman Show*. Just like the real *Late Nite*, Phil's show featured a band, top-ten lists, and stupid camper tricks. Of course, Letterman probably never got booed off the stage by a bunch of nine-year-olds. Nonetheless, we sent a letter to Dave's producers listing the top-ten reasons why we should be invited on the show.

Top Ten Reasons why Phil & Bob should be on Dave's Show

10. Unlike Silly zoo animals, Phil & Bob probably won't urinate on stage.

9. Viewers are sick and tired of Shirley Maclaine.

8. Since Bob & Phil are legally brain dead, NBC can't claim them as intellectual property.

7. Not even Dave could get a speeding ticket with our limo.

6. Viewers might mistake us for John Candy and Chris Farley causing ratings to soar.

5. Opportunity for Dave to discover genetic links to Calvert Deforest.

4. Phil & Bob are only people who would ever go back for seconds and thirds at CBS cafeteria.

3. We'll help clean up after the show.

2. What's worse, a ten minute ratings disaster or ten years of annoying crank calls?

1. Isn't one psychopathic stalker enough for you?

Showing blinding insight, we sent a similar letter to the *Conan O'Brien Show*. While we never heard back from Letterman, Conan's producers actually considered inviting us on their show. Just to be sure that we wouldn't completely fall apart on camera, they insisted on viewing video footage of us before scheduling our appearance. Through a predictable mix-up, we sent them the disastrous ESPN2 tape. Needless to say, they dropped us in favor of the two bozos who portrayed Chris Partridge on the *Partridge Family*.

*   *   *   *

If Colorado's Sal Aunese inspired Orange Bowl run was the greatest football story in school history, Colorado's improbable national championship the following season comes in a close second. Finishing the 1990 season 11-1-1, the Buffs were the most unlikely of champions. Not since Southern Cal captured a share of the '74 championship with a similar record had a team with multiple blemishes been awarded a national championship. Nothing came easy for Colorado. They trailed in ten of their thirteen games, and in eight of those games, they trailed with less than four minutes remaining.

The season started inauspiciously. After blowing a pair of two-touchdown leads to Tennessee and Illinois, Colorado was 1-1-1, and seemingly out of championship contention. If not for Eric Bienemy's game-winning touchdown plunge on the final play of the Stanford game, the Buffs would have been 0-2-1. With their dubious early season performance, they were dismissed as a mediocre team that had performed admirably in the face of extraordinary circumstances.

Their conference opener against Missouri ("Misery" to those familiar with Big Eight football) did little to quell the critics. Trailing the lowly Tigers 31-27, Colorado drove downfield for the potential game-winning score. With less than a minute to play, the Buffaloes converted a first down at the Missouri 3-yard-line. What happened during the next few moments is still bitterly recalled by Missouri fans:

> **1st down:** Quarterback Charles Johnson scrambled the Buffs to the line of scrimmage and downed the ball with 27 seconds remaining.
>
> **2nd down:** Eric Bienemy's rush was stopped short of the goal line. Colorado used its final time out with 18 seconds remaining.
>
> **3rd down:** Bienemy was again stopped short of the end zone with the game-clock still running.
>
> **4th down:** Johnson downed the ball on what he, and more importantly the referees, assumed to be 3rd down.
>
> **5th down:** Johnson snuck into the end zone for what has become known as the "fifth-down touchdown."

Even after the Big Eight rejected Missouri's petition to reverse the decision, there was some sentiment for Colorado to relinquish the victory. Colorado refused, though, reasoning that their play-calling was based on the official down designation. Somewhat justified, they argued that they would have never grounded the ball on fourth down and probably wouldn't have run on third down. Still, Colorado's tainted win actually caused them to drop a couple of places in the polls.

> There is precedent for such a reversal. In 1940, second-ranked Cornell defeated Dartmouth 7-3 on a fifth-down touchdown scored during the game's final moments. When the game film proved that the touchdown came as the result of an official's error, Cornell relinquished the victory as well as their national championship aspirations. Of course, Cornell wasn't playing for a multi-million dollar Orange Bowl bid.

In the wake of the controversy, Colorado continued to defeat their conference foes. A come-from-behind victory over Oklahoma gave the Buffs their first back-to-back triumphs over the Sooners since the mid-'60s. A couple of weeks later, they trailed Nebraska 12-0 at the end of three quarters, only to erupt for 27 fourth-quarter points, giving them their first victory at Lincoln since 1967. The Nebraska victory earned them the Big Eight crown as well as a national championship rematch against Notre Dame in the Orange Bowl.

There was no second half collapse in this Orange Bowl. Instead, Charles Johnson replaced the injured Darien Hagan and sparked a second half comeback. But Johnson's heroics were almost for naught. Leading 10-9 with less than a minute remaining, Colorado was forced to punt from their own 47. Rocket Ismail, arguably the greatest return man in college football history, was receiving for Notre Dame. It should have been a no brainer: kick the ball out of bounds and let your defense continue to dominate the game! Instead, they punted to the Rocket, who returned the ball 91 yards into the Buffalo end zone. However, for once, luck turned against the Irish as the play was called back on a questionable clipping call.

To overcome the nation's most difficult schedule, Colorado needed a fifth-down touchdown against Missouri, an incredible fourth-quarter explosion against Nebraska and a phantom clip against Notre Dame. They may have been the most underwhelming champion of all-time, but whenever it was crunch time, they came through. As a result, they captured a share of the national championship, belatedly granting Sal Aunese his final wish.

*   *   *   *

After their miraculous Orange Bowl victory, Colorado captured the writers' poll and finished one vote behind Georgia Tech in the coaches' poll. The belief that Nebraska's Tom Osborne cast the dissenting vote just adds additional fuel to what is arguably college football's nastiest rivalry. With the winner representing the conference in the last eight Orange Bowls, Nebraska-Colorado has supplanted Nebraska-Oklahoma as the Big Eight's premier contest. In many ways, this game has surpassed rivalry and been elevated to full-scale war, with displays of bad taste and ill will having become commonplace. In Lincoln, "Sal is Dead; Go Big Red," has become a rallying cry. In Boulder, Husker fans are doused with beer, and cars bearing Nebraska license plates are vandalized.

Nebraska became Colorado's rival through the sheer will of Bill McCartney. When he arrived from Michigan, McCartney was dismayed to find Colorado lacking a major rival. After a poll revealed Nebraska to be their most hated opponent, McCartney designated them as Colorado's new arch-rival. On the schedule, the Nebraska game was printed in red while every other game was in black. McCartney banned all red from the football office and declared that when Nebraska fans crossed the border, they were entering enemy territory. He even insinuated that Nebraska's Herbie Husker mascot, a giant blonde-haired, blue-eyed cowpoke, was a satanic symbol.

Nebraskans dismiss Colorado fans as being a bunch of obnoxious rich kids, who, in place of being able to sustain any sort of real football rivalry, manufactured one to suit their pitiful school's esteem needs. In return, the Boulderites claim, "It doesn't matter if you beat us because we're wealthy and having a great time in Boulder, while you're a bunch of corn-huskin', cousin-marryin', bowl-losin' farmboys living in a dust bowl." Even when Nebraska beats Colorado *(Editor's note... which is more often than not)*, it doesn't take long for the Buffalo students to start chanting, "We don't live in Lincoln." For this game, we made certain not to wear any red.

*   *   *   *

There is nothing like gameday in Boulder. With the mountain sunshine shimmering off of six inches of fresh snowfall, you couldn't ask for a nicer day, that is, if you were wearing the right clothing. In our rush to leave Tuscaloosa, Bob carelessly forgot to pack his clothing. Wearing shorts and a T-shirt, he was clearly the worst dressed fan at Folsom field, albeit not the craziest. When Colorado hosted Nebraska during the Aunese season, a local television station offered free tickets to those fans who were willing to do the craziest things. One guy dunked himself in Buffalo dung, and a woman turned herself into a giant granola bar by rolling in honey and oatmeal.

While these one-time actions border on lunacy, we met one guy who has them all beat in terms of pure, devoted perpetual fanaticism. After graduating in 1980, Dallas resident Phil Pilgrim, like some sort of Capistrano swallow, found his way back to Boulder for virtually every home game, in spite of the team's less than stellar performance. Then, when Colorado's program emerged in the late-'80s, Pilgrim's pilgrimages became a compulsion. Despite working overseas in London from 1989-92, he managed to fly home for all but four of Colorado's games. When he was unable to attend, he listened to the games on a 900-number at a cost of close to $350 per game.

One factor contributing to the party atmosphere at Colorado games is that Folsom Field is one of the few collegiate stadiums that still sells beer. Yet, as wild as that can make the atmosphere, the running of Colorado's Buffalo mascot, Ralphie, is even crazier. Before each half, Ralphie's handlers run her down the Colorado sideline, make a U-turn and return down the opponent's sideline. As Ralphie is a 1,300 pound buffalo, it might be more accurate to say she drags her scurrying handlers down the sideline, as they vainly struggle to regain control of the animal. (A showdown of man versus beast not unlike the maitre'd struggling to steer us to our table, as we suddenly spy the contents of the buffet.)

One of Ralphie's handlers told us about the bizarre high of trying to control a half-ton beast while being deluged with lungies from the opposing players. Another handler hinted at an even more bizarre high that he received by snorting dried buffalo excrement, dressing up like a Viking and riding Ralphie (or any other large mammal) through downtown Boulder. We later discovered that while the gentleman who explained this "high" was indeed a handler of sorts, he had nothing to do with leading Ralphie around during games.

Ralphie was inspiring, but apparently not enough to boost Colorado against the big red Nebraska juggernaut. As the game ended, the Colorado student section again rationalized their defeat with the chant, "We don't live in Lincoln." The Cornhusker fans triumphantly littered Folsom Field with oranges. Still, no one was happier with Nebraska's win than the Orange Bowl committee, who had just moved a step closer to hosting a national championship showdown. On the other hand, no one was less happy than us as we dropped another $110 bet, but we shrugged it off. We had bigger and better fish to fry, like losing our remaining money at our next stop. Las Vegas here we come.

Kirkland, Washington
Washington vs. Southern California

Shiftless in Seattle

After ten weeks of being together day and night, night and day, night and night, day and...(well you get the picture), we had had more than enough of each other. We knew it was time for a break. So after several steak buffets and a streak of bad luck in Las Vegas, we separated, with Bob spending the remainder of the week in San Francisco with his favorite sister and Phil juking down to Los Angeles to key his ex-wife's car. If we hadn't separated, either one of us might have given in to the urge of savagely beating the other, until one-by-one, the individual personality quirks that we found so revolting were crushed into oblivion. As sick as Phil was of Bob's slovenly lifestyle (complete with fecal humor and a fascination with his own saliva), Bob was even more fed up with Phil's insistence on using his spent toe-nails as toothpicks and his preoccupation with speaking in rhyme. Surely, without the hiatus, blood would have been spilled.

But after only one week apart, we genuinely missed each other, or maybe we were just completely psyched that our odd-couple-on-wheels experiment was almost over. In any case, we rendezvoused in San Francisco and began the trek north. The drive through the rolling hills of the Pacific Northwest was the most scenic of the entire trip, especially for two guys whose only encounter with the landscape beyond Massachusetts came from a View Master. Stopping for burgers at every Carl's Jr. along the way, we arrived in Seattle on Tuesday afternoon.

The University of Washington, or "U-Dub" in the local parlance, promised an introduction to West Coast football. In the South, hard-nosed SEC fans judge their teams by the simple analysis of wins and losses. But even a mediocre team can win the hearts of their fans as long as they play tough football. Out west, schools have a different approach to the game, and U-dub is a perfect example. Wins and losses matter, but in the laid-back, permissive and more liberal learning environments of Washington, Oregon, San Francisco and Los Angeles, other aspects of the game seem to matter more.

Whether it's the natural effect of the Hollywood glitz or the cultural fall-out from Haight-Ashbury, the West Coast fans love a great show. That said, there may be no better stage than Husky Stadium. In addition to a great football game, show tickets entitle you to a panoramic view of the Seattle skyline, an awe-inspiring vista of majestic Mt. Rainier, and the stadium-abutting, lapping waters of Lake Washington, home of college football's only swim-up tailgate.

       *   *   *   *

We were fortunate enough to visit U-Dub at a pivotal moment in their football history. Washington's football program had peaked the year before our visit, with a resounding 41-7 victory over 15th-ranked Stanford midway through the 1992 season. The 8-0 defending national champion Huskies had supplanted Miami at the top of both the writers and coaches' polls. Since Coach Don James had scrapped his "two back, three yards and a scrape of turf" philosophy in favor of a wide-open, attacking style at the end of the '80s, Washington had become the most dominant team in the West. Having clinched their third consecutive Pac Ten championship, the Huskies seemed destined to battle Miami and Florida State for the title of "team of the '90s," but then everything went haywire.

First came the startling revelation that quarterback Billy Joe Hobert had received a $50,000 loan from a booster. A few days later, Washington was manhandled 16-13 by Arizona's "Desert Swarm" defense and knocked out of the national championship race. A demoralized squad then finished its season with embarrassing losses to arch-rival Washington State and Michigan in the Rose Bowl. In those two games, the vaunted Husky defense surrendered 80 points, the highest two-game total of the Don James era.

Suddenly, a Washington team that had seemed so invincible, appeared to be quite beatable. However, their on-field problems paled in comparison to their brewing off-field controversies. The Hobert loan had spurred investigations by both the Pac Ten and the NCAA. Even though most of the infractions were arguably minor transgressions and the entire coaching staff was absolved of any wrongdoing, the Pac Ten laid down severe sanctions a few weeks before the '93 season began. The Huskies were banned from the postseason for two years and penalized twenty scholarships. Although the school was allowed to play on television, it was required to forfeit one year's television revenues to the conference. Cynical Washington fans noted the conference's hypocrisy: why kill your Golden Goose when you can just steal it's eggs?

Because Washington had historically run a clean program, many fans considered these sanctions to be the equivalent of shooting a dog because of fleas. Like the Kennedy assassination and the Fox Network's cancellation of Chris Elliot's *Get a Life*, these penalties inspired scores of conspiracy theorists. Many believed that the other Pac Ten schools were so sick of losing to the Huskies that they decided to level the playing field by saddling Washington with unreasonable penalties. Accordingly, we saw a campus full of "Pac 9 — If you can't beat 'em, disqualify 'em" T-shirts. Just days before the start of the season, Don James resigned, claiming he could "no longer coach in a conference that treats its players and coaches so unfairly."

The beginning of the post-James era coincided with the beginning of our trip. Washington opened the '93 season against Stanford, whose coach, Bill Walsh, was being vilified in Seattle for calling Washington a "football factory." Walsh accused the Husky football players of being "mercenaries," hidden away in their own compound, isolated from the rest of the student body. He lamented that their collegiate experience left them ill-equipped to cope with the real world. We wondered what Walsh would have thought of our own college experience. Do you think that four years of beer pong, poker and ESPN had prepared us to conquer the corporate world?

The Huskies new coach, former assistant Jim Lambright, made no attempt to defuse the situation. Instead, he encouraged his players to take out their frustrations on Bill Walsh's Cardinal team. Just moments before kickoff, the entire Husky team dropped to one knee and raised their helmets in tribute to Coach James. The fans mirrored the team's salute with a thunderous five minute standing ovation. With James watching from the press box, Washington rolled over Stanford, 31-14.

*   *   *   *

We were itchin' to explore all of Seattle's cultural and scenic avenues, from its espresso bars and grunge rock hangouts to the awesome grandeur of the Space Needle. We even planned a day trip to Vancouver so we could explore life north of the border. Yet, like so many other aspects of our trip, nothing went according to plan.

It wasn't completely our fault; the limo had developed serious mechanical problems, problems that couldn't be rectified with a new radiator hose. When we checked our sputtering vehicle into a service station and told the mechanic that we needed it back for our Canadian adventure on Wednesday, he only needed a minute under the hood to tell us, "The closest you're gettin' to anything Canadian this week is inside that McDonald's Egg McMuffin you're inhalin' right there." We didn't really understand his explanation, but we did realize that we would be stranded at the Kirkland Motel 6, twenty-five minutes from campus.

Despite this setback, we really had little to complain about. If there was one thing that we learned at summer camp, it was how to amuse ourselves when there was seemingly nothing to do. So, what do a couple of well-educated, upstanding young professionals do to entertain themselves? We haven't the foggiest notion, but we were more than content to swill cheap beer, watch low-budget action movies, and most importantly, get in some target practice. Is the reference to target practice surprising? You wouldn't think that two unassuming types from the state that produced liberals like Mike Dukakis and Ted Kennedy would be into weapons, would you? Well, we're not. At least not the type of weapons you're probably thinking about. As far as we're concerned, the NRA and Congress can argue forever over whether to ban AK-47s at nursery schools, but don't even try to legislate away our right to bear water balloons.

After twenty minutes during which we filled and dropped dozens of surgical gloves from our third story perch, our killing instincts were sated. Besides, we had just dropped a particularly nasty glove filled with shaving cream and orange soda, and the resulting splash had taken out the left side of the chamber maid's uniform. She was bigger than us, and we knew that if she made it upstairs, we would have been no match for her. We scampered down the back stairs and headed over to Larry's Market, the same Larry's Market featured on the Visa commercials. There, we combed the aisles snacking on their free and not-so-free samples.

That was the sum and substance of our activities for our first four days in the Pacific Northwest: wake up, watch movies, invade Larry's, take a nap, wake up, watch movies, pillage Larry's, take a nap, you get the picture. We're somewhat embarrassed to admit that those four days may have been the most enjoyable portion of the trip.

*　　　　*　　　　*　　　　*

Even though Don James' 99 conference victories make him the winningest coach in Pac Ten history, he is arguably only the second most successful coach in the annals of Washington football. The top honor just may belong to Gil Dobie. From 1910 to 1918, his Washington Sun Dodgers (that's what they were called then) outscored the opposition 1,930-118. They also compiled an incredible 58-0-3 record, still the longest unbeaten streak in college football history.

Apart from his obvious coaching success, we loved the ingenuity of the "Bink Play" Dobie pulled off against Oregon in 1911. The play was basically an end run, where the right end looped around the offensive line and got the ball and ran down the left sideline. The key, however, was the execution of the deception. When the quarterback yelled hike, the center snapped the ball... into his own gut! The quarterback then took off his leather headgear, tucked it under his arm and began running to his right. As he headed toward the sideline, he threw his headgear into the air. While the Oregon defenders chased the QB's headgear, the right end looped back behind the center, received the hand-off and raced forty yards for the touchdown.

Despite his success, the combative Dobie managed to alienate virtually the entire city of Seattle. "Gloomy Gil" was an irrational perfectionist who lived alone in a room cluttered with empty Chinese food containers, old newspapers and dirty laundry. Oops, that's Phil's room. Dobie's was cluttered with books and football diagrams. He was an abrasive tyrant who was so unpopular that even the alumni booed his teams and pelted him with rotten vegetables as he paced the sidelines. After leaving Seattle under a shroud of controversy in 1916, the enigmatic Dobie enjoyed tremendous success at Cornell, Navy and Boston College before being enshrined in the College Football Hall of Fame.

*   *   *   *

College football takes on a peculiar form in the Pac Ten. It's not as if the essence of the sport has been corrupted by the West Coast. Southern Cal, UCLA and Washington can all claim national championships during their glorious gridiron pasts. More recently, Oregon and Arizona have emerged as national powers. If winning and losing are the only things that matter, western football is certainly comparable with anything played in the South.

Still, we were able to delineate some distinctions between the southern and western brands of football. The West Coast has certain intrastate rivalries that approach the intensity of the southern football experience, but the bottom line is that football does not occupy the same importance as it does in the South. That shouldn't be too surprising, though. Football didn't build the western schools the way it built Clemson, Alabama and Florida State. Also, the West never went through the Civil War and the psychological reconstruction that football success gave to the southern psyche.

But if the western experience lacks the cultural and historical basis of southern football, it more than makes up for it in grandeur. Showmanship makes all the difference in the world of western football. Whether the "show" is the geographical setting of the southern Californian beaches, the dazzle of spectacular half-time shows or the rivalry-embittering pranks, the West puts on some incredibly entertaining displays of Saturday afternoon madness.

Like so many other parts of American pop culture, many sports trends have been born out west. The currently popular "wave" is not just some Richard Simmons-led conspiracy to make sports fans exercise. Its origins can actually be traced back to the University of Washington. (Those harsh Pac Ten sanctions now appear somewhat justified.) Before co-hosting the equally annoying *Entertainment Tonite*, Husky Yell Leader Rob Wellor introduced the wave at Washington in 1981. Interestingly enough, Wellor originally intended for the wave to be done vertically, from the top to the bottom of each section. It only caught on when he transformed it into a horizontal wave by running laps around the stadium imploring each section to stand up.

As popular as it has become, the wave is really just the "cutting edge" version of the more complex card stunts perfected by Pac Eight schools during the '60s. The basic concept of the card stunt involves the placement of cardboard squares on each seat of the student section. At the appropriate signal, the students hold their cards above their head and the result is a huge picture or phrase visible from the opposing stands and the Goodyear blimp.

Of course, it didn't take long for someone to figure out that the card stunts had one serious vulnerable spot. No single person really understood "the big picture." Cal Tech took advantage of this weakness when they sabotaged Washington's card stunts during half time of the 1961 Rose Bowl. By posing as reporters researching a story on card stunts, a couple of the hoaxters were able to learn the mechanics of the stunts while scoping out the Long Beach State dorm room where the 2,232 cards and master instruction sheets were being safeguarded. After several break-ins and a few hundred hours of frantic labor, their diabolical plot was set.

Before a capacity crowd and a national television audience, Washington's first nine stunts went off as planned, but the next three were significantly altered. Millions of viewers were dumbfounded when a Cal Tech Beaver appeared instead of a Husky. Their confusion was compounded when the next stunt, a script "huskies" came out backward as "seiksuh." Undeterred, the card leaders continued on with the show. But when the word CALTECH appeared instead of HUSKY, the flustered card leaders canceled the remaining stunts. Not even Washington's upset victory over top-ranked Minnesota could salve their wounded egos.

Washington shouldn't have been so upset, because Caltech, along with MIT on the East Coast, is the national leader in prank creativity. The definition of prank, at least in the college football rivalry context, is basically the deliberate perpetration of a deception that takes its victims fully by surprise and makes one question why any sane person would have gone through such trouble to create so much unnecessary chaos. Cal Tech and MIT have mastered the art.

MIT received their "fifteen minutes of gridiron fame" during the 1982 Harvard-Yale game. A couple of days before "The Game," several MIT pranksters snuck into Harvard Stadium and laid the makings of a big surprise. Using a remote control, they activated their prank during half-time of The Game. A stunned crowd of blue-bloods looked on in bewilderment as a giant weather balloon bearing multiple MIT insignias arose from an inflation device buried beneath the field. But this was just the beginning of the MIT blitz. Disguised as Yale band members, the Tech band was able to elude security long enough to spell "MIT" on the field. Other Techsters handed out 1,134 flash cards to the Harvard students, claiming they were part of a "Beat Yale" card stunt. Much to the chagrin of both Harvard and Yale, the card stunt read "MIT."

The Cal Tech students have been no less ingenious. Two decades after sabotaging Washington's card stunts, Cal Tech struck again in Pasadena in 1984. Using high tech gadgetry, some Cal Tech hackers sabotaged the Rose Bowl scoreboard. During the fourth quarter of a UCLA blowout, the scoreboard suddenly read, "Cal Tech 38 - MIT 9." While the city of Pasadena unsuccessfully attempted to prosecute the culprits, scores of hi-tech companies deluged them with job offers.

Still, Cal Tech and MIT are only barging in on other schools' football experiences. They're not using pranks to heighten their own rivalries the way the other Pac Ten schools have. Take USC and UCLA, for example. Historically, Southern Cal's Tommy Trojan has been the target of the marauding UCLA students. Besides coating this bronzed shrine to Trojan athletics with blue and gold paint, the Bruin students have repeatedly stolen Tommy's sword. One year, instead of stealing the sword, they merely welded it to Tommy's back. Eventually, the Trojan students banded together to curtail these attacks, but not even the prospect of hundreds of club-carrying vigilantes could deter the Bruins. Some ingenious pranksters obtained a helicopter and attempted to dump several hundred pounds of manure on the statue. Unfortunately, the suction from the blades pulled the manure right back into the helicopter. To discourage further assaults, Tommy Trojan is now wrapped in what could best be described as a giant condom during the week preceding the UCLA game.

The Trojans have been far from pacifists. Their arrogant attitude toward their public school neighbors is probably the single greatest contributing factor to the animosity surrounding this rivalry. But the wealthy Trojan students aren't content with just driving the nicer automobiles; they also want the upper hand in clever pranks. They once distributed fake notices on UCLA letterhead, successfully canceling a Bruin pep rally. Another time, they tapped into the UCLA public address system and broadcasted an endless loop of the Trojan fight song. Pulling a page from the Cal Tech notebook, several USC students clandestinely placed themselves on the committee responsible for the UCLA card stunts. Bruins everywhere were embarrassed as a small "SC" somehow appeared in virtually every card stunt for an entire season.

On several occasions, the pranks have surpassed the bounds of safety and good taste, such as the time some Trojan students planted dynamite in the heart of UCLA's homecoming bonfire. The resulting blast shattered windows in neighboring Westwood. If that wasn't bad enough, another deranged fanatic rigged a land mine under one of the Coliseum end zones. Thankfully, he was caught before he could detonate the device.

*   *   *   *

At 10:30 on Friday morning, we got our car back just in time to finally explore the University of Washington. Unfortunately, our campus visit was cut short after an ill-fated lunch at Schultzy's. Instead of enjoying a quick bite before exploring the remainder of the magnificent campus, we committed yet another ill-advised display of gluttony: we attempted the Schultzy's Challenge. If you can break the record for sausage eating in this no-frills, sit-at-the-counter pork emporium, your food is on the house. The names of all past record holders are displayed on the wall for everyone to marvel at. There was Joe "Fat Boy" Stavis, who busted three shirt buttons on his way to eating ten sausages, and Wally "The Artery Plow" Gunkus, who powered down eleven of the mammoth meat monsters. As we learned the history of these legends, we sat in awe, but our task was even more daunting. We were attempting to break the record of Lincoln Kennedy, the massive Husky All-American who now anchors the offensive line of the Atlanta Falcons. Seventeen sausages. We were confident, yet cautious.

How could anything that felt so right be so wrong? Not only did our combined consumption of nine sausages fall far short of Kennedy's record, but we suffered such severe gastric distress that we were forced to beat a hasty retreat to the Motel 6, where we both lapsed into a pig snout and nitrate-induced food coma. While we may never experience Seattle's famed night life, we did gain further insight into why Lincoln Kennedy's weight has hovered around the 400-pound mark.

*   *   *   *

There is something almost mystical about the Pacific Northwest. Of course, we never got out of our hotel room to figure out what it could be, but everyone always claims there is. After checking out a little Washington football history, we were convinced it was true. There have been some pretty odd occurrences. Even in 1895, the mystical quality must have rubbed off on Vashon College when they ventured north to play the Sun Dodgers. K.C. Nieman's seven touchdowns, including a 97-yard run that is still the longest in school history, sparked a 44-4 Washington victory. What made it bizarre, however, was the fact that Nieman was loaned to Washington by Vashon because Washington had too few players to field a team.

More recently, cheerleader Marilou Franco was tackled and thrown into a sideline snowbank by some Husky players. Apparently, it was more than just raging hormones that inspired this assault; Marilou's pants had caught fire after she brushed up against an electrical heater, or so they claimed.

Maybe the most bizarre incident occurred during the fourth quarter of the 1985 Orange Bowl, when second-ranked Oklahoma kicked a field goal that apparently gave them a 17-14 lead over the third-ranked Huskies. But an illegal procedure penalty nullified the score. However, the driver of the Sooner Schooner (a conestoga wagon drawn by two tiny ponies that gallop onto the field after every Oklahoma score) never saw the flag. When he drove the Sooner Schooner onto the field, an impatient referee assessed an additional 15-yard delay-of-game penalty. Having just moved 20 yards in the wrong direction, Oklahoma had the ensuing field goal attempt blocked. With momentum on their side, Washington scored two touchdowns in a one-minute span, propelling them to a 28-17 victory.

*   *   *   *

As much as we enjoyed our stay in Kirkland, we realized that we still needed some material for the book, lest we publish a four-month diary of buffets, water balloon drops and crank calls. But with our limo in the shop for most of the week, we never really uncovered the characters and traditions surrounding Washington football. Hopelessly confused, we explained our predicament to Seattle (and now ESPN) radio personality, the Fabulous Sports Babe. In her infinite wisdom, she assured us that as long as we spent a few hours tailgating on Lake Washington, we would somehow uncover the aura that is Husky football. The Sports Babe even set us up with a boat ride from one of her listeners.

We were thrilled to be joining Rob Berman's entourage for a three hour tour of picturesque Lake Washington. We figured that a few hours on the water would allow us to squeeze everything we needed to know about Husky football from our crew mates. But once we got into the middle of the lake, we just couldn't keep our minds focused on football. In fact, we talked about everything except football.

Things didn't change much when we arrived at the stadium. We were in such awe of the scenery that we barely paid attention to the game. That just may tell you how unfocused we really are. As scenic as Husky Stadium may be, it's difficult not to pay attention to a game there. With nearly 70 percent of the 72,500 seats located on the sidelines, it's one of the loudest stadiums in the country. An ESPN sideline crew once registered noise readings of 130 decibels during a game. With its thunderous crowd noise, Husky stadium also has to be rated among college football's best home field advantages.

Unfortunately for Washington, the crowd noise wasn't enough to propel their injury-riddled squad past the re-emerging Trojans. As had become par for the course, we dropped another $110, and increased our season losses to $890. During the boat ride home, we just sat admiring the view and pondering: pondering whether or not to purchase one last bucket of Larry's Market buttermilk chicken; pondering whether or not the limo would completely fall apart; and most of all, pondering why the Husky faithful didn't seem too upset after their team's defeat. We had seen outright crying at Georgia, depression at Michigan, a funeral march at LSU, and calls for Ken Hatfield's head at Clemson. Maybe it's just a matter of perspective. Whether the Huskies win or lose, Lake Washington still sparkles clear blue, the grill keeps sizzling at Schultzy's and the sun still sets over the Cascade Mountains.

SATURDAY AFTERNOON MADNESS
FOOD HALL OF FAME

Using the "Four Qs" of buffeteering (quantity, quantity, quality and quost), we selected the following restaurants as charter members of the Saturday Afternoon Madness Food Hall of Fame:

Dreamland: *Tuscaloosa, Alabama*
More addictive than smack, crack or a Hostess snack. Dreamland serves nothing but ribs, white bread and the greatest sauce you'll ever taste. After suffering withdrawal symptoms, we had two cases of Dreamland's ambrosial sauce shipped home to Boston.

Just BBQ: *Clemson, South Carolina*
Our mothers always warned us that pulled pork would make us go blind. Pork was the page of the Chinese menu from which we never ordered. The irony of it all: two Jews discovering that pork was their favorite of the four food groups. Now we know how Luke Skywalker must have felt when he learned that Darth Vader was his father.

Charlie Williams' Pinecrest Lodge: *Athens, Georgia*
A place where too much is never enough. The buffet table is a country mile long and features barbecue, catfish, and fried shrimp, all washed down with some sweet tea and a slab of homemade dingleberry pie. Furthermore, it's even better than a state fair for watching the fatties waddle by.

Crazy Jim's Blimpy Burgers: *Ann Arbor, Michigan*
Not as good as we anticipated, but still the best burger joint we experienced. Gotta love their slogan: "Cheaper than food." If you're in the mood for a hunka hunka burning beef, here's your spot. Where else can you enjoy a quintuple burger with cheese while gazing at pictures of Beaver Cleaver and the Three Stooges?

Palo Alto, California
Big Game: Stanford vs. California

Come Join The Band

You can keep New Year's Day and its thirteen consecutive hours of made-for-television bowl games. Just give us the Saturday before Thanksgiving, the day when most of college football's greatest rivalries are played out. For all but a handful of schools, success isn't measured by the whim of the pollsters, but rather by their performance against their arch-rivals. The Sugar Bowl has virtually no meaning to Alabama if they can't beat Auburn. As long as Harvard beats Yale, they really don't care what happens during the rest of their season. And a victory over those pot-smoking, flag-burning Ducks will make Oregon State completely forget about the harsh whippings they may have received from USC and Washington. In this respect, college football is drastically different from every other collegiate and professional sport. A regular season victory over the Super Bowl champions would be of little solace to a mediocre NFL franchise and North Carolina and Duke's basketball programs are measured by their tournament performances rather than their records against each other.

> **Here are just a few of the classic confrontations often contested on the Saturday before Thanksgiving:**
>
> | | |
> |---|---|
> | Michigan-Ohio State | Clemson-South Carolina |
> | Alabama-Auburn | USC-UCLA |
> | Tennessee-Kentucky | Virginia-Virginia Tech |
> | Washington-Washington St. | Harvard-Yale |
> | Depauw-Wabash | Lafeyette-Lehigh |
> | Arizona-Arizona State | Minnesota-Iowa |
> | Indiana-Purdue | Mississippi-Mississippi St. |
> | Duke-North Carolina | Utah-BYU |

With all these great rivalries from which to choose, what were we doing in Palo Alto? Shouldn't we have returned to Ann Arbor for the Michigan-Ohio State game, a rivalry so heated that legendary Buckeye coach Woody Hayes always refused to pay tolls while driving through Michigan?

Part of the appeal of Stanford-Cal was geographical. A wisecracking Seattle mechanic warned us that a Haitian refugee boat had a better chance of making it through the Rockies than our limo. Furthermore, we were both maxed out on our credit cards and had only some pocket change and McDonalds coupons for the journey home. When Bob's sister Wendy offered us a week of freeloading and chocolate chip marshmallow treats in her Bay Area apartment, we decided that the Stanford-Cal game made the most sense. After being treated to one of college football's classic rivalries, we are certain that we made the right choice.

   *   *   *   *

It is known simply as "Big Game," and as if to underscore the importance of any competition between these two rivals, all activities contested by them share the adjective "Big." When their glee clubs sing together, it's Big Sing, swim meets are Big Swim and diving competitions are Big Splash. Assuredly, a poker contest would be a Big Deal and a series of waltzing competitions would be Big Balls. Grandiose adjectives aside, this rivalry has all the elements of a classic: geographical proximity, sociological and political underpinnings, and more than a few myths and legends to provide a uniquely bitter flavor.

At least one basis for this rivalry stems from the markedly different attitudes that pervade the campuses. Set in the midst of the wealthy suburban enclave of Palo Alto, Stanford is a majestic private institution whose students were insulted when we referred to their school as the "Harvard of the West." While walking through Stanford's campus, we felt surrounded by that uniquely conservative feel of "the establishment." The tranquillity of the campus helps explain why students refer to it as "The Farm."

Cal couldn't be farther from Stanford on the atmospheric and political spectrums. Three decades after its heyday as the birthplace of the free speech movement, Berkeley remains America's most vibrant college community. A walk through Berkeley's Sproul Plaza just may have been the inspiration for Prozac. The philosophical free-for-all was in full swing when we arrived for a day-long visit. "Naked Man" wore nothing but a backpack, sandals and some strategically placed sun block. The off-key caterwauling of "Singing Man" has been known to excite the wildebeests at the local zoo. We even met our own personal savior, an Abbie Hoffman look-a-like whose preachings on Yoshua had all the coherence of Robert DeNiro's final monologue from *Cape Fear*. If his own chemical imbalances hadn't already hindered him enough, he was being unmercifully heckled by what he continually referred to as an "uncircumcised Philistine." The heckler scattered the crowd when he unzipped his pants, demonstrating that he was, instead, a circumcised Philistine. Only one afternoon there convinced us that Berkeley truly deserves its "Berserkley" nickname.

Philosophical differences aside, the competition between the two schools is what drives this rivalry, and it's not just limited to the playing fields. Stanford students will confidently tell you that most Cal students are still bitter about being rejected by Stanford. Berkeley students counter that, while the parents all want their kids to go to Stanford, the kids all really want to go to Cal. They also prod Stanford about being a university of spoiled rich kids, explaining why performances of the Stanford Band are often accompanied by the Cal students shaking "daddy's" car keys.

Feelings of general disdain are at the root of all rivalries, but what really sets apart an epic rivalry are the fans antagonizing opposing fans for no other reason than the pure fun of it. There is no better example of this time-honored tradition than the legend of "The Axe." The Axe has become a symbol of victory to be held over the head of the vanquished, and obtaining the Axe is anything but a trivial goal.

We learned the legend of the Axe the way students at both schools do, at each school's Big Game Axe Rally. Not surprisingly, there are several subtle differences between their respective renditions. The Stanford version shuns the name Cal in favor of the more descriptive "Weenies." No less demeaning, the Cal faithful always spell and pronounce their enemy as "Stanfurd," as in the "Leland Stanfurd Junior College."

There is agreement on certain basics. The Axe has its roots in the Axe Yell, which was born in 1896. According to R.G. O'Neil, in his book *The Stanford Axe:*

"The axe was the most terrible of weapons. Even as an instrument of domestic utility, we think of the axe not as a great boon to the pioneers... but rather as the means for stopping the squawks of excited chickens by one clean blow which severed the head and covered the ground with spurting blood... And the stark-naked truth of the matter is simply this: The Axe is the symbol which most accurately describes the subconscious feeling that those loyal to Stanford and California share toward the other school."

Inspired by this feeling, Stanford's Wild Bill Irwin and Chris Bradley created the Axe Yell. As explained by Hal Mickelson, the long-time voice of the Stanford Band, the yell is performed once slowly and then a second time quickly, "in the classical form as God had intended," as follows:

> *Give 'em the Axe, the Axe, the Axe!*
> *Give 'em the Axe, the Axe, the Axe!*
> *Give 'em the Axe,*
> *Give 'em the Axe,*
> *Give 'em the Axe,*
> *Where?*

Right in the neck, the neck, the neck!
Right in the neck, the neck, the neck!
Right in the neck,
Right in the neck,
Right in the neck,
There!

It wasn't until a few years later that someone wielded an actual Axe to accompany the yell. In 1899, after Stanford lost the first game of a best of three series against Cal for the Pacific Coast baseball championship, yell leader Billy Erb decided to inspire the team by purchasing a rusty broadaxe with a 14-inch blade. At that evening's bonfire, Erb used the Axe to chop the head off of a blue-and-gold clad dummy. So inspired were the students that Erb brought the axe to the ballgame the following day.

During the game, Erb wielded the weapon, threatening the Berkeley rooters and exhorting his fellow partisans into a frenzy. Nevertheless, Cal won the championship with a surprising 9-7 victory. But the Cal partisans weren't content with just their baseball victory; they wanted the Stanford Axe. Seizing the Axe, the Cal loyalists made a run for it, leading a wild chase through the streets of San Francisco, pausing at a butcher shop only long enough to cut off the axe's handle so it could be hidden from the police, who were searching students as they boarded the ferry back to Berkeley.

So frequent and violent were the ensuing efforts to liberate the Axe that the Stanford president declared, "Let no old axe cut off our dignity and self-respect." Still, not everyone at Stanford was content to end things there. If the Axe could be declared Cal's by right of conquest, then surely it could again belong to Stanford by right of subsequent conquest. Or so the logic must have been for a group of Stanford students who were later dubbed "The Immortal 21" (or, according to the Cal version, "The Immoral 21.") For three years, they plotted their scheme, and on the eve of the 1931 Cal rally, they descended upon Berkeley to put their nefarious plan into action.

At the conclusion of the rally, four blue and gold clad Stanfordites, posing as protectors of the prized possession, hopped aboard the armored car transporting the Axe back to the bank vault where it was normally safeguarded. When the car arrived at the bank, four more Stanfordites, disguised as newspaper men, convinced the guardians to pose for a few publicity pictures with the Axe. But the flashbulbs turned out to be tear gas bombs. In the ensuing confusion, the Axe was snatched and whisked away in an awaiting getaway car. Meanwhile, the remaining members of the Immortal 21, disguised as Cal students, organized search parties, each of which was directed in the opposite direction of the getaway. The Cal version of the story claims that the getaway car was about to be apprehended when it reached a drawbridge, where the engineer (allegedly a *summa cum laude* graduate of Stanfurd) was convinced to raise the bridge just after the Stanfurd entourage had crossed.

Reminiscent of the scene at Berkeley thirty years before, the Stanford students gathered for a spontaneous celebration. Classes were canceled and the *Stanford Daily's* headline read "AXE REGAINED," while the *Daily Californian's* screeched "AXE STOLEN." In an effort to head-off what promised to be a continued series of Cal attempts to recapture the Axe, both schools decided to make the Axe the official Big Game trophy. The Axe is now mounted on a handsome hunk of mahogany, which also bears the scores from each year's Big Game.

Members of the Immortal 21 gloat in victory

Making the Axe the official Big Game trophy hasn't completely eliminated efforts to steal it. Besides leading the football series 47-37, Stanford leads 4-3 in successful Axe thefts. Stanford's "Infamous Three" deserve special mention for stealing the Axe several days before the 1973 Big Game. Impersonating the Cal football coach, they convinced the head of the Cal Axe Commission to bring the coveted trophy to a football writers banquet at Ming's Restaurant in Palo Alto. When the gullible Axe handlers arrived, they were ambushed by brothers of the Delta Tau Chi fraternity.

With possession of the Axe, the Infamous Three issued a list of non-negotiable demands to the Stanford administration. In exchange for the safe return of the Axe, they demanded $6,000, Thanksgiving dinner with the university president, admission to the Stanford graduate school of their choice and the services of esteemed legal scholar Lionel Hutz to extract them from the legal predicament that was sure to ensue. Stanford countered something to the effect that if they didn't return the Axe, they would be spending Thanksgiving incarcerated in the Attica school, studying unnatural anatomy under professor Harry Hillbilly. Needless to say, the Axe was returned in time for the Big Game.

*   *   *   *

While students at both schools get excited about Big Game, there is no better example of a rabble rousing force than the Leland Stanford Junior University Marching Band. In its own words, the Stanford Band has "dedicated itself to the lofty pursuit of music and irreverent humor... challenging the powerful forces of dullness, complacency, normalcy and boredom."

The Stanford Band more closely resembles a social club than a traditional extracurricular activity — and an avowedly immature social club at that. Their clubhouse is a dilapidated former ROTC firing range slated for demolition due to its non-compliance with current building standards. Known as the Shak, this refuge from the pressures of a rigorous academic schedule is a disheveled mess of stolen street signs, moth-eaten costumes, half-destroyed props, broken glass and a plethora of other undetermined novelties. Nonetheless, the Band feels at home there. One student told us that the Shak is "the ultimate tree house you always wanted as a kid but lost interest in before you were old enough to build." Another band member explained, "It's what the world would look like if there were no parents."

Although band members claim that there is no rhyme or reason as to what street signs they choose to steal, there seems to be a general theme of sex, drugs and rock & roll. While we were big fans of the "Emergency Pass Out Gate," "Beaver Crossing" and "Moaning Cavern Park" signs, perhaps the sign that best explains the band is the "Child Development and Mental Retardation Center" sign prominently posted on the outside of the Shak.

Judging from its appearance, you might think that the Shak is the product of disorganized minds. Nothing could be further from the truth. Former drum major Greg Louden told us about some classic band pranks, one of the more fiendish of which allowed them to vent their hatred for the militaristic Southern Cal marching band. (Then again, in comparison to the Stanford Band, Peter, Paul and Mary could be seen as militaristic.) Greg assured us that this hatred is shared by all other Pac Ten bands as well as "all good, God-fearing, patriotic citizens of this country, this world and most galaxies." Louden claims that the USC band is so uptight that its members actually receive monetary fines for mistakes made during performances.

Curious to discover whether the USC band was really as disciplined as its reputation stated, several bandsmen littered the field with hundreds of dollar bills, hoping to entice the Trojans into breaking formation during their performance. Although not one Trojan fell for the trick, the band still had a viable backup plan. When the USC football team came out to warm up for the second half, they were dumbfounded to find the dollar bills still lying on the field. More importantly, they had no idea what to do with them. The players collected the bills and handed them to their captain, who did exactly what the band knew he would do: he presented the wad to the game official, as waiting band members snapped photographs for the next addition of the *Stanford Daily*.

Louden succinctly summed up the Band's philosophy: "Sophomoric humor is the divine right of sophomores... and juniors and seniors." As Greg graduated in 1990 and still returns week after week, sophomoric humor also appears to be the right of some alumni. Greg is a virtual fountain of band history, and he entertained us for hours with legendary band stories, many of which occurred on the band's trips to away football games. Most of the signs covering the Shak's walls were copped during these trips in a general display of what happens when you let the inmates out of the asylum.

Greg recalled a memorable flight to Arizona. When the pilot informed the passengers about the "wonderful view of the Grand Canyon to your left," the entire band shifted over to the left side of the plane, causing the plane to dive violently. As a result, the pilot kept all further scenic vista suggestions to himself. On that same flight, two members mixed peanut butter and jelly in a vomit bag, and one of them pretended to puke into the bag in order to draw the stewardess' attention. Upon arrival, the other member reached over and began to eat the contents of the bag. The startled stewardess lost consciousness and had to be helped from the plane. It's safe to assume that the band has been banned from using that airline.

The Stanford Band is not a true marching band. Unlike every other band we witnessed during our journey, Stanford is a scramble band. Instead of marching, they dance, run and saunter from formation to formation. Once they get into formation, they just stand and play. It's not like they can't march; they just choose not to. However, there was one performance for which the band actually taught itself to march in the traditional eight steps to five yards format... sort of.

The fans at Oregon's Autzen Stadium were shocked to see the normally rebellious Stanford Band form two lines and begin marching toward and through each other in perfect synchronization. Of course, the band turned this demonstration of discipline and precision into chaos. When it seemed that the precision demonstration would end successfully, the last two people in each line collided and began a fist fight. Not unlike the assassination of Archduke Ferdinand, this incident erupted into an all-out war, with musicians wielding hammers, axes and boxing gloves and tearing off their uniforms to reveal martial arts outfits and battle fatigues. (Of course, the French horns quickly surrendered.) With only the drummers playing *Allegro Confusiano,* the band continued this battle royal until the field was strewn with dead bodies, weapons and instruments.

Instead of marching practice, the band is usually busy perfecting its musical repertoire. Unlike traditional marching bands, the Stanford Band plays good time rock & roll, deliberately shunning antiquated school songs and salutes to the Carpenters, and as a result, they are as enthusiastic about performing as any of the other bands we witnessed. Concert cellist Tanya Navas told us that she shows up for rehearsals week after week just to play the cymbals.

While their music and lifestyle may be unique to college marching bands, it has been the band's half-time shows that have garnered most of the notoriety. Their formations have run the gamut from scrambled obscenities to not-so subtle sexual references to biting political and social satire. Band members maintain that their shows aren't really in bad taste; they're just misunderstood. When outraged alumni complained about their Flying Genitalia Formation, the band accused their critics of suffering a Freudian misinterpretation of their Linear Accelerators Spewing Particles March. The band's salute to the link-up of the Soyuz and Apollo spacecrafts was marred by similar misinterpretations.

Perhaps those incidents were just honest misunderstandings, but there have been plenty of other times when the band has stood at and exceeded the bounds of good taste. Several years ago, an incensed Notre Dame fan had to be restrained from attacking the band's field leader, who was leading the half-time show dressed as a nun and using a cross to keep tempo. Their *Tribute to Presidential Diseases Show* made light of Ronald Reagan's prostate and Jimmy Carter's hemorrhoids. And when Bay Area heiress, Patty Hearst, was kidnapped, they formed a giant Hearstburger — all bun no patty.

Although they have often delved into the realm of bad taste, the vast majority of the Stanford Band's shows are harmless, and at times, incredibly clever satire. Their "Other Temptations of Christ" included tearing the tags off mattresses and having too many items in the express checkout line. They mocked Iraq's invasion of Kuwait with the *Crisis in the Midwest Show* in which North Dakota annexed South Dakota, claiming that they were historically one people. The civic-minded band even provided the government with a possible solution to the budget crisis. They suggested franchising the Mustang Ranch,

America's most famous brothel, which had just been taken over by the IRS. Accordingly, they played the B-52's *Love Shack* while forming the word "McHo" on the field.

In an era in which college campuses are struggling with political correctness, it shouldn't be surprising that the band's behavior has resulted in two suspensions. After several drunken band members urinated on the field during a nationally televised game at Washington in 1986, athletic director Andy Geiger suspended them for one game, citing "insulting and lewd behavior." Upon returning from the suspension, they took the field wearing halos and marching behind a giant banner that read, "Sanitized for your Protection," while playing *When the Saints Go Marching In*. They also formed a "Geiger" counter with an arm that wavered between "band" and "banned."

Most band members reluctantly admit that their first suspension may have been warranted. It's their second suspension that was controversial enough to spur debate everywhere from the *Wall Street Journal* to the floors of Congress. The band's 1990 *Spotted Owl Show* at Oregon mocked the debate between conservationists and loggers over the protection of timberland to save the endangered spotted owls. First forming the word "Spot" and then dropping off the "S", the band insinuated that the real concern of Oregonians wasn't the destruction of the habitat of some polka-dotted fowl, but rather the destruction of their marijuana crops. When the Oregon fans and administration complained, the Stanford athletic director suspended them indefinitely, citing a "lack of sensitivity." They had been banned for political satire. Voltaire must have turned over in his grave.

Most band members dismissed the suspensions as the price they had to pay for challenging the outer limits of political satire. But just to show they were ready to cast a discriminating eye toward future material, the band published a list of the top ten shows that were rejected for their next performance.

TOP TEN SHOWS
REJECTED BY THE BAND:

10. The Immaculate Conception Show
9. The Jesse Helms Wet Dream Show
8. Goldilocks does Cal
7. The Last Temptations of the Dalai Lama Show
6. The Swear Words in Braille Show
5. The Virgin Mary Tractor Pull Show
4. The Euphemisms for Vomiting Show
3. Eugene: Land of Enchantment
2. The Gummi Products that Didn't Do Well, in Fact They Were Complete Disasters Show
1. The Dilemma of the Blind Gynecologist Show

Obviously, some people appreciate their irreverent sense of humor. They've played for the Democratic National Committee and Queen Elizabeth. (At the last minute, they nixed the *Great British Hemophiliacs Show*.) Somebody even had recorded band music played at his funeral. A number of alumni, however, don't find any humor in the band's antics, decrying their performances as a crude and shameless display of gutter humor.

We choose a far more conciliatory stance. Was it really so bad when their pregame salute to Cal fans featured the friendly salutation "HI FOLKS?" But many Cal fans vociferously complained when the bandsmen who were supposed to be forming the top of the "O" got confused and briefly stood at the top of the "L." If nothing else, the band proudly points to its unbiased stance, boasting that their *Death of Mao Show* offended both liberals and conservatives alike.

From our brief experience with the band, it is clear that whatever you think of their behavior, the band's zest for performing has been a unifying force at the school and has given them their own niche in the Big Game tradition.

*   *   *   *

Big Game has been bizarre right from its inception. Decades before promising a "chicken in every pot," engineering major Herbert Hoover organized Stanford's first football team. The first game was scheduled against Cal for March 19, 1892. Showing the same organizational and leadership skills that later earned him an ignominious distinction in American history, Hoover failed to account for a few minor details.

To be fair, Hoover could hardly be blamed for printing up only 5,000 tickets because no one could have anticipated that 20,000 people would show up for the Bay Area's first ever major football game. It was his second blunder that caused the most commotion (and leads us to wonder if this guy is somehow our distant relative). Hoover forgot to bring a football! The game was delayed for over an hour as the owner of a sporting goods store rode his horse back into town to pick one up. Unable to find one, he stuffed a bladder into an empty punching bag. Nevertheless, Stanford won 14-10. This first game foreshadowed a storied and often bizarre football tradition.

It's a cliché, but when these teams meet, you can throw the record book out the window because anything can and often does happen. Big Game has been defined by fantastic finishes (44 of the first 95 games were decided by 7 points or less), improbable upsets and plays that appeared to have been diagrammed in the Twilight Zone. With that in mind, one particular game stands out above all others: the 1982 Big Game featuring "The Play," the most bizarre game-ending play in college football history.

Even without The Play, the 85th edition of Big Game may have been the most spectacular in this rivalry. Trailing 19-17 with 53 seconds remaining, Stanford had the ball on their own 13, fourth down and 17. We don't have to tell Cleveland Browns fans what happened next. On his final collegiate drive, John Elway did to Cal what he has been doing to AFC defenses ever since. He calmly drove his team to the Cal 18-yard-line, where he called time out with eight seconds remaining. If he had only let a few more seconds tick off the clock before calling time out, Mark Harmon's field goal putting Stanford ahead 20-19 would have been the final play of the game. But when a Hall of Fame Bowl official shook hands with Stanford Athletic Director Andrew Geiger in recognition of Stanford's impending bowl bid, it turned out to be premature.

From the numerous accounts we heard from both Stanford and Cal fans, The Play takes on an almost surreal aspect. Stanford lined up to kickoff from its own 25, the result of a 15-yard penalty for excessive celebration after the preceding field goal. Mark Harmon's squib kick was fielded by Kevin Moen at the Cal 44. Moen wheeled and threw an overhand lateral to Richard Rogers, who then ran a few yards before lateraling to Dwight Garner. Garner's role in the play is still hotly disputed because it was at this point that confusion and mayhem overwhelmed the players, officials and everyone else in the stadium. Garner moved forward about six yards before being gang-tackled by three Cardinal linebackers.

Stanford fans will tell you that the game was over because Garner's knee had hit the ground. Cal fans (and more importantly, the referees) insist that Garner somehow managed to toss the ball back to Rogers. If fans can still manage to debate this point with the benefits of years of instant replay, imagine trying to figure out what was going on if you were a referee or Gary Tyrell, a trombonist with the Stanford Band who was waiting to rush the field in celebration of Stanford's Big Game victory.

As Garner was tackled, the band and Tyrell swarmed the field. Meanwhile, Rogers ran to the Stanford 46 and lateralled to Mariet Ford, who then ran to the Stanford 24 before tossing the ball blindly over his head, praying that a Cal player would be there. Six laterals after originally fielding the ball, Kevin Moen caught the desperation lateral and made a mad dash through the

Stanford Band into the end zone, where he collided with (and absolutely flattened) Tyrell. Cynics joked that the trombones were the weakest section of the Stanford defense. For over an hour after their shocking defeat, the distraught Cardinal players anxiously sat in the locker room, fully dressed, expecting that they would have to replay the kickoff, but they waited in vain. To sum up their feelings about The Play, Stanford replaced the Axe in its showcase with a giant screw.

During the week after The Play, the *Stanford Daily* decided to unilaterally alter history by printing a fake issue of Cal's newspaper. The headline story reported that, after review of incontrovertible photographic evidence proving that an official had signaled the play dead, the NCAA had decided to reverse its decision and award Stanford the Big Game victory. Cal students were seen with tears streaming down their faces after thousands of issues were substituted for the real *Daily Californian* on the Berkeley campus. To this day, Stanford still refuses to acknowledge the defeat, and whenever they win possession of the Axe, they change the score on the trophy to depict a 20-19 victory.

Postgame research revealed that The Play may not have been as spontaneous as it appeared. Cal players had actually prepared for it with their Sunday afternoon games of "Garbazz," a non-violent mixture of rugby, football and keep-away. The essence of the game had players moving a football down the field with a combination of forward and backwards passes. Although players didn't get to deck trombonists every time they scored, the game was still quite popular. Nonetheless, Cal pulled off The Play despite a significant disadvantage: they had only ten players on the field at the time.

Like Billy Cannon's midnight run at LSU and Run Lindsey Run at Georgia, The Play is now part of the collective consciousness of the Cal-Stanford rivalry. Everyone remembers and will recite for you their experience on the day of The Play. But of all the stories we heard, Jim Quillinan's has earned a special place in our hearts.

Jim graduated Stanford in 1970, and because his father went to Cal, the rivalry has always been a part of his family. Jim traditionally would get Big Game tickets for his father, his uncle Norm and their two friends. Although his career caused him to miss most games, Jim always bet $5 on the game with his Uncle Norm.

In 1983, Jim called his father to arrange for the turnover of the tickets. His father hesitated, because his Uncle Norm, stricken with Parkinson's disease, would be hard-pressed to attend. Nevertheless, Quillinan's father instructed him to proceed as usual because they would find some way to get Uncle Norm to the game. Needless to say, on the night following The Play, Jim got a call from his Uncle Norm demanding his $5. Even years later, as his uncle's condition worsened and he had trouble recognizing his own family, he would still recognize Jim and pester him about The Play.

*   *   *   *

Like many other collegiate rivalries, Stanford-Cal is chock full of futile, yet creative endeavors aimed at annoying and frustrating the enemy. The dumping of Cardinal red dye into Berkeley fountains, the painting of blue and gold paw prints on various Stanford buildings, and the releasing of red and white mice into Cal's library are just some the good natured pranks exchanged by the students of these two schools. We overheard a couple of Cal students discussing how three young men came running through their class dressed in nothing but blue and gold paint. Fortunately, it was anatomy class, so the distraction was minimal if not beneficial.

Other stunts have invoked more guile and ingenuity. For example, some Cal pranksters once printed up and distributed notices on Stanford letterhead canceling Stanford's traditional Big Game bonfire. The letter was so convincing that the *San Francisco Examiner* printed a story detailing the bonfire's cancellation. Another incident involved Stanford's kidnapping of Cal's cheerleaders by posing as reporters from the *San Francisco Chronicle*.

Even with campus security out in force, we decided to venture forth on the eve of Big Game in search of a little rivalry mayhem. After catching the Big Game bonfire at Berkeley's Greek Theater, we returned to the Shak for one final visit with the band.

For the entire week before Big Game, the band guards the Shak 24 hours a day to ward off Cal vandals. We don't know why.

There isn't anything the Cal pranksters could do to the Shak that the Stanford Band hasn't already done. If the building's condition had been somewhat disheveled earlier in the week, it now appeared as if an aftershock from the 1989 San Francisco earthquake must have hit. Apart from the usual signage and stainage, the floor was cluttered with various contraptions, for lack of a more descriptive word. During the week leading up to Big Game, band members traditionally construct various engineering marvels only to "grovel" (destroy) them following Big Game.

We were offered a ride on a rope swing/toboggan that had been constructed from some scrap plywood, a grocery store conveyor belt and a couple of old skateboards. But Phil's experience with negligence cases gave him a sixth-sense about accidents waiting to happen. Having gained more than a few pounds since our college days, we didn't want to risk the involuntary collapse of the structure before its designated time.

While we were able to resist the urge to grovel the limo, we weren't above taking part in "rank drink," a tradition where band members concoct and imbibe thoroughly nauseating, yet creative beverages. Some of the favorites include the Tuna Colada (Star-Kist floating in a minty broth of Scope mouthwash), the A-1 SteakShake (Adolph's meat tenderizer is optional), and the Screaming Viking (cucumber should be bruised). However, the acknowledged crowd-favorite is only imbibed prior to the Washington game. Comprised of root beer, dry ice and no less than 17 different alcohols, the Steaming Husky Shit also features two Tootsie Rolls lazily floating on its surface.

While it remains unclear exactly which rank drink we were drinking, we accepted some drunken freshman's challenge of going shot for shot with him. Apparently, he was celebrating the prospect of reaching puberty before graduation. Experience won out as the pencil-necked frosh made the crucial mistake of beginning the contest about ten shots ahead and 140 pounds behind us. The following morning, we found him passed out in a fetal position beneath some moth-eaten costumes.

But before passing out, he invited us to come join the band for the Big Game show. He instructed us to be at the Shak by 7:00 a.m. dressed in white shorts and a black shirt. We were both quite excited about the opportunity to play with the band. What could possibly beat the rush of stepping onto the field and being pelted with frozen fruit by the Cal faithful?

Somehow, we were able to shake off the cobwebs and arrive at the Shak by the designated time. We had already polished off a half dozen donuts before one of the band leaders informed us that a drunken freshman doesn't have the authority to initiate members into the band. Since our musical contributions were not wanted, we retreated back to the apartment to watch ESPN's *Gameday*. They aired a segment about two mutant dropouts traveling across the country in a limo... hey wait a minute, that was us on *Gameday!* Who says television contributes to the delinquency of youngsters?

*   *   *   *

Big Game security was tight, as the Stanford administration was determined to thwart any on or off-field incidents, but with the thought that goes into the pranks between these schools, security is at a severe disadvantage. Take, for example, the projectile technology employed.

When Nebraska beat Colorado securing yet another Orange Bowl berth, Husker fans littered Folsom Field with oranges. But throwing fruit is far too primitive for the sophisticated Big Game fans, especially when they can funnelate frozen fruit. A funnelater is a slingshot that can easily be made from two five-foot pieces of surgical tubing, a lacrosse stick netting and some duct tape. It allows fans to launch missiles at the enemy from over 100 yards away. In past years, the Stanford lacrosse team has been deployed to protect the band from these vitamin-rich projectiles. Band members have also used 8-irons to knock the fruit back into the stands. In a more passive approach, the fruit has been used to mix fresh-squeezed screwdrivers.

As Stanford's Russ Meyer learned, funnelating fruit does have its risks. During 1991's Big Game, Meyer and his cohorts loaded a funnelater with an apple. Two of them secured the tubing, while a spread-eagled Meyer pulled the pouch toward his crotch, five rows back. Their execution had all the makings of a Roadrunner cartoon.

When Meyer released the missile, the pouch turned over on itself, swung out twenty feet and flung the apple back into his groin at a speed in excess of 100 MPH. Meyer told *Cardinal*

Today, "I was OK for the first five seconds, then it hit me. I broke into a cold sweat and collapsed to the ground in agony." Shortly thereafter, he resigned from the Three Stooges fan club and reports to have lost his compelling urge to overuse the television remote control.

*   *   *   *

Our seats were located right next to the Cal student section, ensuring a raucous afternoon of vociferous Stanford-baiting. The Cal students are particularly conscious of anyone daring to wear any color remotely resembling cardinal red in their section. Throughout the game, they continually chanted, "Take off that red shirt," until the offending garment was shed.

We also had a great view of Cal's Golden Bear mascot, Oski. After several students were mauled by bears, Cal abandoned live mascots in favor of Oski. Although he looks like he would fit in well at a Hanna-Barbara theme park, Oski's confrontational style has made him universally hated among the Pac Ten mascot fraternity, but like the much maligned Bill Lambeer, beloved at home. As opposed to the upbeat and whimsical Stanford Tree, Oski is an introspective and often brooding mascot. If they were going to film a Big Game movie, Marlon Brando would be the only logical choice to play Oski (a young Steve Martin would have made the perfect Tree). Shunning the rah-rah role of most mascots, Oski nervously paces the sidelines, only occasionally stopping to give fans a thumbs-up sign when things bode well for his team.

With his true identity protected by the Oski Committee, Oski has had a tumultuous past. Perhaps his most well-known ploy was working a basketball crowd into a frenzy by arming himself with a giant layer cake and pretending to vacillate between throwing it into the Cal student section and tossing it at the opposing fans. Apparently, Oski got a tad carried away one evening and lobbed the cake at some visiting Oregon State fans, resulting in a two game suspension. Reportedly, former OSU point guard Gary Payton still holds a grudge about his parents being covered with gooey layer cake.

By comparison, Stanford's Tree is a far more upbeat and whimsical mascot. A tree as a mascot you may ask? Well, it actually makes a lot of sense. Stanford used to be known as the

Indians until sensitivity to Native American concerns caused a shift to the inoffensive Cardinal (the color, not the bird, religious leader or type of number). Nonetheless, what kind of a mascot can you get from a color? Instead, Stanford adopted the tree as its mascot in honor of "El Palo Alto," the tall tree that served as a landmark to settlers and gave the city of Palo Alto its name.

Earlier in the week, we had a chance to sit down with the Tree, who agreed to "tell us about his roots." The Tree explained that each year, the band chooses a new tree on the basis of "dazzling showmanship, visual wit and mimetic verisimilitude" (smarmy Stanford words). During the grueling application process, applicants have been forced to dress as rabbinical dead-heads and turn themselves into giant sundaes.

Considering the tension that exists between these rival institutions and what bears have been doing to trees in the woods for eons, it's not surprising that Oski and the Tree have had their share of confrontations. Their animosity reached its apex when they got into a fist-fight during the 1989 Big Game. Besides battling Oski, the Tree has often been the target of drunken Cal hooligans. After witnessing repeated attempts to defoliate the Tree, Stanfordites have banded together to protect their mascot. We watched in amazement during the pregame show, as several braindead Cal students attacked the Tree, only to receive a savage pummeling from the band before being led off the field in handcuffs.

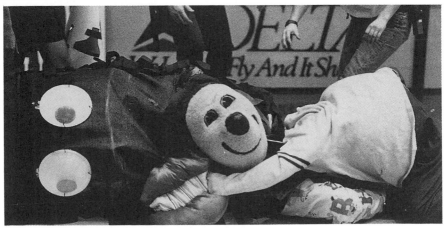

Oski gets the better of the Tree

The Cop gets the better of Oski

The game itself promised to be emotional. Both teams were out of bowl contention and only a Big Game victory could salvage their seasons. Las Vegas had installed Stanford as a 2-point favorite. If we had learned anything during Big Game week, it was to remove those little red peppers before wolfing down a plate of Hunan chicken. We also learned to always bet on the underdog in these types of rivalries. In a rare prudent move, we broke our tradition of betting on the home team and wagered $100 on Cal.

Because of the diversions surrounding Big Game (including Oski's theft and wild ride around the stadium in the security chief's golf cart), we didn't pay much attention to the game. But whenever we did look at the action on the field, it seemed that Cal was scoring yet another touchdown, on its way to regaining the Axe with a 46-17 Big Game victory.

After the game, security massed in front of the Cal student section, valiantly hoping to prevent an advance onto the playing field. In a standoff reminiscent of Berkeley's anti-war demonstrations of the '60s, the police held the Cal students at bay for almost a half hour. Occasionally, a trickle of fans would charge the field, only to be beaten back and arrested by security. Eventually, Cal's numbers won out as a mass of students swarmed the field and tore down both goal posts.

*   *   *   *

As we left Palo Alto, we compared the reality of our experience to our expectations. Easterners often dismiss California as lacking in history and tradition. Whether this criticism is justified or not, it certainly doesn't apply to football. The Big Game is at least as rich in tradition as any rivalry in the country, and the participation of its fans gives it a unique flavor, unattainable anywhere else. As we embarked upon the longest drive of our trip, we now understood a different side of college football. More importantly, we knew that you simply can't get better Mexican or Chinese food anywhere in the world.

College Station, Texas
Texas Aggies vs. Texas Longhorns

Strangers in a Strange Land

What would your call be? If you could attend either the Texas-Texas A&M Thanksgiving Day clash or the following afternoon's Oklahoma-Nebraska slugfest, which would you choose? On the one hand, Oklahoma-Nebraska is *the* traditional Thanksgiving rivalry of our generation. With Orange Bowl berths and national championships usually riding on its outcome, this game is invariably a classic. Many fans still consider the 35-31 Nebraska triumph in 1971 to be the greatest college football game ever played. With Nebraska again in national championship contention, this edition of the game had similar potential. Furthermore, we were both anxious to visit Lincoln's Memorial Stadium (a veritable shrine that becomes Nebraska's third-largest city on football Saturdays) as well as our friend from summer camp, Mark Edge (a veritable Shriner who becomes Nebraska's third-largest idiot on football Saturdays).

On the other hand, how could we possibly traverse America in search of college football's greatest venues and completely ignore the Republic of Texas, a place so football-crazed that even their high schools have spring practice. Where else would you find bumper stickers that read, "My linebacker can kick your honor student's ass." And wasn't it Texas where some deranged woman shot somebody to advance her daughter's cheerleading career? Omitting Texas from our gridiron odyssey would be a blasphemy akin to sampling fast food's greatest burgers without tasting a Big Mac.

After toying with the ludicrous idea of splitting up, watching both games and then reuniting in Graceland, we chose Texas A&M. With the exception of avoiding the moldy shellfish at Big Daddy's seafood buffet, this was the best decision we made during the entire trip. Football may be a religion at many other places, but none of those other religions can match the pageantry and ritual of the Church of Aggieland.

From watching years of college football telecasts, we already knew that the Aggie students stand during games and kiss their dates after touchdowns. (Then again, so do nymphomaniac hemorrhoid sufferers.) However, we were completely unprepared to experience the other manifestations of this so called "Spirit of Aggieland: Yell Practice, Bonfire, Elephant Walk — events which all precede their annual intrastate showdown with the University of Texas.

*   *   *   *

When the student writers at *The Battalion* instructed us to arrive on campus in time for Tuesday afternoon's Elephant Walk, we figured there was no possible way that we could leave Palo Alto Saturday night, traverse 2,500 miles of desert in a broken-down funeral limo and arrive in College Station just sixty hours later. But out of curiosity, we asked them to explain Elephant Walk. When they described it as a massive food fight between the junior and senior classes, we immediately revised our itinerary.

After 40 grueling hours in the limobeast and 6 pounds of drive-through tacos, we arrived at Texas A&M's Kyle Field just in time for the festivities. Nothing could have prepared us for what we experienced. We walked through a tunnel which opened into an end zone and another world. We turned around and saw 8,000 students, not a long haired freak in the bunch, sitting in the bleachers above us. Actually they weren't sitting at all, but they weren't standing either. They were leaning forward with their hands resting on their thighs, assuming, for lack of a better term, the "please-sir-may-I-have-another" position. All of a sudden, the whole lot of them let out this earth shaking yell: "Yeaaaa! Gig'em! Aggies!" The entire procession seemed to be led by three guys clad in overalls and carrying axe handles. For lack of a more descriptive name, we'll call them the "Hee Haw Boys."

As we looked on in complete amazement, one of the Hee Haw Boys stepped up to the microphone and let out a thunderous "Howdy!" We nearly jumped out of our shorts when the entire student section responded in unison with an even more deafening "Howdy!!" Then the Hee Haw Boys told some jokes about the University of Texas, during which, the students continually intervened with assorted yelps, whoops and hisses. To add to the mayhem, many of them were dousing each other with shaving cream, chocolate sauce and an array of other condiments. If this wasn't bizarre enough, every now and then, the Hee Haw Boys would start waving their hands in crazy spastic motions, except that they really couldn't have been totally crazy, because within moments, the entire student section would be making the same inexplicable motions. After finishing their seizures, everyone again assumed the please-sir-may-I-have-another position and let forth another mighty yell. Despite being clueless, we were incredibly impressed.

*   *   *   *

It turns out that we were witnessing a seniors only Yell Practice with the "Heehaw Boys" being the Yell Leaders. In Aggieland, they have neither cheerleaders nor cheers. Yells are led by Yell Leaders, upperclassmen elected to that prestigious position by the Twelfth Man (Aggiespeak for student body) for their burning desire to motivate the Aggies.

The please-sir-may-I-have-another position is known as "humping it." Ever since an Aggie engineer determined that humping it was the anatomical position from which to emit the loudest sound, all yells have been done from this position.

Unlike traditional cheerleaders, the Yell Leaders don't orally communicate with the student body. They simply select a yell and communicate it to the Twelfth Man through the use of hand signals. The students in the bottom row pick up the hand signal and repeat it, passing it up row by row, until the entire

Twelfth Man knows what yell is coming up. Then the Yell Leaders assume the hump-it position and the yell begins.

As we saw for ourselves, yells are taken very seriously in Aggieland. Yell Practices commence right from the beginning of a student's involvement with A&M when the freshmen (Fish) attend freshmen orientation (Fish Camp). Then throughout their four-year stay, there are continuous Yell Practices, the most notable of which are held at midnight on the Friday before each home game. The ritual begins with a torch-lit procession from the Quadrangle to Kyle Field. After the yells and the after-touchdown kiss are practiced, the Twelfth Man sings *The Spirit of Aggieland.* As many as 40,000 Aggies have been known to participate in midnight yells. With all do respect to the other pep rallies we attended, Yell Practice makes them seem like Karaoke night at the Elk's Club by comparison.

In Aggieland, when your team scores, so do you. It's a tradition for the students to kiss their dates following touchdowns. When we asked one student what happens after two-point conversions, he just smiled and winked. Supposedly, during the lean years, Aggies also got to kiss their dates after every first down.

It seems that every Aggie tradition revolves around the Twelfth Man. As any Aggie can tell you, the Twelfth Man dates back to their 1922 Dixie Classic match-up against the mighty Centre College team that had recently snapped Harvard's six-season winning streak. Injuries had so depleted the A&M squad that coach Dana X. Bible was forced to summon Aggie student E. King Gill from the stands. Gill willingly answered this call to duty and donned the uniform of an injured player. Although he never played a down, his readiness symbolized the willingness of all Aggies to support their team. In his honor, Aggie students stand during all football games, waiting to be called into action.

After six decades of patiently waiting on the sidelines, Coach Jackie Sherrill called the Twelfth Man into service. Sherrill was so impressed with the enthusiasm he witnessed during the building of the Aggie Bonfire that he decided to harness this energy for the benefit of the team. With a kicker and ten walk-ons, Texas A&M fielded college football's most aggressive and exciting kickoff coverage team. For eight seasons, these volunteers stymied the opposition, while setting school records for kickoff coverage (In 1983, they allowed a paltry 13.1 yards per kickoff return). But after a Texas Tech player bowled over some skinny engineers for a touchdown, current coach R. C. Slocum reduced the Twelfth Man squad to a single walk-on. As we walked through campus, we noticed an abundance of chalk-written graffiti urging Slocum to bring back the entire Twelfth Man.

Midnight Yell

However, the concept of the Twelfth Man transcends football. It's a willingness shared by most Ags to serve their school, their friends, their country and their God in any way necessary. Having defended America everywhere from San Juan Hill to the Persian Gulf, there is no better example of Aggie service than in times of conflict. With the entire graduating classes of '42 and '43 serving combat duty, Texas A&M provided more World War II officers than any other school in the nation.

*   *   *   *

Much to their dismay, students eventually graduate from Texas A&M, and thus it is inevitable that a student will no longer be a part of the Twelfth Man. That's where Elephant Walk comes in. Elephant Walk is an annual rite of passage commemorating the seniors' final game against Texas as members of the Twelfth Man.

Our arrival at the stadium coincided with the pre-Elephant Walk Yell Practice. At its conclusion, the senior class descended from the stands and formed several hundred lines of fifteen people across. Joined by their closest friends, with their arms draped around each other's shoulders, they followed the Yell Leaders on a symbolic march through campus.

As the seniors wandered through campus like elephants searching for a place to die, the freshman and sophomores were forbidden to view them. Much like Roseanne's visit to the nude beaches of France, there were unsuspecting underclassmen literally covering their faces and ducking for cover as the procession marched by. On the other hand, many juniors have taken it upon themselves to "grode" the elephants to a quicker death. The preferred weapons for groding are eggs and shaving cream, but mustard, syrup and motor oil are also quite common. True to the school's military roots, we witnessed some ingenious methods of groding, such as a group of juniors who were slingshotting baskets of eggs into the hoards of seniors.

But don't think the seniors were unprepared for this onslaught. Although many of them exhausted their armaments on each other during the Kyle Field Yell Practice, they mounted a valiant defense. Nevertheless, the seniors were sitting ducks for the juniors' guerrilla warfare tactics. Much like the Minutemen at the Battles of Lexington and Concord, the undermanned juniors continually took pot shots into the lines of seniors before scattering into the thicket.

Not everyone in Aggieland is thrilled about the relatively new tradition of groding. Many believe that Elephant Walk is a solemn occasion, a time for reflection and reunion, not an excuse for a massive food fight. Later that day, members of the Corps reassembled and conducted their own Elephant Walk. In full dress uniform, they silently marched through campus, single-file, with their right arms resting on the shoulders of the cadets in front of them.

*   *   *   *

Although it has nothing to do with football, Silver Taps is one of the traditions that best reflects the Spirit of Aggieland. Silver Taps is an emotional and solemn ceremony held on the first Tuesday of any month in which a student has passed away during the previous month. Every light on campus is extinguished (cars included), as thousands of students silently gather in front of the Academic Building for the 10:30 p.m. ceremony. The deceased are honored with three rifle volleys of seven shots apiece, following which the buglers play *Silver Taps* three times. Afterward, a tearful Aggie student body silently departs. Thankfully, we didn't get to experience this tradition.

As for the uniqueness of Texas A&M itself, the Aggies say: "From the outside looking in, you can't understand it. From the inside looking out, you can't explain it." Nevertheless, here's our best shot. Until a few decades ago, Texas A&M was an all-male military institution whose graduates were held in such high esteem that General Patton once boasted, "Give me an Army of West Point graduates and I'll win a battle. Give me a handful of Texas Aggies, and I'll win the war." It's a place where words like honor, code and loyalty are the backbone of a life devoted to defending something worthwhile, not as a punch line to some joke. While other schools may talk about traditions, the citizens of Aggieland continue to religiously practice theirs.

Even though the Corps of Cadets only number 2,000 at this 40,000 student institution, they remain the heart and soul of the university. But what separates A&M from the other military academies (and for that matter, every other place on earth) is its seemingly incomprehensible combination of militarism and friendliness. With all Ags considering it their duty to extend a "howdy" to visitors and friends alike, Texas A&M is the only school where you run the risk of being howdied to death.

The Twelfth Man also engages in Yell Practices after all home games. Victories are celebrated by ceremoniously dunking the Yell Leaders into the "Fish Pond" before breaking into a triumphant Yell Practice. After being outscored, the Twelfth Man remains in the stands for a postgame Yell Practice. Apart from preparing them for the next game, these Yell Practices symbolize their continuing support for the team. Pictured is a post-victory Yell Practice. Notice the Aggies "humping it" in the background and the Yell Leaders signaling the upcoming yell.

The animosity between A&M and their rivals in Austin was obvious right from the beginning. Because Texas A&M is the oldest public school in the state, they refer to their rivals in Austin as texas university (t.u. for short) while Longhorns call their school The University of Texas. Semantics aside, the University of Texas, with its location in the state capital, is the more powerful of the two schools. When oil was discovered on land belonging to the University of Texas system in 1923, a fund now worth close to $4 billion was established. It was decided that the fund's interest would be split between the two largest of the Texas schools, with two-thirds going to the Longhorns and one-third going to the Aggies. To many Aggies, it doesn't matter that A&M has received hundreds of millions from this windfall, what matters is that those conniving Longhorns somehow managed to get twice as much. With the Longhorns in control of the legislature, A&M always seems to be treated like a second class institution.

Still, there's much more to this rivalry than one school's struggle for parity with their snobby rivals. The fundamental differences that exist between partisans of these two schools may have been best summed up by the following editorials from their respective school newspapers. An Aggie columnist called Austin an "urban psychosis of steroids, acid, and drag worms" and asked its "decadent, socially-diseased" residents if they have noticed that "College Station continues to grow, while the only meager activity in your city is the piss-ant protesters demonstrating for the cause of the week." The Longhorn columnist was no less vitriolic, claiming that every true Longhorn should thank God for not being a "crew-cur-wearin'-fried chicken-eatin'-sheep-lovin'-Republican-votin'-boot-wearin'-Aggie."

But despite the animosity inherent in this rivalry, Texas A&M still strives to be the friendliest school in the world. When Longhorn safety Freddie Steinmark lost his leg to cancer in 1969, the Ags wired him a 60-foot long get well telegram.

When Elephant Walk came to an end, we came face to lumber with Aggie Bonfire. We stood there silently, jaws agape, completely overwhelmed by the mammoth proportions of this wooden colossus, and it wasn't even finished yet! Comparing Aggie Bonfire with other Bonfires is like comparing lightning with a lightning bug. While their tea-sippin' rivals were burning draft cards during the '60s, the Ags were building Bonfires that reached fantastic new dimensions. In fact, their 109-foot Bonfire in 1969 earned a spot in the *Guinness Book of World Records.*

Out of concern for safety, the school now limits Bonfire's height to sixty feet, but judging by the size of the stacks that stood before us, this limit doesn't seem to be strictly enforced. A few years ago, some engineers tried to measure Bonfire's heat by sticking an industrial thermometer into its core. The thermometer melted. Bonfire burns so hot that the fire department warns all residents within a square mile to water down their roofs, clean their gutters and remove all flammables from their yards. After dozens of neighbors had holes burned in their roofs, Bonfire was moved to a spacious field on East Campus.

Bonfire symbolizes every Aggie's undying love for Texas A&M as well as their burning desire "to beat the hell out of t.u." With every aspect of its construction administered by the Twelfth Man, Bonfire has become the ultimate testament to what Aggie teamwork and motivation can accomplish. On fall weekends, hundreds of students wake up at the crack of dawn, put on their nastiest work clothes, hop into the back of pick-up trucks and ride out to the cutting site. Using axes that, like so many of the Aggie traditions, have been passed down from generation to generation, the students cut and top the trees by hand.

Obviously, a great deal of organizational skill is necessary for such an undertaking. Much like the characters in some Orwellian novel, each Aggie's function is determined by the color "pot" (helmet) on their head. At the top of the hierarchy stands the eight senior and eight junior Redpots. Their red helmets are so coveted in Austin that it is rumored that any Longhorn capable of stealing one would receive an automatic bid to the fraternity of his choice. While none of the students we encountered could remember any "tea-sip being that stupid," John Maher, in his book *Bleeding Orange,* recalled one foolhardy Longhorn from the '70s who grabbed a red pot and made a mad dash for his car, only to get an axe handle through his windshield.

The creation of Bonfire begins early in the semester. As soon as the first bundles of logs are delivered to campus, the senior Redpots take up residence in a large tent at the Bonfire site. Their presence is intended to prevent those "long-haired Hippiehorns from accidentally lighting it on fire in one of their frenzied pot parties." There is always at least one senior Redpot guarding Bonfire at all times. Supposedly, there's a $10,000 bounty in Austin for any Longhorn capable of prematurely torching the Bonfire. Some fool once tried to douse the stacks with gasoline only to be savagely pummeled by a six-pack of Aggies before the dastardly deed could be completed. Nevertheless, the senior Redpots remain forever vigilant.

In addition to the sixteen Redpots, there are also six "Climbers" who wear silver pots, five senior "Brownpots" and four "Centerpolepots." Each male dorm has one Yellowpot and each unit of the Corps has a maroon "Buttpot." There are even "Pinkpots" who provide refreshments for the hungry workers. As we watched the pots busily attending to their duties, we were reminded that the only colored pot in Austin was "green with red hair."

Bonfire resembles a sixty-foot, six-layer, chocolate wedding cake. While all Ags may contribute to the first four stacks, the junior Redpots are responsible for the fifth stack, and the senior Redpots, the sixth and final stack. Atop the sixth stack sits an outhouse, symbolic of "the best fraternity at Austin."

Although the Bonfire outhouse is constructed on campus, this wasn't always the case. It was once customary for Ags to steal them from unsuspecting residents of the Brazos County countryside. In his book *Good Bull: 30 Years of Aggie Escapades,* John Hoyle sheds some light on why this practice was stopped.

One year, a few Ags spotted the perfect outhouse, but were afraid that they would be caught if they took the time to load it onto their vehicle at the farmstead. Instead, they decided to lasso the outhouse, drag it a half-mile away, and then load it onto their truck. As planned, they drove up, lassoed the outhouse and sped away. But as they were driving down the road, they heard some banshee-like yells coming from inside the outhouse. About 300 yards later, they stopped to investigate the disturbance. Much to their chagrin, there was a fiercely agitated 75-year-old man with his pants at his ankles, screaming bloody murder.

Aggie Bonfire

Not all citizens of Aggieland are thrilled with the Bonfire. Some believe it's a major embarrassment to the university. They complain that students spend more time at the Bonfire than in the classroom. In *I Bleed Maroon*, Frank Cox lambastes those in the academic world who are "unable to understand that the valuable, useful, and lasting values of cooperation, communication, organization, leadership, hard work, and accomplishment gained through an adventure such as building the Bonfire are very useful and needed tools in the work world."

The environmental killjoys have also thrown in their two cents. For some reason, they have taken exception to the concept of cutting down 10,000 trees, soaking them in jet fuel and burning them in a wild pagan ritual. They bemoan that at least the Amazons destroy their rain forests to earn a living. At College Station, it's a pep rally. The critics find it ironic that 40,000 "patriots" can sing *God Bless America* while needlessly burning one of America's forests. In response to these environmental concerns, the Aggies have started the tradition of replanting two trees for every one cut down. They also point out that most of the land cleared for the Bonfire had already been slated to be cleared for mining or cattle-raising anyway.

*   *   *   *

On Wednesday, the day before the game, we again checked out the progress of Bonfire's construction. Of course all that wood and the thought of the fire which would soon arise from it made us think of only one thing: barbecue. Hungry for a small taste of Texas culture and a large taste of brisket, we headed over to Tom's Barbecue. Tom's featured a simple lunch, and we opted for the ribs and links combination. You get ribs, links, a slab of cheese, some onion slices, a pickle and some white bread. There's no plate, because its served on wax paper, and you don't need a fork, assuming you have fingers. The concept of cholesterol control has obviously never been featured in any of the *Field and Stream* magazines that the patrons of Tom's read (or for that matter, any of the *Mad* magazines that we read).

After sleeping off Tom's beef infusion of earlier that day, we headed toward the field for the Bonfire celebration. Despite freezing rains, there were over 40,000 people in attendance. As we watched the Redpots struggle to light the Bonfire, we wondered if some ingenious tea-sips hadn't somehow doused the stacks with asbestos. But when the Bonfire finally caught, a cold damp night was instantly transformed into a toasty inferno. Tradition says that if the Bonfire collapses before midnight, the Aggies will be outscored by the Longhorns. By not lighting Bonfire until 11:00, the Aggies assured themselves of another Thanksgiving Day triumph.

Another one of Texas A&M's non-football related traditions is "muster." Each year on April 21st, the date Texas won its independence from Mexico, muster ceremonies are held around the world to pay homage to the Aggies who have passed-on during the year. A roll call of the departed is read, with all those who knew the deceased answering "here" to the name. A candle is also lit for each departed Aggie. At the conclusion of the ceremony, a firing squad fires three volleys of seven shots and *Silver Taps* is played three times. Besides memorializing the departed, muster is a time for all Aggies to renew their pledges of loyalty and friendship to each other and to Texas A&M.

*　　　*　　　*　　　*

Thanksgiving Day arrived cold and rainy. With the embers still smoldering from the Bonfire, the cadets marched into Kyle Field to the wild cheers of 15,000 fans and the shivering claps of two whiny Yankees. While each unit was greeted with heavy applause, the loudest cheers were reserved for Company E-2, the unit responsible for the care of Reveille, A&M's beloved collie mascot. Owned by no one, yet belonging to all Aggies, Reveille has been the first lady of Aggieland since being accidentally run over by a carload of marauding cadets in 1931. After the unfortunate accident, the cadets brought the injured pup back to campus to care for her. When the bugler blew reveille the next morning, the pup began barking and howling. She was immediately christened as Reveille and adopted as the official mascot of Texas A&M.

According to her official biography: "Reveille made every Yell Practice and all the games. She had a strong preference for cadets in uniform and was known to bark at civilians. She loved to heckle Joe College, Peruna, Bevo, bears, owls and frogs. Reveille was very snooty to other dogs and respected by all Aggies." Being a true Ag, Reveille proudly served her country during World War II, eventually attaining the rank of general in the K-9 Corps. When she died, she was accorded a formal military funeral and buried at the entrance to Kyle Field. She and her successors, Reveille II, Reveille III and Reveille IV, are buried together, all facing the scoreboard so they can watch the Aggies outscore their opposition.

Reveille is the highest ranking member of the Corps of Cadets, outranking even the commander. Because of her rank, she is allowed to eat her meals in the mess hall and has free reign of all campus buildings. The care of Reveille is a very serious matter, with the mascot corporal being one of the more prestigious positions within the Corps. Each year, there is a formal "passing of the leash" to a new sophomore cadet who has demonstrated the requisite knowledge of the facts and history surrounding Reveille. It takes a special person to care for Reveille because she is incredibly intelligent. She can even spell "A-G-G-I-E-S" by barking six times, once for each letter.

Freshmen are watched carefully to ensure that they demonstrate the proper respect to Reveille. The only acceptable greeting for her is, "Howdy, Miss Reveille, Ma'am." Although they may not refer to her as a dog, the term canine is acceptable. Furthermore, they can't touch her or have their eyes linger on her. After football games, the freshmen form a human wall to escort Reveille out of the stadium. Due in part to their vigilance, Reveille is the only mascot in the Southwest Conference that has never been kidnapped.

Editor's Note... *The streak had to end someday... Reveille was pilfered from a Cadet's backyard in Dallas while the Aggies were preparing for the 1994 Cotton Bowl. Of course, the Longhorns were responsible for the heist. She was recovered several days later in Austin, thus ending "doggie-gate."*

Conversely, the Longhorn's Bevo has traditionally been one of college football's most slovenly mascots. In his its ignominious career, Bevo has been stolen and branded by its rivals, sedated by its own school, knocked down by Earl Campbell and bonked in the head by an irate SMU cheerleader. Aside from serving as the special guest of honor at team banquets, Bevo has made few meaningful contributions to the school.

The University of Texas adopted its first longhorn steer mascot in 1916. Because of the cost of maintaining the ornery beast, he quickly fell out of favor on the Austin campus. To create additional enthusiasm, Bevo's handlers decided to brand it with the 21-7 score from the team's 1916 victory over A&M. But the resourceful Aggies beat them to the punch, instead branding the steer with the 13-0 score from A&M's 1915 victory. To mask their shame, the steer's handlers altered the 13-0 to resemble the letters BEVO. The name stuck.

If Reveille received the most applause while marching in, the Aggie Band finished a close second. With over 300 members, they are the world's largest precision military marching band. As anarchic as the Stanford Band was, the Aggie Band displayed an equivalent level of discipline. Supposedly, they are so disciplined that they once marched off the field in disgrace because a single cadet screwed up. A few years ago, the band leaders purchased some software to help them choreograph their marching formations. When they entered their signature piece, the "Maroon Tattoo," the computer claimed that it was impossible. But what's impossible for ordinary folks is just routine for the Ags. Even while watching the Maroon Tattoo, we couldn't figure out how lines of bandsmen could walk through one another without crashing into each other.

*   *   *   *

We were fortunate enough to be witnessing the 100th meeting between these ancient rivals. Although Texas held a commanding 64-30 lead in the series, A&M had dominated the recent meetings, having won 7 of the last 8 games entering the '93 contest. With a Cotton Bowl berth on the line, the 9-1 Ags were a three touchdown favorite over the 5-4-1 Longhorns. But in the face of 40 MPH wind gusts and a bonechilling rain, the Longhorns mounted a valiant struggle. If not for a late goal-line stand and a Leeland McElroy 100-yard kickoff return, this might have been the greatest upset in the history of the series. Nevertheless, the Aggies prevailed 18-9, earning their third consecutive conference championship and continuing the greatest run of dominance in SWC history. Fortunately, our bookie took Thanksgiving off, preventing us from dropping anther $110.

*   *   *   *

As we left College Station in a mad dash to Gainesville for Saturday's Florida-Florida State showdown, we really weren't sure what to think about Aggieland. On the one hand, we both realized that we were tea-sips at heart. Who needs duty and honor when you can sleep late and play beer pong all day? On the other hand, we have nothing but the highest respect and admiration for the Ags and their university. There is no other school that we visited where the students and alumni ("former students" in Aggiespeak) share such pride and unbridled love for their university. Despite its less than majestic landscape, College Station is an extraordinary place. They say that the wives of professors would break out in tears upon arriving in College Station, only to break out in tears again when it was time to move on a few years later. Likewise, we both departed Aggieland with a bit of sadness, as we wondered whether we would ever be privileged enough to return.

The Maroon Tattoo

The Meadowlands
Army vs. Navy
Wow!

With the thunderous shots of the Aggie victory cannon still reverberating in our ears, we departed Texas A&M. After a harrowing journey in which our tail pipe fell off, we arrived in Gainesville, just two hours before the kickoff of the Florida-Florida State game. Despite the national significance surrounding Florida State's annual showdown with Miami, Florida is by far Florida State's most hated rival. How could it be otherwise with less than two hours of interstate separating the state's two largest public universities?

Two hours may not seem like a lot, but still, we had enough time to enjoy some tailgate cuisine with the Gator and Seminole fans. After plying us with pork and hops, they had little trouble convincing us that this was *the* game in Florida. To reinforce the point that the rest of the world doesn't matter when the Gators and Seminoles clash, one fan (we recall his name as being Butch) told us about a demonstration that took place on Florida State's campus during the hostage crisis of the late '70s. A group of Iranian students staged a rally in support of their country, with only a massive police force preventing them from being attacked by the angry mob of onlookers. But as the tension reached a climax, the mob's "USA! USA!" chants miraculously became drowned out and eventually replaced by cheers of "Go to hell Florida! go to hell!"

In light of this animosity, we wished that we could have arrived earlier in the week and received a better taste of the Sunshine State's most bitter rivalry. From what we saw, though, the Seminole faithful had really cranked up the party and the national championship machines for this game, putting their efforts during the Kickoff Classic and Miami game to shame. Conversely, the Florida fans were also whipped into an equally frothy frenzy, hungry for the chance to spoil Florida State's national championship season. Orange and Blue-clad Gatorbackers screamed pro-Florida cheers and anti-Seminole epithets at anyone who came within earshot. Seldom on the trip had we witnessed such a genuine hatred for the opposition. In this case, the familiarity of living two hours apart really did breed contempt.

After wallowing in the animosity and pageantry of this intrastate rivalry, we made our way to the stadium. Through some sort of bizarre chain of events, Florida's sports information department granted us sideline passes for the game. Perhaps they wanted us to experience "The Swamp" and its awesome crowd noise from a player's perspective. Or more likely, they wanted to keep us away from the press box buffet.

While most of the details from Florida State's 33-21 victory have faded from our memories, The Swamp's awesome crowd noise left an indelible impression. If Michigan's bowl-shaped stadium funnels noise away from the field, The Swamp's brick, shoe-box configuration directs the noise back at the players. If we couldn't communicate while standing just a few feet apart, imagine how difficult it must be for opposing offenses to pick up the quarterback's audibles. Not surprisingly, Florida State jumped offside several times that afternoon. When Florida scored a third-quarter touchdown to pull within 6 points, the 85,507 fans cheered with such thunderous approval that Florida coach Steve Spurrier actually covered his ears to block out the deafening noise. Without a doubt, Florida's Swamp was the loudest stadium that we experienced.

Toughest Visiting Venues

1. The Swamp, *Florida*
2. The Orange Bowl, *Miami*
3. Kyle Field, *Texas A&M*
4. Doak-Campbell Stadium, *Florida State*
5. Death Valley, *LSU*
6. Death Valley, *Clemson*
7. Memorial Stadium, *Nebraska*
8. Husky Stadium, *Washington*
9. Jordan-Hare Stadium, *Auburn*
10. Notre Dame Stadium, *Notre Dame*

*   *   *   *

With the Seminole faithful still celebrating their state championship, we pointed the limo north in anticipation of the military mayhem surrounding the Army-Navy game. As we motored toward Annapolis, and in the spirit of this classic rivalry, we debated the relative merits of the Army's Sergeant Bilko versus the Navy's Captain Binghamton, at least until our attention was diverted by the hundreds of "South of the Border" billboards lining the Carolina interstate. The billboards for this glistening tribute to capitalism began beckoning us from ninety miles away with messages like, "Kids, keep screaming, They'll stop!" Ninety miles later, our voices raw from screaming, we arrived at South of the Border: a monstrous neon truck stop, located in Dillon, South Carolina, just south of the North Carolina border on Interstate 95.

After a few heart-stopping rounds of miniature golf at "Pedro's Golf of Mexico," we purchased one last memento for our limousine, an official South of the Border severed leg. For the rest of the trip, people following our limo could not only read our bumper stickers, but also wonder about the condition of the carcass connected to the bloodstained foot dangling from the trunk. With leg in hand, we headed for our final regular season game.

*   *   *   *

Upon arrival at the Naval Academy, we were amazed by the complete lack of understanding we had for their existence. Unlike Texas A&M, which beguiled us with its militarism and Twelfth Man tradition, yet still retained the typical collegiate lifestyle, the military and naval academies exist in a world of their own. Sure, we shared a commitment, but somehow pledging to uncover college football zaniest characters and traditions paled in comparison to the life and death pledge taken by these men and women.

Not surprisingly, it took us some time to acclimate ourselves to the military surroundings. We were never greeted with a simple, "Hi, how're you doing," or the all-too-familiar, "Excuse me, but the homeless shelter is three blocks that away." Rather, the Middies opted for the more formal, "Welcome aboard." When Bob mistakenly referred to one of the students as a Cadet, he was curtly admonished that Naval Academy students were known as Midshipmen and Military Academy students were known as Cadets. He was also warned, "I'll explain that to you once, but the second time, I'll beat you for it." Needless to say, Bob didn't make the same mistake again.

While giving us a tour of Navy's scenic coastal campus, one of the Middies told us that he was going to be assigned to the South Pacific after graduation. The thought of being posted near the motherland, China, with all of its Mandarin and Szechwan delights made us green with envy. Jokingly, we asked him if we could still get commissioned to the Academy. Staring at our guts, he mentioned that Middies must always be prepared to pass the Physical Readiness Test (PRT). While he might have been stretching the truth a bit, he claimed the PRT consisted of pushups, screaming, pushups, running, pushups, sit-ups, pushups, and calisthenics. The only other time we had ever heard the word pushups as many times was when the ice cream man drove by.

While we certainly wouldn't be able to go pushup for pushup with the Middies, they probably would be hard pressed to handle our version of the Physical Unreadiness Test (PUT). Let's see these shining beacons of physical fitness strip a flock of chicken wings clean to the bone and eat a sack of pork rinds while watching an entire 14-hour *Bewitched* marathon — featuring both Darrens!

With our guts full of PRT stories, we next headed over to watch an event that typifies Army-Navy week: a pizza eating contest. Here, at last, was something with which we could identify. In fact, here was something about which we could feel superior. They were on our turf now, and they had chosen a format that was even more to our liking: total pieces eaten within a one hour time limit. Those pencil-necked naval types wouldn't stand a chance against our likes, even if it was only the two of us against their four man teams.

The first rule of military engagement must be to recognize when you're outflanked, because they refused to let us participate. We weren't upset. In fact, we enjoyed watching this grueling competition. For the most part, the participants got out of the gate quickly, but slowed to a grinding halt at the thirty-five minute mark. Marathoners refer to that point as "breaking through the wall," because if you can push through it, the rest of the race is a mere formality. Experienced eaters call this point "breaking through the intestinal wall," because if you can eat through it, things loosen up quite a bit.

*   *   *   *

The Army-Navy game has as prolific a history as any rivalry in all of sports. Played at a neutral site three weeks after the final regular-season games, this contest has the look and feel of a bowl game. Season records don't mean a thing in this game, as the same characteristics that make the Middies and Cadets our nation's finest, also enable either team to win on any given day. As the Academies prepared for the 94th meeting, the series was tied 43-43-7.

While the Naval Academy was founded almost a half-century after West Point, Navy began playing football a decade before Army. In fact, football was frowned upon at West Point, where Cadet Philip Sheridan was severely reprimanded in 1850 for kicking a football around the barracks. Even when General Sheridan became a Civil War hero, football remained barred as a hindrance to discipline. However, when the Navy challenged the Army to a game of football in 1890, the sport immediately earned a niche in the annals of military history.

With the vast majority of the West Pointers never having played the game, the Navy dominated the first contest 24-0. The

Cadets were so unfamiliar with the game that after Navy scored a touchdown on a fake punt, Army vociferously protested, claiming, "It was clearly a false official statement for an officer and a gentleman to announce that he was going to kick the ball and then do something else with it."

The intensity and animosity escalated during the next few seasons. After the controversial 1893 game, a general and an admiral challenged each other to a duel, which fortunately ended without injury. In the interest of national security, President Grover Cleveland suspended the series. Nonetheless, the game was resumed five years later as a memorial to the soldiers killed in the Spanish-American War. Among the dead was Dennis Michie, the Cadet credited with bringing the game to West Point and whose name graces Army's football stadium.

By the '20s, Army-Navy had emerged as the premier rivalry in all of sport. In fact, this rivalry's popularity is credited with giving rise to the first ticket scalpers. These schools had such a national following that their 1926 contest was moved to Chicago's Soldier Field, where a record crowd of 110,000 fans watched them battle to a 21-21 tie. Two years after their epic tie, the series was actually suspended for two seasons because of eligibility disputes. Since then, not even World War II and the assassination of President Kennedy could stop this game.

Although World War II didn't stop the series, it did give it a unique twist. When wartime economic restrictions prevented West Point's Corps of Cadets from traveling to Annapolis for the game, President Roosevelt ordered that half of the Naval Academy be assigned to cheer for the Army.

Although the modern-day games no longer have national championship significance, their importance is not lessened. General Douglas Mac Arthur may have summed up at least a part of the reason, claiming, "Upon the field of friendly strife are sown the seeds that on the other days, on other fields, will bear the fruits of victory." Former players hail the game as a pinnacle experience. Roger Staubach once told Tom Callahan of the *Washington Post*. "I loved my five Super Bowls. But, I'd take the Army-Navy game without question." It's no wonder that all over the world, military personnel from admirals to generals to PFCs make bets on the game, nothing illegal, just uniforms or services, because pride is on the line. And for those who have attended these Academies, pride means far more than national rankings.

*   *   *   *

During Army-Navy week, discipline takes a backseat to good-natured pranks, allowing Middies and Cadets to vent steam before the end of the semester. This week is particularly difficult for the transfer students. It is considered an immense honor to be chosen to spend a semester at the rival academy, and only the top students are chosen to do so. On the other hand, these "honored" students receive tremendous abuse during game week. One Cadet told us he was checked every 30 minutes to make sure that he wasn't getting any shut-eye. Other Middies assured us that this guy had already had his uniform stolen, and by the end of the evening, he would have no mattress and no doors on his room. Nevertheless, the Cadet maintained his resolve. His company officer offered to let him sleep in his office all week, but this proud soldier refused, claiming, "What fun is that?" He probably regretted that decision, because we were told that other Middies planned to kidnap him and leave him naked, taped to a torpedo monument.

During the course of this rivalry, pranks between the two service academies have ranged from the benign to the technologically complex. On one end of the spectrum, there are simple demonstrations of spirit, such as spirit posters made from bed sheets exhorting the team on to victory. But unlike other schools, where publicity-seeking students make a simple sign featuring the call letters of whichever television network is broadcasting the game, spirit posters usually consist of giant messages drawn on 20 to 30 bed sheets which have been sewn together. It's even more complex than that, because a spirit poster is only effective if it can be seen. Making the sign visible is what this activity is all about. To this end, the Cadets and Middies go on "recons" to hang the posters in strategic places, preferably at the rival camp. At the Naval Academy, the signs are hung on the houses of the highest officers, but other times, they have been hung at Times Square and even outside Colin Powell's office at the Pentagon.

Moving along the spectrum of pranks, the next most elaborate might be termed "stunts." Stunts consist of doing something to the other service branch that seems relatively innocent, ludicrous and almost impossible. A great example of a stunt is when the Middies awoke to find an F4 Phantom rolled up next to the statue of Tecumseh in the center of their campus. In 1991, the Midshipmen took stunts a step further. A squadron actually flew up to West Point and bombarded the Cadets with thousands of ping pong balls inscribed with "Beat Army."Another favored Naval prank involves sending boats up the Hudson to spray the Cadets with water during their evening formations.

The next step up the ladder of audacity borders on the criminal. It's bad enough that they have stolen each other's mascots on numerous occasions, but the Middies claim to have kidnapped the Corps Cadet Commander and one of the Army's four mules and deposited them in Canada before the 1992 contest. No one at West Point would confirm the story.

*   *   *   *

Having spent three days at Navy, we felt we wanted to give equal time to Army, so late Thursday morning we strolled into West Point's Office of Public Affairs. In the midst of an office covered with "Beat Navy" and "Slam the Squids" signs to remind us why we were there, we spoke with Brigade Spirit Officer Daniel J. Kdurna, (One Adam-12, be on the lookout for a missing vowel) who assured us that although the Naval Academy has the rowdier reputation of the two, there is nothing bland about West Point's Army-Navy week. While standard dress for the Cadets is conservative gray slacks, white Oxford shirts and ties, the dress during game week reflects the arch-rival mentality of this series. Almost everyone dresses in fatigues "preparing for battle all week," as Kdurna explained.

Just like at the Naval Academy, the grounds of the Army campus take on the flavor of the big game. The tunnel between Eisenhower Hall and Grant Hall had been painted over with the ubiquitous phrase, "Beat Navy." One wall listed the scores of every Army victory over Navy, and even featured the confident "Reserved for 1993" just below the 1992 score. During this week, all first year Cadets are required to greet all upperclassmen with a salute and "Beat Navy, sir!" Even the menu has been changed: pizza is, of course, "Beat Navy pizza;" pretzels are "mule-kicked pretzels;" and nuts are "crushed goat nuts."

Army also promotes annual spirit-building activities, such as leaving a cannon on the front lawn of the Superintendent's house and the creation and placement of spirit posters. One Army prank recounted for us has to rank as one of the great spirit poster hangings of all time. In 1992, some marauding Cadets somehow snuck onto the USS Intrepid and hung a massive "Beat Navy" spirit poster over the ship's side.

Does this all sound a little crazy? Maybe so, but Kdurna insists that the team on the field can sense the emotion in the stands. "The players told us that the fans pulled them through last year," when a final-second field goal capped a furious comeback victory. With support like this, we knew we were in for a great day of football on Saturday.

*   *   *   *

On Thursday afternoon, we witnessed yet another traditional Army-Navy week contest: the Goats-Engineers football game. West Point's junior class is annually split into two teams, those above the median grade point average (the Engineers) and those below the median (the Goats). The game was played in full pads and uniforms, with practically the entire academy in attendance. With ABC's Brent Musberger calling parts of the game over a 1930s-era PA system, the brute strength of the Goats overcame the shiftiness of the Engineers. None of the Engineers seemed too disappointed, though, for tradition says that if the Goats win, Army will defeat Navy.

*   *   *   *

After a week of military mayhem, gameday finally arrived. The tailgate scene lacked some of the extravagance that we saw across the South in terms of all-out, bust-ass cuisine preparation, but it did have a mystique of its own. This aire emanated from the manner in which the two groups appeared and behaved. Groups of Middies dotted the stadium grounds dressed in their traditional black uniforms and white hats, intently awaiting the battle call. Cadets also milled about in their dress-grays. They too seemed poised for action.

From inside the stadium, we watched the students from both Academies assemble and "March On" into the stadium. Each branch has assigned seats on opposite sides of the field. Just prior to kickoff, the schools held a formal exchange of POWs as the transferees from both schools were marched to midfield and exchanged so that they could enjoy the game with their classmates. We were told that from that moment on the game was all-important. No family, friends or girlfriends are allowed to mingle with the Cadets or Middies during the game.

Awaiting the usual type of beginning to a football game, we were astounded by the Navy Seals that parachuted into the stadium with the game ball, just as a group of F14s did a fly-by. The game, played for the Commander-in-Chief's trophy, looked as if it was going to be spectacular. Unfortunately, the weather didn't lend itself to the spectacular. It poured throughout the game, and while it didn't dampen the spirits of the Cadets or Middies in attendance, it made the play and Phil a bit sluggish. A missed Navy field goal from short range decided the game in the final seconds. The Cadets were predictably ecstatic, and the Middies were despondent.

*   *   *   *

That was it! Four months on the road came to an abrupt end. We suddenly found ourselves back at Tang Dynasty in Massachusetts — not really remembering the uneventful trip back home. We met some friends for dinner at a "welcome home" party. They were starved for tales from our trip. As the stories flowed out of us (almost as fast as the Mai Tais and Chinese food flowed into us), we realized that a book could and would have to result. There was simply too much insanity to keep to ourselves. Sure, there was still a trip to the Orange Bowl and the national championship game on the horizon, but at that moment we were content to talk with our friends and enjoy the sweet smells of chicken wings. All other thoughts were temporarily shelved.

Our Favorite Things About College Football

Best Fightsongs: Notre Dame *Victory March* and *Michigan's The Victors*

Best College Towns (no particular order)
Chapel Hill, Boulder, State College, Madison, Austin, Berkeley, Saratoga Springs, Columbus, Athens, Eugene.
Favorite Place on the Planet: Baton Rouge

Best Party School: Florida State
Penn State may be the most underrated.

Loudest Stadium: The Swamp, Florida

Best Halftime Show: The dotting of the "i" at Ohio State
Beano Cooke claimed he would rather dot the "i" than become president.

Best Tailgate: LSU

Best Stadium: Notre Dame Stadium

Most Scenic Stadium: Husky Stadium (Washington)
honorable mention: Folsom Field (Colorado) and Michie Stadium (Army)

Best Mascot (live): Ralphie the Colorado Buffalo

Best Mascot (costumed): Stanford's Tree and Cal's Oski

Best Pregame Tradition: Walk through the Grove at Ole Miss

Best Bands: Stanford and Texas A&M
Only because we missed the Battle of the Bands between Southern and Grambling.

Best Pep Rally: Texas A&M Bonfire

Most Knowledgeable Fans: Alabama
They're even knowledgable by southern standards

Best Cheerleaders: Southern Cal

Best Campus Eatery: Dreamland, Tuscaloosa Alabama

Best Campus Bar: Rathskeller, State College

Most Devoted Fan: Giles Pellerin
He has attended every Southern Cal game since 1926

Miami, Florida
The Orange Bowl: Florida State vs. Nebraska

The Last Waltz

During the three weeks between the Army-Navy game and the Orange Bowl, we met daily to work on our book, but we accomplished nothing. We didn't write one single page of material, never contacted a publisher, and never even thought about how we were going to pay our massive trip debts. We were too busy debating about how we were going to get to the Orange Bowl.

With its sputtering carburetor, we didn't think the limo would make it to Connecticut, never mind Miami. Luckily, there were other alternatives. Phil's Acura certainly could have negotiated a journey down the Atlantic Seaboard, and with the recent fare wars, flying to Miami would have been surprisingly economical. Yet, there was something blasphemous about completing the jihad without our beloved limo.

So we took yet another ill-advised risk and headed south in our trusty limo. Surprisingly, we made it to the Sunshine State with little difficulty. It must have been those good luck charms we purchased at South of the Border.

On arrival in Ft. Lauderdale, we descended upon the Carquest Bowl's media hospitality suite, where a friendly woman handed us a pair of commemorative Carquest Bowl carrying cases and invited us to partake in the free media guides, yearbooks and newspapers. We ignored the media materials, instead stuffing our bags with croissants, candy bars and beer from the complimentary food and beverage bar.

Before escaping with our ill-gotten booty, fate again interceded on our behalf as our hostess invited us to attend that evening's media dinner: a luau at a tiki and balsa wood memorial to Polynesian cuisine known as the Mai Kai restaurant. Just thinking about those troughs overflowing with Asian delicacies triggered Pavlovian fits of orgasmic lust.

Upon arrival at the luau, we blitzed the buffet table in search of the noble chicken wing. Instead, we were accosted by some guy named Charlie, who had that all-too familiar glazed look in his eye — that same quizzical look that most people get when they listen to us detail our odyssey with a combination of football history and allusions to the *Beverly Hillbillies*. But Charlie was also swaying, swaying to the degree that we couldn't help but think that there was either seismic activity below his waist or he had thrown down a few too many Mai Tais. What happened next remains fuzzy.

Editor's note... As any lawyer could tell you, what happens at a crime scene is often perceived by eyewitnesses in strikingly different ways. Bob described Charlie as a rugged 45-year-old ex-prize fighter who launched some vicious anti-Semitic epithets in Bob's direction. Despite the imposing Goliath before him, Bob claims to have successfully defended the faith with a series of pugilistic maneuvers that would have made Hulk Hogan envious.

While Phil agrees that Charlie deserved to be pummeled, he has a slightly different recollection of the fracas. According to Phil, Bob deployed the stoogesque, "you got something on your shirt trick," to gain an unfair advantage over an old man who had the sickly look of someone experiencing rejection following a liver transplant. After Bob dumped Charlie amidst a tray full of sweet and sour chicken,, Phil recalled laughing hysterically when a waitress threw Bob into a hammerlock and bounced him from the restaurant.

*   *   *   *

Unfortunately, the Carquest Bowl couldn't live up to the excitement of the media dinner. A sparse crowd of 15,000 showed up at Joe Robbie Stadium in Ft. Lauderdale to watch Boston College defeat Virginia in a game that possessed all the drama of a Bulgarian film festival. Nevertheless, the Carquest Bowl was just an appetizer for that evening's national championship showdown between Nebraska and Florida State.

We drove down to Miami, parked the limo and engaged in one final tailgate party. With two of college football's perennial bridesmaids battling for an elusive national championship, the atmosphere was electric. We saw one hawker trying to scalp tickets for $500 apiece, yelling:

> *Who needs a pair*
> *To see Charlie take to the air?*

Hell, for $500 you could rent a helicopter and see Charlie Ward from the air.

Amidst a frenzied sea of garnet and gold, we took our seats. Although Nebraska was ranked atop both polls, they were a two-touchdown underdog. In recent years, the Huskers had rolled through the regular season, only to annually get demolished in their bowl game. Conversely, Florida State had been college football's most potent postseason team, having gone undefeated in an unprecedented 11 consecutive bowl games.

However, the Cornhuskers played inspired football and actually took a 16-15 lead late in the fourth quarter. But Charlie Ward drove the Seminoles down to the Nebraska 5-yard-line where Scott Bentley kicked a field goal to put Florida State ahead with just 21 seconds remaining. As the kick sailed through the uprights, we looked at each other in bewilderment. Having followed Florida State's triumphs right from the very first game of the season through their victories over Miami and Florida, our dream season had mirrored theirs, and Bobby Bowden's long awaited national championship seemed imminent. Or did it?

With just seconds remaining, Nebraska mounted a desperation drive, one that appeared to fall short when Trumane Bell was tackled at the FSU 28-yard-line. When the clock ran out, we joined the Seminole partisans in a cathartic championship celebration. As we were exchanging high fives and hugs with the surrounding fans, our attention was drawn to the confusion on the field. After a few minutes of frantic discussion, the referees determined (rightfully so) that there was still enough time for Nebraska to attempt a game-winning 45-yard field goal.

But the kick sailed off "wide left" and a second, even more raucous, celebration commenced. For a few glorious moments, we shared in the Seminole euphoria. Our joy quickly turned to sorrow, however, when we were smacked by the harsh realization that our dream season was now over.

With the massive anchor of reality dragging down our spirits, we shuffled back to our vehicle. All that was left to do was return home, and even that wasn't easy.

As we drove through Georgia contemplating another stop at South of the Border, we cranked up some Elvis Presley tunes on our cassette player. At first, we thought we were listening to a new version of *Hound Dog*, one with an extra drummer... a rhythmically-challenged extra drummer. Unfortunately, it was the limo's engine providing the base line. As the coughing turned to a slow knocking, we struggled to muffle the noise by rhythmically matching the engine noises with Presley ditties. First, *Return to Sender* worked, but the engine's cadence shifted again. We compensated with *I Can't Help Falling in Love with You*, but the beat and the car slowed to a crawl. As the black monster stalled altogether, all we could hear was Elvis singing *Don't be Cruel*. We were the victims of one final automotive nightmare.

After 15 minutes of futile calls to AAA, the car miraculously started. With one foot on the accelerator and the other on the brake, we somehow limped into Richmond Hill and the friendly confines of Motel 6. Appropriately, Elvis sang *Heartbreak Hotel*.

A jug of "sweet Georgia wine" and a $450 carburetor later, and we were back on the road. A blizzard had blanketed the entire eastern seaboard, making our ride north particularly harrowing. Almost five days after Florida State's incredible Orange Bowl victory, we finally crossed into Massachusetts. The snow had subsided, leaving only one final hurdle to overcome, the Massachusetts Turnpike toll collector. Our unexpected travel costs had left us with only a $1 bill and three pennies to pay a $1.30 toll. Inside the front seat cushion, we found a chocolate encrusted dime. What a break. We were now only 17 cents short, and we were able to scrape a little snack off the coin too. A foray into the ashtray uncovered a lint-covered nickel. When Bob's jeans, an old sneaker and the glove compartment yielded another 7 cents, we were only a nickel short. Phil found a dime in his suitcase and we sped through the toll. Our dream journey had ended... with five cents to spare.

Greatest Bowl Games
of the Last Quarter Century

After the shock of our ride home wore off, we reflected on what a great Orange Bowl we had witnessed. While it may not have been a pretty game from a technical standpoint, the drama surrounding Florida State's national championship march down the field and Nebraska's valiant last-second drive make the 1994 Orange Bowl worthy of mention amongst the greatest bowl games of the past quarter century.

1995 Orange Bowl: Nebraska 24, Miami 17
Redemption! The Cornhuskers took care of the unfinished business from their heartbreaking loss in the 1994 Orange Bowl. They snapped a decade-long string of bowl futility by wearing down Miami, the team that delivered Nebraska so many of its harshest defeats, in the Orange Bowl, a stadium where so many of those whippings took place. After two decades of running one of college football's classiest programs, Tom Osborne was awarded his first national championship.

1992 Sugar Bowl: Notre Dame 39, Florida 28
Coming off embarrassing back-to-back losses to Tennessee and Penn State, Notre Dame was a heavy underdog against third-ranked Florida. Critics joked that the difference between Notre Dame and a bowl of Cheerios was that Cheerios belong in a bowl. But like so many times before, Notre Dame had the last laugh as they rebounded from a 16-7 half-time deficit for a shocking 39-28 triumph.

1990 Orange Bowl: Notre Dame 21, Colorado 6
Riding the emotion of quarterback Sal Aunese's tragic death, Colorado shocked the nation with a perfect regular season record. Playing for an improbable national championship, the Buffs controlled the first half, but failed to score on three golden scoring opportunities. Notre Dame dominated the second half, giving Colorado a disappointing finish to an incredible season.

1987 Fiesta Bowl: Penn State 14, Miami 10
It was more than a postseason showdown between football's two best teams; it was the swagger of Miami clashing against the understated dignity of Penn State. Despite being outgained 445-162, Penn State upset Miami, giving Paterno his second national championship.

1984 Orange Bowl: Miami 31, Nebraska 30
Trailing 31-24, top-ranked Nebraska scored a touchdown with just a minute remaining. If Nebraska had kicked the point-after, they would have walked away with a tie and the national championship. But Tom Osborne elected to go for the decisive victory and the title of "Greatest Team of All-time" with a two-point conversion.

1979 Sugar Bowl: Alabama 14, Penn State 7
In a national championship showdown, Alabama stopped Penn State on three consecutive plays from inside the 2-yard-line in what may have been the greatest goal line stand of all time.

1975 Rose Bowl: Southern Cal 18, Ohio State 17
It was Woody Hayes vs. John McKay and Heisman winner Archie Griffin vs. Heisman runner-up Anthony Davis. It was also one of the most exciting Rose Bowls ever. Trailing by seven points late in the fourth quarter, Southern Cal mounted an incredible 83-yard touchdown drive. A successful two-point conversion gave the Trojans a share of the national championship. Their 1980 rematch, in which USC prevailed 17-16, was also a classic.

1973 Sugar Bowl: Notre Dame 24, Alabama 23
With a national championship on the line, a missed two-point conversion proved to be the difference in this first ever meeting between two of college football's most storied programs. We spoke with countless fans who remembered this as the most exciting game they ever saw.

1971 Cotton Bowl: Notre Dame 24, Texas 11
Joe Theisman's Notre Dame knocked off the undefeated top-ranked defending national champion Longhorns, ending their 30-game winning streak.

Epilogue

Eighteen months have passed since our harrowing journey home from the Orange Bowl. Our book still isn't finished, must less picked up by a publisher, and Michael Jordan has already endured an entire baseball career and returned to basketball. Nebraska is college football's national champion, as Joe Paterno again laments another undefeated season without a trophy, and we still don't have a book.

For better or worse, we are back in the real world. The assimilation has not been pretty. Bob has pursued numerous wild business opportunities, some of which may have even been legal. Phil rejoined his old law firm long enough to repay his trip-related debts, before again leaving the profession in disillusionment.

During the first few weeks after the jihad's completion, we met almost nightly at Tang Dynasty, the same restaurant that gave birth to our crazy scheme, and futilely attempted to pound out a viable book. With seemingly irreconcilable creative differences, the writing process became painfully unproductive. As the weeks marched on, our meetings became more and more infrequent, until we completely stopped talking to each other by the summer.

Working alone, we each attempted to write our own versions of *Saturday Afternoon Madness*. Then fate intervened. Just days apart, we each sent our rough drafts to Wayne Ellis, one of our few semi-literate friends. Wayne convinced us that if we could somehow combine the travelogue aspects of Phil's book with the college football history of Bob's book, we just might get something decent. With Wayne serving as our referee, we began the grueling process of assimilating the two books. Bob would give his version to Phil. Phil would revise it and give it to Wayne, who would revise it and give it to Bob, who would... ad infinitum.

There continue to be fights between us, and our friends laugh at our ineptitude. We are continually asked about the status of the book and have become quite good at deflecting the queries or distracting the questioners. But we couldn't help asking our own questions. Had we really been so crazy thinking we could get this thing done? Certainly not. It's not like we were trying to write *War and Peace*. It's just a book about college football. Did we make a mistake trying to appeal to sports-watching couch potatoes? Simple answer: O.J. Simpson Trial.

And the most vexing question of all: "What was the point?" not just the point of the book, but the point of the whole trip? Were we just trying to exalt the stature of college football in American culture? Others could do that without traveling across the country, and they could probably describe it more poignantly. Were we trying to demonstrate the dangers of four months of idle time on the minds of two men facing a premature mid-life crisis? Maybe a little, but we knew that before we left.

Maybe the point of this thing really wasn't so profound after all. We saw a chance to live out a dream, and we took a shot at it. Whether the whole story gets published or not, forty years from now, we'll be able to sit down with our grandchildren and, like so many of the storytellers we met during our journey, we'll be able to recount our magical odyssey through the wonderful world of college football. The memories will be blurry, and we wouldn't be surprised if it all kind of blended together into one incredible day of college football, of Saturday Afternoon Madness...

Saturday Afternoon Madness

The brilliant sunlight floods our mountain-top retreat. The flatirons of Boulder streak skyward, filled with expectation of the game. We pillage the free breakfast line, the fifth such cost-free morning in a row. I don't think we paid for a meal the entire trip. Leaving the hotel, our sturdy, maintenance-free chariot purrs as we parade through another of America's charming college towns. The four-hundred foot-tall Touchdown Jesus carved into the flatirons watches us head toward the stadium like a proud father seeing his children head off to school. The day only gets better.

By the time we arrive at the stadium, Notre Dame Stadium, bursting at the seams with tradition and success, the tailgating was in full swing. We valet park the limo, admiring our mighty vehicle as the attendant drives it away. Just as we are about to enter the eclectic tailgating scene, Chico Moore of LSU fame pulls up in his purple and gold amphibious Tiger Machine. His wig, tuxedo and boots shine with the hope of another LSU season. He beckons us to climb aboard because we're all heading to Lake Washington for a little pre-pregame partying. Chico drives right off the end of the dock, we hit the water and the party begins. Suddenly, his limo transforms into a houseboat party platform.

Even though its barely 9:30 a.m., and we've already eaten, the waitstaff appears carrying trays of boudin. We cannot resist. Chico's guest of honor is none other than Sharon Stone. She instructs the party on boudin etiquette. We watch as she deep-throats not one, not two, but three entire boudins. She grins a toothy, meaty grin and tells the party to dig in. We squeeze the meat tubes, expecting the sweetness of boudin, surprised and delighted to find that the casings contain Dreamland rib sauce.

After four hours of stuffing our faces and wishing we had a toothpick for Ms. Stone, we land near the foot of the stadium. We are ablaze with excitement and meat farts. Today's game features two of college football's greatest coaching legends: Joe Paterno and Bear Bryant. This match-up is especially delicious because the Bear has proven immune to The Paterno's psychic abilities. We made our way through the tailgaters (most of whom proudly display the colors of their favorite southern team), wondering how so many of them managed to make it all the way to Boulder for the game.

282

We enter the stadium, making a mental note not to dispar-age the military because Notre Dame stadium is filled to capacity with cadets and midshipmen. The crowd noise is deafening. It's Florida's Swamp without the humidity. Even though the decibel level would make Roger Daltry blanch, we can still make out the rhythmic calls of Texas A&M. Our eyes and ears follow the noise until we locate the Yell Leaders, complete in overalls, silently leading the calls with their uncanny miming skills. Then, in the far corner of the stadium, we spot the inevitable red army, the Cornhusker faithful who cannot pay enough to follow their team wherever they may go. On all sides of the red spot, keys are being waved, some by Coloradoans, some by Berserkley maniacs. Never has such a diverse crowd assembled for a game. And why not, this will be the mother of all games.

The teams take the field just before the National Anthem. Liberace is wheeled out to the fifty-yard line, accompanied by the Stanford marching band, and proceeds to whip off a ragtime version of our country's song. As Liberace continues to rock, the band takes the shape of a DNA strand. Through a series of intri-cate and potentially fatal maneuvers, the band creates a 220-person-strong genetic string. It towers over the stadium. The majorette at the top waves to Touchdown Jesus, who winks back. It's game time. The crowd erupts. Somewhere a trombonist goes down.

All eyes follow the referees and captains to midfield. Surprisingly, The Paterno elects to start Charlie Ward for today's game. The Paterno moves in strange ways. Bear, on the other hand, knows the immensity of this game and decides to go with Doug Flutie, college football's ultimate big game quarterback. The coin-flipper for today's contest is Keith Jackson. Keith tosses the coin, Flutie calls heads, splash. Whoa Nellie! Somehow, the coin lands in one of Frank Howard's cups of chewing tobacco juice. After fishing out the goobery coin, Flutie's team elects to receive.

After the coin toss, we join Bob Ufer and Grantland Rice in the press box. Not just a press box, this exotic retreat would make Robin Leach envious. Cocktails, shellfish and po'boys are the bill of fare. The game is an epic struggle, coming down to the final play. Of course, Flutie connects for a touchdown, but he still needs an extra point to tie. Offensive coordinator Tom Osborne convinces the Bear to eschew the kick in favor of a potential game-

winning two-point conversion. Flutie rolls out right and tosses back to the left. Gerard Phelan makes a diving catch, two points. The Bear wins. Saturday Afternoon Madness spreads into the dusk.

Yep, that's how we'll probably remember it. No trouble, no debt, no heartaches. The hardships just won't matter. What will matter is that for one magical season, we lived out our dreams to the hilt. How many people can say that?

We wouldn't be foolish enough to make
the same mistake twice, would we?

More Saturday Afternoon Madness, possibly?
A seaon of college hoops, maybe?
Major League baseball, never?

What about a year in sports?

About the authors

Bob Waldstein
After receiving his M.B.A. (Major Basketball Aholic) from Duke, Bob traded in his three-piece suits for a gridiron jihad through the heartland of America. He may not know anything about the intricacies of the two-deep zone, but he is imminently qualified to describe the subtle regional variations in tailgate cuisine.

Phil Silverman
After graduating Dartmouth and San Diego Law School, Phil spent four years bailing out Boston's most notorious deadbeats as a bankruptcy attorney. He did some other stuff that he's not real proud of. Now he's better.

Wayne Ellis
Brought in late in the game as editor/referee, Wayne was burdened with the ponderous task of boiling down the information contained in Bob and Phil's notes, bar napkins and food wrappers. At times though, Wayne's clearly deteriorated into a Sisyphus-like role, as time and time again his edits were reinserted by Bob and Phil. This undermining of his literary authority, coupled with a fanatical passion for his native Nebraska Cornhuskers, has resulted in the occasionally spurious editor's notes that are sprinkled throughout the book.

The Saturday Afternoon Madness Road Trip

The Kickoff Classic: Florida State vs. Kansas

State College: Penn State vs. Minnesota

Ann Arbor: Michigan vs. Notre Dame

Baton Rouge: LSU vs. Auburn

Clemson: Clemson vs. Georgia Tech

Athens: Georgia vs. Arkansas

Tallahassee: Florida State vs. Miami

Tuscaloosa: Alabama vs. Tennessee

South Bend: Notre Dame vs. Southern Cal

Boulder: Colorado vs. Nebraska

Seattle: Washington vs. Southern Cal

Palo Alto: Big Game: Stanford vs. Cal

College Station: Texas A&M vs. Texas

Gainseville: Florida vs. Florida State

The Meadowlands: Army vs. Navy

The Orange Bowl: Florida State vs. Nebraska